KV-004-999

Revolutionary Cuba
and the
End
of the
Cold War

David C. Jordan

UNIVERSITY
PRESS OF
AMERICA

Lanham • New York • London

Copyright © 1993 by
University Press of America®, Inc.
4720 Boston Way
Lanham, Maryland 20706

3 Henrietta Street
London WC2E 8LU England

All rights reserved
Printed in the United States of America
British Cataloging in Publication Information Available

Library of Congress Cataloging-in-Publication Data

Jordan, David C.
Revolutionary Cuba and the end of the Cold War / by David C.
Jordan.
p.   cm.
Includes bibliographical references and index.
1. Cuba—Politics and government—1959–   2. Cuba—Foreign
relations—1959–   3. World politics—1975–1985.   4. World
politics—1985–1995.   I. Title.
F1788.J62   1993   327.7291—dc20   92–40550 CIP

ISBN 0–8191–8998–7 (cloth : alk. paper)

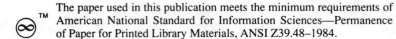

The paper used in this publication meets the minimum requirements of
American National Standard for Information Sciences—Permanence
of Paper for Printed Library Materials, ANSI Z39.48–1984.

To

Anabella, Stephen,

Victoria, and Anne

Table of Contents

Preface

When I first thought of writing about Cuba I asked myself the question: is it really necessary to write yet another book on Cuba? Hasn't everything been said already in countless studies and publications? The extraordinary events of the last two years present new questions as to how these events will impact on the future of Cuba. This book deals with the three attempts of Cuba to be a free state within an imperial international environment. The first attempt was the post-Spanish independence era when Cuba sought to emerge from U.S. dominance. The second era was characterized by Cuban efforts for an autonomous role backed by the Soviet Empire. The third attempt is in the post-Cold War environment where Cuba finds power relationships in flux but still opposes U.S. hegemony. Cuba is now approaching a new historic opportunity to establish itself as a new independent state in the era of the post Soviet empire. How Cuba enters this new era is of crucial importance for a prosperous and free future.

In writing this book I owe my principal debt to my students. Two of my graduate students, Chris Sabatini and William Prillaman, I wish to thank for helping to prepare the graphs on Cuba's changing trade patterns. The eager interest of my students and their efforts to understand the Cuban dilemma gave me the impulse to complete this work.

I especially want to thank my colleagues Adam Watson and Alberto Coll for sharing with me their deep knowledge and understanding of the Cuban experience. Adam Watson was kind enough to read this manuscript and to share with me his writings and insights after his tour as the British Ambassador to Cuba. We agree in seeing Castro more as an authoritarian and an eclectic fascist than is generally accepted by the conventional wisdom. From Alberto Coll, I have been reinforced in my identification of Castro with a military and strategic agenda of conquest. Of course, none of them is responsible for the conclusions of this book.

My deepest debt, however, is to my son Stephen, without whose research and cooperation this work could not have been completed. Lastly, I want to thank my family for their support, patience and consideration. My wife has helped me enormously in proofreading this study. I am also grateful to Pat Dunn for preparing the manuscript for publication.

Introduction

Cuba has been caught in the great tumults of the twentieth century. The country has been one of the key indicators of the battle between the hemispheres, and especially between the United States and the powers of Europe. It has also been caught in a dynamic struggle of ideologies against the backdrop of the idiosyncratic political culture of its people. Both economically and politically, Cuba has had institutions which have imperfectly articulated Cuban desires for freedom, autonomy, and nationalism. Instead, Cubans have been saddled with governments and economic structures, not least under Fidel Castro, which have forced them to confront subjection, dependence, and colonialism. Cuba has been in crisis almost throughout the twentieth century, as it has sought to find an equilibrium which would allow it to achieve both economic and political freedom.

Cuba, in the wake of the fall of the Soviet Union, is in a very precarious position. A Marxist-Leninist state in an era where Marxism-Leninism has lost its intellectual and emotional cachet, Cuba has become increasingly isolated in the wake of the enormous changes taking place in its patron state, the Soviet Union. Cuba is in a period of transition, caught between its erstwhile dependency on the USSR and an unknown future.

Unlike previous eras of imperial or alliance shifts however, the United States has an opportunity to restructure its relations with Cuba in such a way that it can reconcile some of the historic animosities which have plagued the two countries. The problems are very nuanced. Because there are multiple possibilities in regard to how events might unfold, any political analysis of this situation must of necessity, be very complex.

The history of other dependent countries within the Soviet alliance, and the fall of other dictators around the world have taken

1

many different shapes, and have had subsequently different tracks of development. What has happened in Rumania over the past two years is far different from what has taken place in Poland, and neither is similar to East Germany. What we must look for is not one perfect solution for all cases, but contingent solutions for a variety of situations, especially conscious of the particular conditions which apply to Cuba.

Some critics might argue that change may not be very likely until after the death of Castro. However, in the 1988-1991 period, we have seen a number of rulers swept out of power who appeared to control their countries very firmly. Nicolae Ceaucescu of Rumania and Erich Honecker of East Germany both held preeminent positions in their countries. Now the former has been executed, and the latter was smuggled out of his country by the Soviets.

Related experience is one indicator that Castro's grip on his country may not be as strong as once was thought, but there are other factors which are equally important. The first is the failure of the command economy, both in Cuba and in its former patron state, the Soviet Union. The failure to allocate resources efficiently, declining productivity, and crushing state bureaucracies acting as impediments to innovation and soaking up needed resources, have led to a growth in debt, a decline in the standard of living, and the increasing inability of these governments to satisfy the most basic needs of their people. Communist leaders are confronted with the fact that they can no longer compete economically in the international arena, and this realization has had far-reaching political and military implications.[1]

The admission of these problems has led to a crisis of faith in the legitimating ideology of the regime. Marxism-Leninism is no longer seen to be the inexorable ideological force that it once was. Its promises of equality and well-being for all have been replaced by the spectacle of the establishment of the *nomenklatura* or "new class" and generalized misery for the many who do not belong to it. A tacit consensus has developed, affirming that some mixture of market economic measures which include incentives to compete, innovate, and produce, now strikes at the very heart of Marxist-Leninist doctrine.

The political consequences have been profound. While Marxism-Leninism is formally grounded in economics, it has never been in substance, an economic doctrine. Rather, it has served as an intellectual apparatus for social world views of formal egalitarianism. These views in turn, have justified statist dictatorships and the closure of the political process. With the crack-up of its ideological justification, the Soviet Union was forced to grope for alternative justifications for its political power tactics and finally failed.

The Brezhnev Doctrine was repudiated, and most of the external Empire has either been able to detach itself or reorganize its relations to the Soviet Union with the Soviet Union itself, disintegrating into its constituent nations. The Warsaw Pact was formally dissolved in the first six months of 1991, and Poland, Hungary, and Czechoslovakia to a lesser degree, have enacted dramatic economic and political reforms. Even the lower tier of countries, Bulgaria and Rumania, have made efforts toward transforming the political and economic nature of their regime, albeit with less success than the "Little Tigers" to their north.

Within the Soviet Union, the demise of Marxism-Leninism may have been heralded by the last convulsions of the August 1991 coup, but the situation is very complex. Just as the external empire has come apart, so internal unity now is threatened. The USSR's constituent republics have begun to press for more autonomy as the forces of nationalism have surfaced throughout the country. Meanwhile, the country continues to struggle with its outmoded economic model and its bloated bureaucracies. Although the break-up now seems definitive, reactionary coups within the new Republics cannot be ruled out.

But the crisis facing Cuba is not solely a ramification of the demise of Marxism-Leninism in the Soviet Union or its imperial system. Cuban Marxists like to claim proudly that their revolution was indigenous. They argue that there is a difference in the ability of Marxist-Leninist regimes to sustain themselves, depending on whether they were imposed or indigenous. They argue that because the revolution was popular in its roots, that it remains popular now. Hence, they claim that their regime is far more stable than the imposed regimes of Eastern Europe.

Nevertheless, despite (or perhaps because of) Castro's ability to develop a sense of the rootedness of communism in Cuban soil, the total collapse of Marxism-Leninism is further illustrated by what has happened in the island nation. Its economy has been destroyed, the state has been militarized and its government has become corrupt. Its society has been reduced to a culture of fear and distrust, and its newest members have become disillusioned with the entire process.

As one of the Soviet Union's dependent satellites, Cuba has endured many of the same problems that the Soviet Union has faced. It also has lacked the natural resources, and is in a far worse geopolitical position than its giant patron, because it relied on the Soviets to sustain it. The end of the Soviet imperial commitment has left the Cubans in an even more precarious position. Communist regimes have collapsed in Asia, Africa, and the Middle East. With the breakup of the Warsaw Pact and the elections in Nicaragua, Cuba has very few ideological counterparts in either Europe or Latin America. In the current international system, it has very few alternative markets or patrons, and is groping toward a new modus vivendi.

Given this situation, we have set ourselves the task of analyzing how Cuba came to this state of affairs, how its relations became so intertwined with those of the USSR and the United States, and what are the prospects for change. Superficially, Cuba is a client state attempting to discover a formula for its own sovereignty, but it is also a state caught up in the process of state and social change which characterize the modern materialist revolutionary movement.

The Cuban drive for autonomy has taken place in three distinct international environments. The first was the post-Spanish independence era in which Cuba sought to develop an independent nation in the context of North American dominance. The pattern of Cuban independence was gradually emerging, but collapsed in the revolutionary regime of Fidel Castro. The second era was the drive for an international revolutionary role drawing on the Soviet alliance and economic dependency. The third era, which is just beginning, is the fate of revolutionary Cuba in an international system in which the Soviet power projection has collapsed, and the

Cubans seek to find a new way to maintain autonomy while developing a more accountable system of government.

Can Cuba emerge from its history of dependency and statism into a flowering of democratic sovereignty? This objective is not at all inevitable. One of the most interesting challenges for United States foreign policy in the next decade will be whether or not a transition in Cuba can be brought about while Castro lives (assuming he is not killed or dies prematurely), and whether or not it can be accomplished without bloodshed. Given Castro's history and attitudes towards the United States, for many analysts such a transition without U.S. intervention and without protracted internal strife seems to be a fantasy.

It is important to establish the basis of Castro's regime in Cuba, in order to explain both its indigenous and external support mechanisms. Cuba is, to recast a loaded term, "a semi-sovereign" state. It is dependent for its international security on the sufferance of other powers and political power does not derive from the consent of the people, but rather from a tiny elite. In this light, it is important to show how both internal and external factors combined to create the conditions for Castro to found his regime and sustain it for thirty years.

In addition, this study seeks to explore the prospects for such changes in Cuba as have occurred in other formerly Marxist-Leninist states, and for possible policies the U.S. might pursue for understanding and facilitating a Cuban democratic transition. We will explore the Soviet-Cuban relationship since Castro came to power, and in particular, the trends in that relationship during the Gorbachev era. Soviet perspectives on the changing international environment as a whole during the Gorbachev era will be examined, and we will see what implications that perspective has on the Cuban situation in the Americas.

Because of the Castro regime's dual centers of power, it is important to analyze the other factors which would lead to its overthrow. As its external support base becomes increasingly tenuous, it is important to investigate what kind of triggering crises might provoke a regime transition, and what kind of regime we might expect to emerge from the various transition possibilities.

The issues which confront Cuba are of vital importance, not only to her people, but in how they reflect the ongoing conflicts which plague the state system. As an adversary, Cuba exploited and amplified many problems within the United States and between the United States and Latin America. Now, as an increasingly impotent international derelict, Cuba provides a vivid case study for understanding the problems of a state system fundamentally antagonistic to the social ethics, economic practices, and political understandings of western, capitalist democracy.

Furthermore, as the international system changes with the breakup of the Soviet Union, the United States is faced with the task of examining its policies to former Soviet clients in the context of what relations it seeks in an area where the states have historically been sensitive to external U.S. dominance. Not only is Cuba's own development problematic, so are the relations which the United States and other actors in the international system will have with her. This study therefore intends to explore the conditions which have culminated in this period of transition, and indicate some of the enduring conditions in Cuba's internal politics and her relations to the international system.

ENDNOTES

1. This viewpoint at least has wide currency in the United States. A brief scan of the popular journalism reflects the growing sense of crisis in Cuba, despite the continued apparent strength of the Castro regime. Cf. Tad Szulc "Can Castro Last?" *The New York Review of Books* vol. 37, pp. 12-15. May 31, 1990; Charles Lane, "Low Fidelity" *The New Republic* vol. 204, p. 25. January 7-14, 1991; Lisa Beyer, "Fidel's Race Against Time" *Time* vol. 135 pp. 22-24. March 5, 1990.

PART I

UNDERSTANDING CUBA AND CASTRO

Many of the actors in the conflicts which have plagued Cuba in the twentieth century can date their inspiration to José Martí. Prior to José Martí and his generation, Cuba had existed as a loyal, albeit unruly, appendage of the Spanish empire. Since Martí's death and the end of the War of 1898, Cuba has struggled to be an independent, democratic nation. From this beginning there have been powerful forces opposing that drive for independence and democracy, none more powerful than Fidel Castro and the government which he has imposed on the Cuban people for the last thirty years. To paraphrase Rousseau, how did it happen that Cuba which was born with the desire to be free, was enslaved? How did it happen that Cuba's democratic institutions did not flourish, despite the wishes of the vast majority of the Cuban people?

On the one hand, there was a nationalist stream within the country whose defining characteristic was its opposition to foreign imperialism. On the other hand, the emerging democracy was saddled with a tradition of statism. This was a characteristic phenomena of Latin American development, but it proved an impediment to the emergence of a healthy democratic political culture.

Castro, as we shall see, capitalized on the anti-imperialist, pro-statist current in Cuban politics at the same time that he took advantage of the basic aspirations for democracy of the Cuban

7

people. This ideological mix would form the intellectual core of his domestic center of power. The Castro regime derived its domestic strength from a synergy between the nationalist tradition which Castro represents, the organizational capacity of his Marxism-Leninism, and his own powerful personality.

The result has been a government in conflict with its society and in conflict with history. The Castroite government is an extension and outcome of autocratic, materialist values which are inconsistent with the historic aspirations of Cuban society but nevertheless have their roots in Cuban political experience. Castro's government is the culmination of a historic anti-democratic political tradition carried along by the struggle for democracy and nationhood.

CHAPTER I

The Rise of Cuban Nationalism

What kind of civil society can the people of Cuba form, and how has the United States impacted on the development of that society? In order to begin to answer the first question we need to look at Cuba's political heritage. In order to answer the second we need to investigate her revolutionary tradition.

In many ways, Cuba's political tradition is inextricably bound up with her Hispanic heritage. What makes Cuba's civil society unique is that Cuban society represents a confluence of several different traditions. Cuba has a population of 10.5 million, and is largely made up of mestizo, Hispanic, and African stock. There was an indian population of over 100,000 inhabitants when Columbus came to the island in 1492. Over the next century that number dwindled dramatically, and Cuba was heavily hispanicized.

Over the next several centuries, Cuba was colonized through two distinct processes. One was the free immigration of Europeans and the other was the forced importation of African labor. The original Spanish settlers were very rarely accompanied by women. Throughout the sixteenth century, European women represented less than ten percent of the total Cuban population with the result that a significant mestizo population soon developed.[1]

While the ongoing racial changes occurring within Cuba would have profound consequences in the twentieth century, for the most part the political heritage of Cuba derived from a dual tension between competing traditions within her Hispanic roots, and the creole attempt to fashion a new distinctly Cuban political order in opposition to that Hispanic heritage.

Because of Cuba's status as a colony apart from the mainland, the question of governance and of relation to Spain was always of paramount importance. Was Cuba an integrated part of Spain or was she subordinate to Spain? In the first scenario she was entitled to equal representation in the Cortes and the same degree of self-governance as any province inside of Spain. In the second scenario, she was not considered as being equal to Spain, and therefore could be dictated to by royal emissaries sent from Madrid in order to impose the royal will on the colony.

The conquistador epoch was well-known for its combination of God and King. Dissent, whether religious heresy or political schism, was violently suppressed in the name of spiritual and political unity. Hispanic political culture was always more authoritarian than the English experience, but it was also surprisingly democratic. Not perhaps, in the sense that every individual had a right to vote, but every individual was regarded as a metaphysical entity with specific rights and duties entailed through the Spanish Catholic tradition.

Prior to the accession of the Bourbon dynasty to the throne of Spain after the Treaty of Utrecht in 1713, Spain had a very well-developed parliamentary tradition (far better than that of France), and a much more clearly defined sense of the limits of the power of the monarchy than the French did. Cuba, because of her sparse population and geographic isolation, was well on her way toward developing self-governing principles, although in keeping with the Spanish authoritarian and orthodox political tradition.

With the accession of the Bourbon monarchy in the eighteenth century, the development of Cuba entered into a new phase. The American colonies were founded and developed their independence in the context of a still-vigorous, still-rising British imperial system. Cuba on the other hand, began to develop her identity within the context of the decay of the Spanish empire. The driving forces of the Spanish imperial mission, religious unity under the Roman Catholic Church, and political unity under a "benevolent" absolute monarch, came under severe intellectual attack. These principles were challenged by forces within the Empire and opposed by states outside of the Empire.

The Bourbon monarchs did not understand their role within the polity. Instead of adapting to the changing geopolitical, religious, and socio-economic realities of the era, the Bourbons attempted to maintain their position through centralization of the command process and a reliance on a form of the intendant system which they had imported from France. The legendary mismanagement of finances and the lack of developed commercial classes, or even of a positive work ethic, meant that Spain was becoming increasingly marginalized in the race for economic development.[2]

At the same time, Spain's political class became increasingly corrupt and short sighted. The religious establishment as well had a very difficult time in adapting to the new intellectual challenges which the Enlightenment posed. The breakdown of the Spanish imperial model led to ideological fragmentation and the growth of political cleavages not only between every class and political grouping, but within each class and political grouping. Internal decay coupled with rising external threats in England and France meant that Spain also became increasingly marginalized in the international political arena.

In light of this crumbling imperium, the political dynamic within Cuba came to be shaped by three different inter-connecting cleavages: political affiliation, culture, and organization.

The first cleavage revolved around Cuba's sense of identity. Was she an independent state or was she a subordinate entity to a larger political configuration—originally Spain, but increasingly the United States? The upper and middle classes to a large extent, did not think of themselves as an independent unit, but saw themselves as an extension of a larger civilization, whether Spanish or "Western." There was sentiment in Cuba against self-government because of the lack of resources and because of a lack of trust in the indigenous political culture. On the other hand, the creole population began to see itself as increasingly disconnected from Spain. The creoles saw Spanish experience as increasingly alien to their own, and they did not see their political interests as necessarily coincidental with those of the Spanish throne.

The second cleavage revolved around the issue of Cuba's political culture. What role should religion play, if any, in government? What this meant in practice was what attitude should the Cuban government take toward its people, and with what attitude would they approach it. In this great fight were ranged free masons, Enlightened thinkers, and modernists on one side, and the Catholic church on the other.

The secularists wished to devalue Catholicism intellectually and politically. They saw it as the substantive base for the justification for the establishment of the monarchy, and as an impediment to their drive to establish a coherent civic culture. Not only was the church attacked because it was a support of the monarchy, but because it was an institution which preserved the possibility of sanctioned disloyalty to the state in the name of a higher metaphysical good.

The church in turn, was divided in its loyalties to the Spanish regime. Significant sectors of the clergy which saw their mission as rooted in the special conditions of the island, supported the Cuban independence movement. That part which was loyal to the Empire however, saw its mission as being one of integration, and attacked the secularists not only for their secularism, but for their moral and political values.

The lack of coherence of the anti-secular forces was readily apparent. An ideology of Cuban Catholic nationalism did not emerge as strongly as the increasingly dominant Martían secular nationalism. There was too much historical identification with the empire and too much decadence within the church for it to continue to maintain its level of participation in the Cuban political process.

The third great cleavage revolved around the structure of political organization. In the thirteen North American colonies, the deliberative assembly model developed very clearly, but the Cuban situation was far different. There were sporadic attempts at establishing a parliamentary system, and appeals for admission to the Spanish Cortes such as in 1813. However, the parliamentarian tradition was far weaker in Cuba than the authoritarian tradition, whether the "man on horseback" or the military governors sent over by the Spanish rulers.

What emerged by the end of the nineteenth century was an independent country which was secular and authoritarian in its orientation, but in which other political traditions still maintained powerful currents. Spain's decadence, the growth of the indigenous creole class, the inability of the Roman Catholic Church to articulate a persuasive counterattack to that of the secularists, and the rise of other powers with a direct interest in the freedom of Cuba, particularly the United States, all contributed to inherent tension in Cuban politics.

ENDNOTES

1. Louis A. Perez. *Cuba* (New York, 1988) p. 46. Perez goes on to write that due to the "relative absence of women from Europe, women of color played an increasingly prominent role in the island's development. Through the *repartimiento*, the *conquistadores* distributed among themselves Indian women (*naborías*) as personal servants and permanent concubines. The first generation creoles were largely the offspring of European men and Indian women...Miscegenation began with the conquest, and it never ended. Out of these relations emerged a portion of a new and significant population of free people of color." p. 47.

   These historic and ongoing practices make it problematic in determining the exact racial breakdown of the country. Carlos Moore's *Castro, the Blacks, and Africa* (Los Angeles, 1988) contains an excellent discussion of the problem of demographics in Cuba. There have been estimates that have placed the black population in Cuba as high as seventy percent historically. One breakdown that has received some currency is that Cuba is fifty percent mestizo, thirty percent white, and fifteen percent black. Whatever the figure, the general consensus is that Cuba has a majority population of mixed descent. Cf. Moore, pp. 357-365.

   One of the ongoing themes of the Castro regime has been its handling of racial politics. Nominally it claims to have abolished racism and it has made many international pro-Black African postures. This policy has simultaneously generated support among African communities abroad and placated the Afro-Cuban population domestically. But the Castro regime has effectively wiped out the black middle class and employed a system of racial tokenism to maintain the appearance of its toleration.

2.   Cf. Montesquieu's scathing portrait of eighteenth century Spanish mores in his *Lettres Persanes*. One of the great questions of development is not why countries develop capitalist systems, but why capitalism does not develop. The Weberian insight that ethical structures and social mores impact on the structure of economic development is nowhere more accurate than in the development of Hispanic-American economic structures.

CHAPTER II

The Legacy of José Martí

Cuban nationalism began as an effort to throw off Spanish colonial rule. The spiritual leader of this movement was José Martí. Ever since his martyrdom at the hands of the Spanish, he has come to be perceived as the foremost apostle of Cuban nationalism. After the overthrow of Spanish rule with the aid of the United States, Martí has continued to be invoked, even against his former allies. As a result, the most basic forces of the Cuban identity have been antagonistic at times, to the country which abetted the foundation of Cuba as an independent nation.

Following Spain's defeat, Cuban nationalism began to form around a growing anti-American theme, and not without some justice. The United States, which had fought on the side of Cuban independence against Spain, paradoxically lost its role as the defender of Cuban nationalism shortly thereafter.

The central ambiguity of the behavior of the United States lies, perhaps, at the root of the problem. On the one hand, the Teller Amendment of 1898 clearly showed the U.S. desire to help the Cubans procure their freedom.[1] Aid to Cuba was seen as a vindication of the Monroe Doctrine, not just because of the traditional U.S. opposition to European powers on the continent, but also because of the uniquely American linkage of freedom from colonial rule with democratic self-government. Cuban independence served both long-term American strategic foreign policy principles, and the regime philosophy which undergirded those principles.

On the other hand, the Platt Amendment of 1902 incarnated an entirely different current in U.S. attitudes toward Cuba.[2] As one astute observer put it, the United States "wanted an independent Cuba, but with strings attached."[3]   By the turn of the century, the U.S. had invested over fifty million dollars in Cuba, and by 1930 (the high point of U.S. investment in the island), that investment would grow to over a 1.5 billion dollars.

Not only were powerful business interests agitating for a greater U.S. presence, but there was also a strong paternalistic sense at that time, that Cuba did not have enough of a mature political culture to govern itself effectively without slipping into more bloodshed and conflict. Indeed, the second U.S. governor of Cuba, Leonard Wood, reported to William McKinley in a famous passage that

> People here, Mr. President know that they are not ready for self-government . . . We are going ahead as fast as we can, but we are dealing with a race that has steadily been going down for a hundred years and into which we have got to infuse new life, new principles and new methods of doing things. This is not the work of a day or of a year but of a longer period.[4]

This argument referred back to the perennial issue in Cuban politics concerning the extent the people could exercise effective self government. It also underlined the problem of the extent political elites and foreign powers might aid or hinder the development of a democratic political culture.

It was the common sense of many observers of the Cuban political scene, that the Spanish rule of the nineteenth century, creole political irresponsibility, and the long periods of violent opposition had led to a degeneration in the Cuban political culture. In this context, the Spanish Royal Order which reduced Cuba to submission to the arbitrary power of a Governor General sent from Spain had profound long-term effects. Short-sighted, and at times, despotic Spanish rule, led to creole political irresponsibility and disengagement from the process of self-government. The long periods of violent conflict within the society, especially during the ten years war of 1867-1877 leading up to the War of Independence, had the effect of polarizing the country and breaking down its social structures. The civil wars brought to the fore elements of the population which were not interested in democratic self-government, but which would, unless controlled in some measure by U.S. intervention, lead to continued and protracted civil war on the island.

Revisionist scholars would seize upon these attitudes with a critical effect. Such actions as the hoisting of the American flag over Santiago, the Guantánamo facility, and the Platt Amendment, were interpreted as showing that the United States had not helped free Cuba from Spain, but had rather imposed its own imperial agenda upon Cuba instead.[5] If Cuba was de jure free, she was de facto an American protectorate, and the energy which had been devoted to destroying the Spanish hold over the island was redirected in some measure against the United States.

The Platt Amendment not only provided a justification for periodic U.S. intervention in Cuban affairs, it also had a profoundly negative psychological impact on the island. Even though it was imposed by U.S. fiat, it still required two ballots in Cuba to be ratified. One delegate, General José Lacret, shouted, "Cuba is dead; we are enslaved forever."[6]

It is clear that important sectors within Cuban society profoundly disagreed about the course of its political destiny. The ruling classes were divided between loyalty to Spain, reliance on affiliation with the United States, and autonomous independence or autarchy. There was doubt at that early stage, if Cuba could form an independent state, but the actions of the United States paradoxically confirmed it in its independence, even as the United States seemed on the point of bringing Cuba under its imperial mantle.

The victory over the Spanish and the subsequent dismantling of the colonial apparatus eliminated the Spanish colonial option. At the same time, the ambiguous signals of the Teller-Platt Amendments effectively eliminated the practical political possibility of Cuba joining the United States.

The next thirty years have been characterized by some critics as the era of the Platt Amendment.[7] Though abrogated in 1934 by the U.S. Congress, the Platt Amendment created a national inferiority complex in Cuba. Political actors in Cuba developed a lack of a sense of political accountability to their domestic constituents. The shadow of the United States was such that political figures knew that so long as they circumscribed their behavior to conform to basic U.S. interests that they would remain in power, because those U.S. interests would work to sustain them.

While this framework works as a simple model, the realities of the situation were more complex. U.S. foreign policy was not synonymous with its economic interests only. The U.S. would not prop up a dictatorship like Gerardo Machado's, just because he supported U.S. sugar producing interests. During the 1933 revolution, Sumner Welles, the U.S. Ambassador to Cuba intervened, and proved to be the deciding factor in forcing Machado from office. But this anti-dictatorial action was not enough for the Cuban leftist nationalist movement. The fact that Welles threw his support behind the Conservative Party further fanned the flames of left-wing nationalist anti-Americanism.

The Importance of José Martí

It is from the Machado period, that many people date both the rise of the cult of José Martí and the leftist revolutionary tradition in Cuba. The principal figure of Cuba's independence movement from Spain, José Martí, was sought by the various nationalist currents in Cuba to undergird their agenda for the type of regime Cuba should have and the foreign policy Cuba should pursue.

The symbolism of his martyrdom made Martí the great patron of Cuban nationalism. Martí's death was in effect, a deliberate suicide; the example of weaker physical force conquering even in defeat, through higher, moral means.[8] Georgie Anne Geyer writes about Martí's last battle, noting that "he rushed into the middle of the Spaniards, on a white horse, and was not unexpectedly shot dead."[9] As C.A.M. Hennessy wrote, the cult of Martí during the 1930's and 1940's

> betrayed many of the characteristics of a sect mentality, providing a psychological compensation for a middle class lacking both power and faith in its own ability to change a society corrupted by United States' influence. It provided a flight into a world of fantasy where, in the

style of Rodo's *Ariel*, Cuban spirituality was contrasted with United States' materialism and greed.[10]

Martí's overall identification as the apostle of Cuban nationalism and independence made his appropriation of great importance for any nationalist leader. The complexity of his writings was therefore used to support a variety of positions, and his appropriation became a commonplace in Cuban polemical writing. He is undoubtedly, the major figure in the pantheon of heroes of all of the anti-imperialist movements of modern Cuba.

Despite the elements of anti-Americanism in Martí's thought and later expressions, there is much more admiration than criticism, and more affinity than distance in his appraisal of the Cuban relationship to the United States. However, it is also true that Martí's revolutionary posture had enough radical elements in it for an appropriation by Marxists to be made with some plausibility.

In corroborating this appropriation by the secular nationalist movements of the country, it can be said that Martí was influenced by the liberal and anti-scholastic political tradition in Cuba. There is some speculation about Martí's affiliation with masonry, which in Latin America has a long tradition of being associated with these groups.[11]

The main thrust of this intellectual current was to identify Martí with the liberal ideological orientation toward national consciousness. This consciousness is very much in the Jacobin tradition in which man is the center and interpreter of the universe. On this rationalist premise, the nation is seen as a self-developing, self-conscious construct of the human mind. Martí fueled the understanding that Cuba could be a tabula rasa; the country could have a new start once it threw off the yoke of Spanish colonialism.

The nationalist movements of Cuba were largely associated with the secular liberal tradition. There were divisions based on religion, but anti-clericalism did not develop in Cuba to the extent that it developed in other parts of the Latin world. Concomitantly, Catholic action groups did not develop beyond being loose associations in comparison to the explicitly Christian political parties which developed in other Latin countries. This is not to say that subterranean religious elements did not play a role in the development of Cuban nationalism. Santeria, the syncretist religion of a section of the Afro-Cuban community, may have played a role in anti-Catholic agitation,[12] but with the disestablishment of the Catholic Church at the turn of the century, religion was not one of the cleavages around which nationalists rallied.

Furthermore, all of the nationalist forces agreed on Martí's paramount significance for Cuba as an independent state. Where they diverged was on the type of regime Cuba ought to have, and on Martí's significance for Cuba's relations with the United States, Latin America, and beyond the hemisphere. Obviously, it was Castro's intention to appropriate Martí for his authoritarian regime, and link his myth to a predominantly anti-United States foreign policy.

It cannot be denied that Martí provides support for a radical anti-American nationalist foreign policy. One of the quotes the radical nationalists most like to use is Martí's hostile judgment of the United States which he wrote shortly before he died. He declared "I have lived inside the monster [the United States], and I know its entrails; my sling is David's."[13]

It was part of Castro's genius, that he was able to capitalize on this combustible, anti-Americanism and weld it into a permanent imagery and ideology that was one part José Martí, one part Marxism-Leninism. In this way, he was able to hijack Cuban nationalism, and attach it to an ideology that was at once internationalist and non-democratic. Far from freeing Cuba, he forged the instrument of her submission to a statist bureaucracy and single party dictatorship under his control.

Castro used this latent, potentially volatile anti-American sentiment to establish a David and Goliath relationship. Anti-Americanism in Castro's hands, became a tool for his continued legitimacy. It served to integrate the people against a perceived common enemy, and gave his government an external bogeyman to blame for the domestic failures of his regime.

Consequently, Cuban radical nationalism developed in such a way that it led to consistent anti-Americanism on the one hand, and to dependency on an extra-hemispheric power on the other. Martí's name has been invoked to justify a state of affairs to which he was diametrically opposed, namely, the subjugation of his country to an anti-democratic, internationalist, hegemonic state.

ENDNOTES

1. Article IV of the Teller Amendment stated that the United States "hereby disclaims any disposition or intention to exercise sovereignty, jurisdiction, or control over [Cuba] except for pacification thereof, and asserts its determination, when that is accomplished, to leave the government and control of the island to its people."

2. The Platt Amendment stated that: I. The government of Cuba shall never enter into any treaty with any foreign power which will impair or tend to impair the independence of Cuba nor permit any foreign power to obtain lodgment in or control over any portion of the island. II. The government shall not assume or contract any public debt for the ultimate discharge of which the ordinary revenues of the island shall be inadequate. III. The government consents that the United States may exercise the right to intervene for the preservation of Cuban independence, the maintenance of a government adequate for the protection of life, property and individual liberty, and for discharging the obligations with respect to Cuba imposed by the Treaty of Paris on the United States, now to be assumed and undertaken by the government of Cuba. IV. All acts of the United States in Cuba during its military occupancy are ratified and validated. V. The government will execute and, as far as necessary, extend the plans already devised or other plans to be mutually agreed upon for the sanitation of the cities of the island. VI. The Isle of Pines shall be omitted from the proposed constitutional boundaries of Cuba, the title thereto being left to future adjustment by treaty. VII. To enable the United States to maintain the independence of Cuba, and to protect the people

thereof, as well as for its own defense, the government of Cuba will sell or lease to the United States lands necessary for coaling or naval stations at certain specified points, to be agreed upon with the President of the United States.

3. Ramón Eduardo Ruiz, *The Making of a Revolution* (Amherst: University of Massachusetts Press, 1968), p. 24.

4. Wood to McKinley April 12, 1900; Leonard Wood Mss. Library of Congress.

5. One noted nationalist, Dr. Portell Vila wrote in this regard: "The frustration of the Cuban revolution—of its formidable effort and its awakened national consciousness striving to make a truly new state—was the work of the United States, dictated by those with an appetite for annexation. No nation has been so victimized without [developing] a deep resentment in its resistance to the aggressor, a resentment which permeates the organization of its society and its very life." Reprinted in *Background to Revolution* ed. by Robert Freeman Smith, p. 73.

6. Ruiz, p. 33.

7. Cf. Emilio Roig De Leuchsenring *Historia de la enmienda Platt* (La Habana: Instituto Cubano del Libro, 1973) and Louis A. Perez, Jr. *Cuba Under the Platt Amendment 1902-1934* (Pittsburgh: University of Pittsburgh Press, 1986).

8. Georgie Anne Geyer, *Guerrilla Prince: The Untold Story of Fidel Castro* (Boston: Little, Brown, & Company, 1991) p. 27.

9. Ibid.

10. *Background to Revolution* op. cit. p. 28.

11. McGaffey and Barnett *Twentieth Century Cuba* (New York, 1965) assert baldly that Martí was a mason and that this affiliation had a profound impact on the shaping of the secular

nature of the revolution. "Masonic doctrine asserted the existence of universal moral truths which were accessible to the individual intellect without the intervention of ecclesiastical tradition . . . In his writings Martí thus summarized the anticlerical doctrine: 'Christianity has died at the hands of Catholicism . . . There is no better religious rite than the free exercise of human reason.' Freemasonry also provided much of the symbolism of the nationalist movement, including the national republican flag designed in 1849." p. 239.

Also, it is probable that Martí was influenced by the leading intellectual currents of the time including Felix Varella y Morales (1787-1883), the anti-scholastic writer, and Enrique José Varona (1849-1933) the Cuban positivist. Rafael Maria Mendive (1821-1886) passed on directly to Martí the influences of these men and that of José de la Luz y Caballero (1800-1862).

12. The history of Santería's relations to the political developments in Cuba remains to be written, but the fact that the attack on the Moncada Barracks took place during the santería Carnival in Santiago de Cuba, and many of Castro's supporters in the Sierra were santeros, shows that the religion played a certain, if ambiguous role within the revolution. Georgie Ann Geyer writes that as Castro made his triumphal entry into Havana that "many of the guerrillas had, alongside the rosaries and religious medals, Santeria bead collars of various bright colors. Castro would also come to be called *El Caballo* or 'The Horse.' This animal was number one on the Cuban lottery, so it had importance in that sense, but it also had mysterious Santeria dimensions. The priest of Santeria is known as the 'horse' of the saints, and during the Santeria initiation, the saints are believed to take possession of their initiates by literally 'mounting' them." Geyer, op. cit. p. 205.

13. Pamela S. Falk, *Cuban Foreign Policy* (Lexington: D.C. Heath, 1986), p. 5.

CHAPTER III

Statism and Dependency

One of the chief sources of unrest which the nationalist, anti-American Cuban movement tapped into, was the perception of widespread poverty and oligarchic or foreign control of the economy. Cuban nationalists began to subscribe to theories of dependency, and to see their movement in terms of economic liberation and autonomous control of their own welfare. Capitalism came to be seen as an anti-Cuban form of economic organization, despite the fact that the economy was clearly in a early stage of capitalist development.

Dependency theory is essentially based on a Marxist-Leninist theory of international capital relationships. In an updated form, this theory was developed by the Economic Commission for Latin America (ECLA) under the leadership of the Argentine economist Raul Prebisch.   ECLA derived two schools of thought: developmentalism and dependency. The key ideas were that the terms of trade were unfavorable for the developing countries and that central planning and a regional common market could offset the developing countries unfair relationship with the developed countries.

The developmentalist school took this analysis to mean that rapid industrialization guided by a central planning system, could lead the developing countries to a more favorable relationship with the developed nations. The objective was to divert profits from the sales of primary products to the government and to native industrialists.   In addition, developmentalists looked to the international lending community for loans to such progressive governments.

The dependency school was critical of this developmentalist solution. One of the principal theorists of dependency, Fernando Enrique Cardoso, argued that the developmentalist solution was exploited by international corporations. These corporations responded to the protective tariffs set up by the so-called progressive governments by still underselling national industries. While other competition was blunted, foreign technical prowess and economies of scale prevented the development of a nationally owned industry which could compete in international markets.

Cardoso charged, in effect, that monopoly capitalism had been able to circumvent the developmentalist solution to imperialism. Instead, developmentalism had created a further dependency on the great corporations of the developed world. The implications of this analysis were that ever greater state control of the local economies—including the nationalization of foreign economic interests—was a positive development. In this tendency there was, therefore, a coincidence or rapprochement between leftist nationalist movements and Marxist-Leninists.

The meeting point for this synchronism between nationalism and communism, came from the common perception of underdevelopment and modernization. The nation was seen as peripheral, its government weak, and dependent on external centers of power which frustrated true modernization. This perception led to a revolutionary nationalist and Marxist fusion, as the nationalists came to interpret the struggle for development in Marxist terms.[1]

The problem with this analysis is that it identified the economic structures in Latin America as profoundly capitalist where the state's protecting of independent landowners, industrialists—and foreign monopolies above all—was seen as capitalism rather than statism.[2] In reality, the economic structures which developed in Cuba were only capitalist in embryo if they were capitalist at all in the sense of self-generating national capital markets deriving from autonomous enterprises. The core ideas of capitalism include the guarantee of private property, the development of an independent economic sector self-protected from encroachment by the predatory state, the freedom of the open market to allow prices to fluctuate to meet supply and demand, a civil society with national capital forming capabilities, and the articulation of government policies which prevent market inefficiencies like monopolies from occurring. According to this interpretation the economic structures which developed in Cuba prior to 1959 were misidentified. (The very fact the United States had passed the Platt Amendment underscored the U.S. recognition that imprudent government fiscal and budget policies were characteristic of statist policies.)

Rather than a separation of economic and political power, there existed side by side with genuinely capitalist endeavors, a form of economic state corruption. Central oligarchic economic interests used their influence to limit the development of open markets and meshed the power of the state with their own economic apparatus. Where democratic capitalism is profoundly anti-statist, there was a strong strand in the early capitalist structures existing in Cuba which were oligarchically pro-statist. Sweeping concessions to foreign investors infuriated the nationalists, but they were only one ramification of the economic mind-set which ruled the country. Even more ironically, the nationalists by adopting the intellectual apparatus of the Marxists inherited this statist approach to the economy, albeit in a disguised and adulterated manner.

Indigenous capitalist elements were allowed to exist to a sufficient degree that they were able to sustain the economy. Foreign companies were able to provide the bulk of the economic support that the statist regimes needed in order to survive. In this way, foreign ownership was another safety valve, preventing the establishment of a politically independent economic class and providing needed capital. (The same phenomenon in an ever more extreme form is occurring again, with Castro's tourism concessions being a prime example.)

This is not to say that capitalist structures did not exist. Economic figures prior to Castro show that Cuba was actually doing relatively well in a region where early capitalism was widespread and producing state transformations. Cuba ranked fifth in Latin America in terms of annual per capita income in the late 1950s, third in life expectancy, fourth in literacy, third in university students per capita, and fourth in doctors per capita.

Before the Castro revolution, Cuba could not be labelled an undeveloped country in the sense that Asian or African countries were. Cuba was ranked higher in its living conditions than many

East European states, and was showing signs of developing an industrial capacity. It had the highest capitalization rate per capita of any country in Latin America, and industrial production accounted for a larger percentage of the economy than sugar. Cuba produced for its own market 90 percent of its shoes, and had to import less than three percent of its textiles. At the time, the nation's population was predominantly white and mestizo, with a black and mulatto minority somewhere between twenty five and thirty percent of the population.

Unfortunately those who interpreted the distortions that existed in the economy blamed them almost exclusively on the degree that the Cuban state was dependent on American capital. The charge was that American capital had turned Cuba into a vast sugar plantation, and had prevented industrialization and balanced growth. Yet the realities were far different. At the start of 1930, the American share of the Cuban economy was much greater than it was in the 1950s. By 1958, 121 of the 161 sugar mills were owned by Cubans, and Cubans had large stakes in the other mills. The U.S. share of the six billion dollar investment in the industrial, commercial, and agricultural sectors was about fourteen percent of the total, and Cuban banks controlled the majority of Cuban finances. Clearly, Cuba was beginning to have the prerequisites of autonomous capital markets and self financing private enterprises.

Nonetheless, the Cuban regime was capable of insulating itself from direct popular wishes because a substantial part of the economy was still sustained by foreign—particularly American—interests. What continued to distort the activist anti-American minority view of the trends in the Cuban economy was the island's dependency on U.S. trade. In the eyes of many analysts of Cuba, the intertwining of Cuba's sugar monoculture economy with United States interests was seen as a distorting mechanism preventing the diversification of Cuba's economy.

On the other hand, sugar was the premiere crop in which Cuba enjoyed a comparative advantage. By trading on the international market, Cuba was beginning to enjoy an increasing standard of living brought about by international investment in the island economy. Cuba perhaps, was on the threshold of joining the global economic interdependent system as a substantially autonomous actor, rather than being subjected merely to the whims of the American market.

Dependency theorists however, noted the continuing imperfections of the early capitalist system. They saw the continuing existence of large scale foreign involvement as the defining tendency of capitalism, rather than seeing that a competitive environment would open the island economy increasingly to diversified economic development. The concessionary business arrangements between the Cuban government and the foreign business community were a constant sore spot. Anti-American anti-dependency critics did not realize that those arrangements were declining relatively to the nation's own developing enterprises. These arrangements provided employment, substituted for imports, provided revenues to the government and earned foreign exchange. Nonetheless, while the pre-Castro governments did not prohibit indigenous business rivalry to the statist political and economic nexus, the foreign business interests created an environment which encouraged the Cuban private sector to establish close links to the government, paradoxically contributing to a statist mentality in anti-American forces.

Despite this mixture of capitalism and foreign-assisted regime independence from the wishes of the local population, the Cuban economy did progress substantially. That the regime was not dominated by a democratic culture sustained by Cuban domestic private capitalists was true. Enhancement of the state's power further at the expense of the local Cuban entrepreneurs would only increase Cuba's foreign dependency and further erode its democratic culture. Paradoxically, Cuban nationalism was moving in the direction to scapegoat the foreign capitalist interests and not the state's expansion in the domestic economy, and therefore driving Cuba towards greater rather than lesser foreign dependency. The only difference was that this dependency shifted its structure from a declining reliance on foreign investment on the island to a growing reliance on state borrowing from external financial sources.

The ideological thrust that depicted Cuba as impoverished because of its relationship with American imperialists and a small private oligarchy, was inaccurate. If carried to its logical conclusions, it was an attitude which could contribute to arrest the country's emerging capitalist independence and its rising democratic capacity to take greater control over its own affairs.

Given this understanding, a reevaluation of dependency needs to be considered. According to traditional dependency theorists, the relationship is usually an economic one. Industrialized, capitalistic society is seen as exploiting an undeveloped country for its raw materials, cheap labor market, and lack of autochthonous markets. The United States is usually seen as the chief aggressor in these kinds of scenarios, and in Cuban oratory continues to play this role.

This perception of dependency based on the interests of the 'patron' state nevertheless serves as a distraction from the even more fundamental dependency generated by a reliance of the regime on statist policies. Not only did Cuba not become independent as a result of the termination of its relationship with the United States, but it created a whole set of justifications for its 'non-imperialist' dependence on the USSR for its economic livelihood.

In retrospect, it now seems that during the pre-Castro period, Cuba was actually in a capitalist take-off stage, with mixed elements of capitalism and pre-capitalism still predominating. Her dependence on the United States and her reliance on sugar and tobacco were clearly declining. Her manufacturing base was increasing as was the expansion of her international markets and investors. Cuba fit the general outlines of a pattern which W.W. Rostow has elucidated.[3] While in Cuba's case the principal economic conflict was between oligarchic capitalists and free market capitalists, it is apparent that Cuba was caught between trying to implement a social welfare state and satisfying expanding consumption needs which required a more pro-business consensus.

Rostow also noted that

> it is in such a setting of political and social confusion, before the take-off is achieved and consolidated politically and socially as well as economically, that the seizure of power by Communist conspiracy is easiest; and it is in such a setting that a centralized dictatorship may

supply an essential technical precondition for take-off and a sustained drive to maturity: an effective modern state organization.[4]

Castro's economics promised to create a welfare state and promote Cuba's external power and influence at the expense of the nascent capitalist movement in the country. This schism between statism and capitalism would have profound implications for the economic development of Cuba. Economic nationalists should have realized that dependency theory offered false choices. Statism and autarchy were not synonymous, just as dependency was not necessarily the outcome of continued international trade. In a sense, Castro's government would prove to be the culmination of the statist tradition in Cuba, and the consequences would prove to be disastrous for the Cuban people.

ENDNOTES

1. Not only were Cuban indigenous movements attracted to this understanding of Cuba's economic relationship, theorists have also noted the attraction the Soviet Union has for these types of nationalism. Anthony D. Smith writes for example: "The Soviet Union...is seen not simply as a source of development recipes, but as a model of military, political and social development; an engine for generating vast resources of will and energy through an efficient elite organization allied to popular commitment and resources that have made it in fact, and not just nominally, independent of any rival constellation." *Nationalism in the Twentieth Century* (New York, 1979) p. 130. Fidel Castro's ideology is frequently seen as the best example of this revolutionary nationalist and Marxist fusion.

2. Cf. Fidel Castro, "A Historic Analysis of the Cuban Revolution" in Ben Turok, *Revolutionary Thought in the Twentieth Century* (London; Zed Press, 1981) p. 137.

3. Rostow writes that a pre-capitalist situation is one "in which the society has acquired a considerable stock of social overhead capital and modern know-how, but is bedeviled not merely by the conflict between residual traditional elements and those who would modernize its structure, but bedeviled as well by conflicts among those who would move forward, but who cannot decide which of the three roads (pursuit of external power and influence, the creation of a welfare state, expansion of consumption levels) to take, and who lack the coherence and organization to move decisively forward in any sustained direction." W.W. Rostow, *The Stages of Economic Growth* (Cambridge, 1971) p. 163.

4. Ibid., This process may have taken place in the Soviet Union. Despite the expectations of the Castroite leadership the case of Cuba was far different. Instead of advancing, Cuba has suffered a severe economic retrenchment under Castro's governance.

CHAPTER IV

The Cult of the Caudillo and the Cuban Party System

The Cuban practice of making economic interests dependent on state patronage had profound political consequences, but it was only part of a larger Latin American trend toward the growth of the state at the expense of the society. In this regard, the caudillo system,[1] the corruption of the democratic process, and the pliancy and corruption of the political parties which characterized the pre-Castro era all contributed to the shift of the balance of power from its reserve in the political society to its actuality in the political institutions.

These phenomena derived from a profound lack of a sense of political equality within the society as a whole. In a healthy, working democracy, the actors who comprise the state understand their role as one of service to their electorate and constituencies. In a clear political understanding, representatives hold themselves accountable for their actions to the rest of the people. They do not feel as though they are above the law, but rather hold an understanding of the universality of the law. When a lack of a sense of accountability occurs, it is produced because the governors do not feel that they have to uphold any standards external to themselves. On the one hand, this phenomena may create a culture of greatness and a cult of great personalities. On the other hand, it leads to a lack of a sense of political responsibility, and a segregation of society into those who control the state and those who are controlled by the state.

This segregation goes even further than a distinction between rulers and ruled. In the U.S. understanding of capitalist democracy this same kind of distinction exists. Not every one is a member of the House of Representatives or a Captain of Industry, but no one within the ruling class of the system is able to keep the ruled from exerting political or economic rights. When functioning properly, this inherent dynamism has led to extraordinary turnovers of power within the system, and has not led to violent shocks outside of the system.

The Cuban system was, and is far different, with politics following a "boom and bust" cycle of entrenchment, graft, and extra-democratic forced ousters. The political parties were not the spontaneous and organic creations that their propaganda would indicate, but imposed political entities controlled by breakaway factions of the elite strata of the society. Because of their rhetoric and their affiliations, they gave the illusion of being mass-based. They were successful at coopting the lower classes to what were traditionally statist, quasi-socialist solutions for the country's problems. The Machadistas, the Batistianos, the Auténticos, and the Batistianos again, all employed this same cycle. One observer writes:

> Economic power did not produce political power. Rather political power created the opportunity for enrichment and offered the basis for the emergence of a new elite. The state thus served at once as a source and instrument of economic power. The principal configurations of the republic took form early: foreigners prevailed over production and property, Cubans preoccupied themselves with politics.[2]

Agusto Machado, for example, began his career as a people's candidate. Once in power however, he struck a deal with the United States and with the military to enable himself to stay in power. Freed from a sense of accountability to the people, his government became increasingly corrupt. Because of this corruption, it was forced to use ever harsher methods of repression in order to battle dissent. The twin evils of corruption and cruelty which came to characterize his regime would prove to be a recurring plague in Cuban politics.

At the same time, the Machado government popularized the practice (which the Batista government would also adopt) of trying to corrupt the population by buying off segments of it or enacting politically popular legislation which would undermine responsible, principled opposition to the regime. This action of coopting the lower classes by giving them privileges without giving them freedom would be a frequent tactic used by the authoritarian governments of the island.

Lack of political equality and regime legitimacy combined to produce a political culture of arbitrary rules, privilege, corruption, and patronage. The student system was a rule and a power unto itself. The business community operated under a different set of codes, the landowners under still yet another. In comparison to these private laws and private powers, the Cuban government differed in degree and not in kind. The difference was that it arrogated the control of ultimate wealth and force to itself. It destroyed or coopted whatever institutional challenges to its authority it could find, in the understanding that it was shielded from extreme consequences by the United States as a referee of last resort.

In this kind of climate institutional legitimation, in the sense of an establishment of a universally applicable and enforceable legal code, was not only not a reality, it ran counter to the entire political configuration of the country. Prior to the accession of Castro, Cuba witnessed an increasing fusion of statism at the top, and private law at the bottom. The result was that the political elites were completely removed from a sense of accountability to the people, and the people were increasingly frustrated by their inability to have responsible government. In this understanding, Fulgencio Batista plays a seminal role.

A light-skinned mulatto, who rose from his rank as sergeant in the army to dominate Cuban politics, Batista exacerbated the statist tendency without illuminating for the revolutionary thinkers in Cuba what was necessary for the further economic growth and autonomy of the nation. Batista came out of a revolutionary military tradition which emerged in the chaotic circumstances of the Great

Depression. In the circumstances of the highly conflictual environment in which uprisings abounded and revolutionary parties flourished, Batista began his authoritarian rule in December 1935. He hoped to initiate social reforms and attempted to depict himself as a democratic leader combatting the Partido Revolucionario Cubano Auténtico (the Auténticos for short), which also competed with him for revolutionary credentials.

To fight the Auténticos, Batista allied himself with Cuba's communist party and placed communist leaders in charge of Cuba's newly established trade unions. Ostensibly democratic, Batista was also seeking allies among the most committed statist revolutionaries on the island. He moved nonetheless, towards a liberalization of his regime, and permitted reasonably free elections for the National Assembly which drew up the 1940 Constitution.

That constitution combined liberal articles protecting freedom of the press and association with socialist articles calling for an inalienable right to work. (The state would have an obligation to provide it if the free market could not.) Property was declared to have a social function and mineral deposits were declared the inalienable property of the state. *Latifundias* were prohibited, and the state could expropriate property on the basis of paying adequate compensation. In this respect, the 1940 Constitution incorporated many of the features that had existed in the Mexican Constitution of 1917.

After Batista's term in office ended in 1944, the Auténticos came to power under their traditional leader Grau San Martín. The Auténtico administration of the 1944-48 era, introduced numerous social reforms, but was also remarkably corrupt. It was estimated that just one official of the Grau government embezzled about $174 million.[3] One observer put it this way:

> Embezzlement, graft, corruption, and malfeasance of public office permeated every branch of national, provincial, and municipal government. The public trust was transformed into a private till. Politics passed under the control of party thugs, and a new word entered the Cuban political lexicon: *gangsterismo.*[4]

This corruption substantially hurt the Auténtico party. While Carlos Prío Socarriás and the Auténticos still managed to win the 1948 elections, the actions of the Grau San Martín government significantly undermined his party and undermined the political system as a whole. Auténtico disaffection led to two developments: the growth of another party within the system, and a conviction among certain sectors that the entire system was bankrupt. If the most pro-democratic party in the country could succumb to the temptations of power, the whole system seemed to be structurally flawed. In this climate, the most important party became the Ortodoxos. Under the leadership of Eduardo Chibás, the Ortodoxos split with the Auténticos, in protest of the crooked practices of the Grau San Martín administration. Another ramification of this development was that the student movement became increasingly radicalized and antagonistic to democratic solutions.

Chibás was considered the most brilliant politician of his era and the best hope for democracy by many people within the country. He pioneered the use of radio to mobilize a mass audience, and stridently called for democratic reform. Unfortunately, Chibás grew disillusioned with trends that he saw within the country and committed suicide after a radio broadcast in August 1951 in a dramatic effort to arouse the people against the country's sorry economic and political conditions. Following in the footsteps of Martí, the dramatic martyr-like act stimulated immensely the popularity and attractiveness of the political leader and his party.[5]

In these confused and conflicting political circumstances, Batista launched a coup in March 1952. He proceeded to move once again to mount a socially responsive dictatorship. On the basis of the public opinion polls taken prior to Batista's coup, probably better than sixty percent supported either the Auténticos or the Ortodoxos. Batista failed to recognize that despite the democratic parties disarray, the Cuban people still supported democracy.

Again, the U.S. played a divisive role in Cuban politics. In this context, it was argued among the Cuban activists that the United States by recognizing Batista, not only was not concerned about Cuban democracy, but pursued a foreign policy which was inimical to the interests of a majority of the Cuban people. Nationalists perceived this government as serving U.S. interests, and they argued that U.S. influence was the principal cause of the nation's lack of autonomy. At the same time, Batista's government, in an attempt to win popular support continued to implement social measures. Nevertheless, it was viewed increasingly, not only as a U.S. puppet, but as corrupt in its own right.

Despite the death of Chibás, the Ortodoxos continued to gain in popularity. They were seen to be the only party not tainted by corruption. The socio-economic agenda of the Ortodoxos was relatively similar to that of the Auténticos and even of the Batista government. The cleavages which did appear were based on the attitudes toward the United States, and the greater or lesser extent to which the state should be authentically democratic and economically nationalist.

The opposition to Batista therefore, was primarily an effort to reestablish democratic processes which had been brought to a halt by the Batista dictatorship. Castro's 26 of July Movement was only one of a number of opposition groups to Batista. The vast majority of the population sought a return to an uncorrupted democratic government. What hurt Batista was his repression of the democratic movement, far more than the structure of the economy.

There were a variety of militant groups besides the 26 of July Movement. These opposition groups were wide-ranging in their ideological orientations, but none of them were openly communist or communist-sympathizing. The official communist party for most of this period, was openly opposed to Castro's insurgency, and the elements who were communist kept a relatively low profile within the 26 of July Movement. Several senior communist party leaders cooperated with Batista. Indeed, several of their senior leaders entered Batista's party and collaborated with him. The party was able to publish its journals, and on the whole criticized Castro not for his motives or goals, but for his tactics as playing into the hands of Cuban anti-communists.

Castro's accession to power was a fundamental departure from Batista's (and Machado's) example because he eliminated the climate of anarchical order that allowed diverse power centers to flourish, but in other ways, his accession represented the apotheosis of a disguised combination of the worst elements of this tradition.

If we accept Virgilio Tosta's definition that caudillismo is "the union of personalism and violence for the conquest of power,"[6] then Castro is a caudillo. His unstable hierarchical network, his inner core formed by personal alliances, and his mass appeal all fit the pattern of caudillismo. Just as the caudillos of the past had sought to achieve political unanimity, Castro has as well, but he has gone far beyond that to demand social uniformity subservient to him.

In the name of political equality, Castro institutionalized profound inequality. The first part of this process emerged in the purge of all those elements of Cuban society who disagreed with his regime in any way, shape, or form. The second part followed when all political dissent was eliminated, and comprised the distinction between the Cuban *nomenklatura* and the rest of the population.

Furthermore, Castro achieved the complete subversion of the rule of law, and converted the government into the only source of power on the island. Just as the first measure that the ancient Chinese dynasties traditionally implemented upon ascending to power was to eliminate the conditions for conspiracies, so Castro eliminated the conditions which allowed him to gain power. He abolished the freedom of the university, he established new controls in the prisons, and he purged the government of rival centers of power. The will of the party (controlled by Castro's will) became law, with no objective counterbalance to it, not even externally from its patron, the Soviet Union, because the USSR was organized on the same governing principles.

Castro was therefore rooted in the caudillo system, but he was also in dialectical relationship to it, just as the PSP was in the same relation to its governing party predecessors. With the people supine and repressed, there was no check to his power, no accountability, and no opposition. It was as though the Cuban system swung progressively back and forth, until the political elements collapsed in the law of extremes. Absolute power produced absolute inequality and absolute lawlessness.

Castro's lack of recognition of any political limits, his materialistic outlook on life, and his engagement with the people all mark his difference from the caudillo tradition. The caudillos had a sense of their own finitude, and the understanding that if they were above the political laws, they were not above the fundamental laws of their society. Machado subverted his second-term elections, but he did not abrogate them. Batista waged coup upon coup, but he still tried to return to the democratic process, and even devolved power in the 1944 elections. Castro did not want to change just the *Cuba legal*, but the *Cuba real* as well.

Furthermore, despite their violent excesses, the Cuban big men were not as ruthless. Batista had several chances to eliminate Castro, but he refused, saying, "I don't want to be accused of the assassination of Fidel Castro."[7] They committed execrable acts, but they did not do them with the same feeling of justification nor even of righteousness that Castro was able to bring to bear, on the basis of his materialistic ethic which had assumed mystic dimensions.

Furthermore, Castro stepped outside of the Big Man tradition, because he escalated the level of violence and engagement. He did not want a simple coup, because he did not want a simple transition of elites. Prior political transfers had created some elite transfers, but had not disturbed the social structure of the country. With Castro, elite transfer became an either/or proposition. In essence, he destroyed the structures which had created the social bases for the prior elites (and which had produced him). In their stead, the revolution established new elites, premised on the new political order and centered ostensibly on the masses, but in reality, ordered from the top down. Castro's challenge was not to the other members within the elite structure, but to the entire elite structure as it was then constituted. In other words, Castro's ascent to power marked a culmination of Cuban political tendencies toward personalism and party corruption, but his exercise of power has fundamentally altered that historic political culture.

ENDNOTES

1. The caudillo system as used in this book is seen as an expansion of the "man on horseback" nineteenth century tradition. In this understanding, it is used to describe the strong man governments based on the veiled (or not so veiled) use of force of Machado and Batista particularly. A case could be made that Grau San Martín, with his giant system of patronage and same lack of regard for the substance of the constitutional system, could be seen as a variant of this system. Prio Socarrias is the most democratic leader that Cuba has had in the last seventy years.

2. Louis A. Perez, *Cuba Between Reform and Revolution* (New York: Oxford University Press, 1988).

3. Boris Goldenberg, *The Cuban Revolution and Latin America* (New York: F. A. Praeger, 1965) p. 110.

4. Perez, *op. cit.* p. 284.

5. It should be noted that Castro joined the Ortodoxo movement. He saw it as the most progressive of the labor parties and the principal movement for the political renovation of Cuba, and he conceived of the 26th of July Movement as the vanguard of the Ortodoxos.

6. Quoted in Robert L. Gilmore *Caudillism and Militarism in Venezuela* (Ohio, 1964), p. 47.

7. Geyer, p. 162.

CHAPTER V

The Cuban Left

One of the most sterile controversies is over whether or not Castro was a communist before he came to power on January 1, 1959. On the one side, it is argued that he was always a crypto-Marxist. The other point of view is that he had eclectic intellectual tendencies and personal ambition. These tendencies drove him to opportunistically embrace communist ideology and Soviet power in order to enhance his position as a lifetime dictator of the island. What these arguments obscure, is that the communist ideology is but one strand of a generic revolutionary tradition supported by a materialistic, naturalistic, and elitist ethic which had come to Cuba even before Martí's generation came to the intellectual forefront. This ethic has been prevalent in the West since the French Revolution. Indeed, we might refer to Castro's ideology as an intellectual descendent of French Jacobinism.

Many observers of Cuba, and indeed of the entire political environment, have been unable to recognize that the naturalistic and materialistic revolutionary ideology has many different forms. All of these forms are essentially useful to an elitist intelligentsia which has sought to insert itself in developing and developed states as a self-selecting and self-perpetuating arbiter of cultural, political, and economic norms.

This phenomena helps explain why a Castro would be well-received by an elitist intelligentsia in the United States, Latin America and Western Europe. The French existentialist, Jean-Paul Sartre's embrace amply illustrates this tendency, as does the Colombian novelist, Gabriel Garcia Marquez's unconditional support. Modern intellectual Jacobinism presents a critical face toward democratic practices. It can be perceived as justifying a philosopher-authoritarianism such as Castro's over his unenlightened people.

This Jacobinism is a secular gnosticism which transcends Marxism-Leninism, and lends itself to a much larger revolutionary ethic, even as it provides a mechanism for elite control. It should be understood as a theory of the salvation of a people on this earth in historic time by the knowledge and understanding of a superior, educated elite. Clearly, Lenin in his *What Is To Be Done?* was a particularly extreme example of this type of justification of a self-appointed, self-perpetuating elite with a mission of resolving the problems of the working class. He wrote in this regard,

> *There could not have been* Social-Democratic consciousness among the workers. It would have to be brought to them from without. The history of all countries shows that the working class, exclusively by its own effort, is able to develop only trade union consciousness...The theory of socialism, however, grew out of the philosophic, historical, and economic theories elaborated by educated representatives of the propertied classes, by intellectuals.[1]

But this ideology has been prevalent in the more extreme nationalistic movements with their ideological proponents throughout the twentieth century. There are of course, other internationalist gnostic movements and leaders, but the gnostic movement need not be cosmopolitan by any means. In many respects, Castro's takeover had many qualities of romantic nationalism, rather than of deterministic Marxist-Leninism.

It would only be an intelligentsia and a leadership class that was highly sensitive to the over-all gnostic threat to accountable government that would warn against such a leader. To the degree those who make such warnings have to label the proponent of such an ideology a communist, they place themselves at an enormous disadvantage because the communist label may be refuted on technical grounds. "Gnosticism" however, encompasses a far larger number of elitist dictatorial types.

Cuba lacked such a leadership class because of the definitions established at the outset of her independence. Anti-clericalism precluded widespread awareness of the deleterious effects of overweening materialism. Her statism and large underclass created a socio-economic structure in which there was extensive dependency and a reliance on political solutions to what were in reality, civic problems. Thirdly, the presence of the United States was too strongly felt for all of the wrong reasons. The preponderance of the United States divided the sense of accountability that the political leaders felt as to who was their real constituency, and it radicalized the opposition to the government at the same time that it created antagonism to the values of the United States.

Once it is understood that the revolutionary, materialistic, elitist will seek any allies to oppose the democratic principles of a constitutional order, a fertile ground is prepared for megalomaniacal figures like Castro. It should have been recognized that this kind of threat represented a fundamental threat to Cuban society and to democratic values, despite the lack of an explicit communist ideology or alliance with a specific external enemy of the United States. However, such elitist revolutionaries have allies within the American political culture and system as well as with Western Europe because western intellectuals are at war with themselves. All of the developed and underdeveloped countries have substantial sectors of their intelligentsia permeated with messianic, materialistic and utopian ideas. In this light, Marxism-Leninism is only one current within a broad stream of revolutionary, anti-democratic sensibility, and it should not come as a surprise that these movements would be able to work in tandem together. The trend of having distinct Jacobin gnostic movements working simultaneously is repeated in Cuba from the very beginning of its struggle for independence.

Origins of the Twentieth Century Cuban Left

Because of the labor sympathies of Martí, and his sympathetic obituary of Karl Marx, he has sometimes been considered a marxist in everything but name. While this assertion would be stretching the truth beyond recognition, it is true that some of his colleagues within the independence movement were marxists, and worked to establish socialism in Cuba.

The Partido Socialista Cubano, the first socialist party in Cuba, existed briefly in Havana during 1899. It subsequently reemerged as the Partido Obrero Socialista de Cuba in 1904, but that was also a failed experiment. One of its leaders, Carlos Baliño, would work his entire life, both in Cuba and in the Key West exile community to establish a socialist party in Cuba, and he finally succeeded in 1925, with the help of Julio Antonio Mella (a charismatic student leader at the National University and the Party's first Secretary General) to found the Cuban Communist Party.

This movement was mirrored by the evolution of the labor unions. Organized at first under anarcho-syndicalist ideological guidelines, the communists worked to take over the Federation of Cuban Workers which was created in 1911 by Machado, then serving as Minister of the Interior, to control the labor movement. The Trotskyites took it over, and the orthodox communists established the National Confederation of Cuban Labor (CNOC).

The genesis of the FTC by Machado was an augur of things to come. Machado and then Batista, both sought to coopt the communist movements rather than oppose them directly. As a result, the communists occupied an ambiguous position in that they were formally anti-system, and yet they were pliantly pro-system in practice.

Batista made this practice of cooptation an art-form. Under him, the communists consolidated their leadership of the labor movement, (they controlled the amalgamated union system [CTC]), they sent six delegates to the 1940 Constitutional Convention, polled almost ten percent of the population during the 1940s, and several prominent communist leaders occupied cabinet posts in both the first and second dictatorships.

Growth within the system had a profound impact on how the Cuban Communist Party viewed the system. In a sense, the party became part of the system, and one of the reasons that it initially had an ambivalent attitude towards Castro is that it had a stake in the Batista regime.

This relationship between Batista and the party may seem odd at first, but they shared anti-democratic postures, and elitist, paternalistic views of the masses. Batista, like many historic Cuban political personages, did not seem to have much of a fixed political ideology beyond the acquisition of power and its maintenance. He used the military as an institutional support base for his drive for power, but he also wanted to broaden his support base throughout the country. For this reason, his socio-economic policies subverted the democratic aspirations of the people. Instead of fostering a climate of political independence and creating free market conditions, Batista acquiesced to selected communist demands which led to nominal increases in social benefits for the poor, and empowered elements of the communist leadership. At the same time he maintained enough of a foreign business sector to ensure foreign exchange and finance his domestic policies. Batista respected the ability of the communists to control the labor movements. The communists in turn, recognized that they could accomplish much of their agenda—short of gaining political power themselves—through him.

The communist party had its roots in the independence movement and the tobacco and sugar industries, and its major support come from the labor movement and Afro-Cubans. In contrast, the 26 of July Movement had its roots in the ferment of the student movements. The Cuban student movement developed on the basis of the Latin concept of the University as sanctuary. Castro was a known agitator as early as the Bogotazo of 1948, but he did not emerge as a possible left wing political savior until the Sierra Maestra period of 1957-58.

It is from this period that Castro developed his core and peripheral supporters.[2] The core was the small group with him in the Sierra, and the various scattered groups of rural guerrillas, mostly peasants with a considerable proportion of them mulattoes or blacks who he considered his most reliable followers. The second group often denoted as 'the Plains', in contrast to 'the Sierra', was the urban guerrilla groups formed mostly of white students and professionals of the Cuban middle class.

This latter group did most of the actual fighting against Batista, and Castro has never considered them to be as loyal as his less educated following from the Sierra. Most of the official Communist Party was connected with this urban group, and it never had as much influence as the Sierra Group of the 26 of July Movement.

Castro saw the PSP as a vehicle to implement his agenda of consolidating power. He wanted to coopt it, just as Batista had done, not have it coopt his movement. What brought the two groups into alignment was Castro's drive to sustain his power, his anti-Americanism, and his pragmatic adaptation of Marxist-Leninist rhetoric to his own revolutionary language.

Part of the problem in discerning Castro's motives involves the varied nature of the deception of his guerrilla campaign. The guerrilla campaign was waged on multiple fronts. Overtly, it was a resort to violence in opposition to the dictatorship of Batista. Its subtle sub-text was its intention to coopt the Cuban people and the various institutions of the civil society. In this regard, the Moncada Attack Manifesto and the "History Will Absolve Me" pamphlet (Castro's reworking of his trial defense speech), were both geared for external mass consumption. They were not internal programs. The Moncada Attack Manifesto explicitly stated that Castro's revolution was "not a revolution of castes," and proclaimed an "absolute and reverent respect for the Constitution given to the people in 1940."

Carlos Franqui and Haydee Santamaria, two of Castro's supporters, drew up the *Tesis Programática* as another document clarifying the movement's ideology. Franqui later asserted that "the Tesis was never discussed by [Castro] for the simple reason that Fidel was against an ideological definition of the Movement. He felt that an ideological definition would obstruct the participation of the greatest possible number of people in the struggle. He also felt—and rightly so—that the less one said, the less that was outlined ideologically, the greater the audience of our Movement."[3]

Castro also stated in a famous quote in *Revolución* (the magazine that Franqui edited during the 1960s) that all of his pre-revolutionary writings were tailored to create as wide a mass base for his positions as possible. "If we had not written this document [the Manifesto of the Sierra Maestra] with care, if it had been a more radical program . . . the revolutionary movement against Batista would not, of course, have gained the breadth that it obtained and made possible the victory."[4]

Theodore Draper notes that the most striking quality of Castro's statements between 1956-1958 is their "increasing moderation" and "constitutionalism."[5] Inside the July 26 cadres however, there was another story. Che Guevara, and the Sierra group were, by and large, committed Marxists in contrast to many of the fighters in the "plains." A bitter internecine struggle soon developed which led to the purge of non-Marxist elements from Castro's command structure.

Castro came to power ably using the non-Marxist label. He was apparently committed to the traditional Auténtico/Ortodoxo platform of social welfare and democratic constitutionalism, yet he had a rigidly disciplined marxist core of support that was not affiliated with the PSP. Castro was therefore ideally positioned to take advantage of what the political climate offered. Indeed, Huber Matos argued that Castro at this point could have created a democratic republic if he had so chosen. Matos said, "I don't think that Fidel was a Communist philosophically. I believe he saw two alternatives—he could bring about a democratic or a Communist revolution. He opted for the latter because it offered him the opportunity of becoming the undisputed ruler of the country for the rest of his life."[6]

In this regard, Castro was the Trojan horse by which Marxism-Leninism was introduced to Cuba. Eloquent evidence of this Castro-Communist relationship is in Armando Valladares' account of his imprisonment. Valladares wrote that the reason for his imprisonment was his refusal to endorse the slogan "If Fidel is a Communist, then put me on the list. *He's* got the right idea."[7] In this regard, the ideological ascension of communism was built around Castro's cult of personality, not around doctrine. As another critic put it, Castro's axiom "'la jefatura es básica' ('leadership is basic') was far more closely related to 'leadership-principle' movements such as fascism or Peronism than to an ideology-and-party-conscious movement such as Communism."[8]

As can be seen, the Cuban left had two bases of support. The intellectual leftist elite looked to the labor movement, especially the tobacco industry, for its manpower, and to the universities for its leadership cadres. It was never cohesive in its development, and as an intellectual movement was coopted by the political aspirations of the July 26 movement away from orthodox Marxism-Leninism. Yet, the general intellectual current lent itself to precisely this kind of seizure of power. It very quickly embraced the revolution, despite its lack of conformity to an orthodox Marxist-Leninist line.

ENDNOTES

1. Vladimir Lenin, *The Lenin Anthology*, Robert C. Tucker, editor. (New York, 1975) p. 24. Italics in the original.

2. Carlos Alberto Montaner, *Fidel Castro and the Cuban Revolution: Age, Position, Character, Destiny, Personality, and Ambition* (New Brunswick: Transactions Books, 1989) pp. 15-17. Montaner provides the best description of the circles of supporters around Castro and their degrees of loyalty to him.

3. Moore, op. cit., p. 8.

4. *Revolución* Dec. 2, 1960.

5. Theodore Draper, *Castroism Theory and Practice* (New York, 1965) p. 15.

6. Geyer, op. cit., p. 8.

7. Armando Valladares, *Against All Hope* (New York, 1987) p. 5.

8. Draper, op. cit., p. 9.

CHAPTER VI

Understanding Castro

Within academia and history in particular, it is argued that the 'Great Figures' approach to politics fails to take into account larger structural economic, political, and social factors in accounting for political developments. Some social scientists would like to argue that one factor or another prove to be the proximate cause for historical development. In this way, Marxists would like to argue that the economic conditions in Cuba led to the inevitable overthrow of the Batista government, and the accession of Fidel Castro to power. In this analysis, the description of the historical event creates an aura of legitimacy and predestination for the political developments which occurred. The contingent possibilities which might have emerged as the realities confronting Cuba are more easily ignored in this manner. While such 'inevitablist' schools of thought create convenient academic categories, they end up being reductionist and exclusionary of events which do not fit within their intellectual models.

This study originates from a different philosophical understanding. History is a dynamic synergy between political actors operating on a personal level, and social forces acting through them. The political actors may be conditioned by the social forces around them, but are not determined by them. Fidel Castro was not only a member of the 'vanguard of the proletariat,' but an independent political actor shaping events as much as he was shaped by them.

As we have alluded to before, there was a great heritage of Cuban charismatic leaders shaping the will of the people, and incarnating great movements which led to their subsequent mythic status. José Martí was the prototype of this phenomena. J. A. Mella, the student leader who co-founded the Cuban Communist Party with Carlos Baliño, had the "face and figure of a young god and a magnetic flight of oratory," and could have been the first incarnation of Fidel Castro. Eddie Chibás, the Ortodoxo leader, even followed this pattern when he committed suicide after his dramatic radio address.

In this light, we would argue that Cuban communism owes its idiosyncracies, not only to the macro-political conditions confronting the island people, but also to the micro-political maneuverings of its leading political actors. In other words, we cannot understand the evolution of the Cuban state, nor its current dilemmas if we do not understand Fidel Castro.

A Brief Biographical Sketch

Fidel Castro was born August 13, 1926 on a small ranch from the illegitimate union of the landowner, his father, and the household cook, his mother. Fidel's father, Angel Castro, was born in Galicia, Spain. The elder Castro first came to Cuba as part of the Spanish army which sought to crush the Cuban independence movement. After the war, he returned to the island and moved to the province of Oriente. He soon rose to have substantial holdings through a combination of ruthlessness and a shrewd business sense.

Angel's first wife bore him two children, but apparently she left him because of his liaison with the young cook, Lina Ruz. Lina Ruz came from the western part of Cuba, probably when she was about fourteen years of age. She bore six children, of whom Fidel was the oldest.

When it came time to educate Fidel beyond the provincial elementary schools, he was sent to a secondary school run by the Jesuits in a suburb of Havana. This high school of Bethlehem, (Colegio de Belén) brought Fidel into contact with youths from the urban upper classes. Belén seems to have sparked both his resentment of his irregular origins, and his fierce competitiveness. The priests who taught him were particularly struck by his drive to compete, dominate, and excel.

Castro was subsequently packed off to attend Havana University in 1947 at the age of 17. At the university, Castro joined the Unión Insurreccional Revolucionaria. In this violent militant group, acquaintances pointed out Castro's attraction for extremists of both the right and the left, especially among the left. There he formed a close friendship with Alfredo Guevara, the young communist leader of the Juventud Socialista.

The Juventud Socialista was the youth organization of the Communist Party, set up to maintain a following among Cuban youth because the official party had cooperated with Batista in exchange for two cabinet posts. The parallel unofficial party was the Partido Unión Revolucionario or PUR. The PUR was designed to absorb that part of the youth in the Juventud Socialista which opposed cooperation by the official party with Batista.

While at the University of Havana, Fidel was joined by his younger brother Raúl, who also became close to Alfredo Guevara. Raúl became well known as a communist and visited Prague in 1953, where his connections with East Bloc intelligence were solidified. Fidel Castro joined the Ortodoxos led by Eduardo Chibás.

Castro nurtured himself in the revolutionary student tradition. He imbibed its conspiratorial views, and obscured the question of his true agenda by at least nominally endorsing the democratic institutions and social reforms espoused by the Ortodoxo party. Nevertheless, it seems clear that Castro had joined the pro-communist wing of the Ortodoxos, and was part of its militant section. He was involved in the aborted invasion of Santo Domingo and later participated in the riots in Bogotá in April 1948, where his affiliation with extreme left-wing militants came to the attention of the FBI. In 1951, Castro was present at the funeral of Eddy Chibás, where he apparently tried to instigate a democratic coup at that time. Subsequently, he ran for election in the lower house of the legislature on the Ortodoxo ticket.

Even though Castro may not have specifically read Lenin, his mode of operation was very similar. He created public uncertainty with regards to his true agenda. At the same time he exploited the grievances of all strata of society and attempted to be in the vanguard of those appearing to redress those grievances. He used the mass media to propagate his views, and maintained a secret core of revolutionaries who manipulated all of the various fronts.

Castro's constitutionalist initiatives ended with the Batista coup. Reverting back to a more revolutionary approach, Castro organized a militant, clandestine cadre to implement his plans. These operations bore fruition in the most famous event in July 1953, when Castro initiated a raid on the Moncada Barracks in Santiago de Cuba, the capital of Fidel's native Oriente province. The attack on the barracks was a grotesque failure—Castro himself noted that it was a massacre. Like Hitler however, whom Castro had studied very closely, and whose Beer Hall putsch the action imitated, Castro was able to turn the military defeat into a propaganda victory. His "History Will Absolve Me" speech at his trial defense even plagiarized some of Hitler's speech before the Munich tribunal in 1923.

The action highlighted two recurring patterns in Castro's modus operandi: the Martiano symbolism of deriving long-term glory out of disastrous defeat, and Castro's affinity for extremist solutions of any sort. The day of the attack became the date Castro would use to identify his movement throughout his career: July 26, 1953.

From the beginning, Castro was protected by interests both at home and abroad. After the raid on the Moncada Barracks, Fidel ended up in jail, but was subsequently pardoned by Batista. He then went to Mexico, where he reconstituted his guerrilla movement and began to expand his sphere of contacts throughout the western hemisphere. In Mexico he stayed at a farm called the Santa Rosa. The farm was rented through contacts with the pro-Communist Mexican labor leader Lombardo Toledano and the Spanish communist Alberto Bayo.

Mexican security police raided the ranch on June 22, 1956 and found considerable communist literature, including the guerrilla warfare manual that the Soviet Alexei Fyodorov had prepared. Among those apprehended at the raid were the Castro brothers, Ernesto "Che" Guevara—the Argentine guerrilla leader, not to be confused with Alfredo Guevara—Alberto Bayo, and Ramiro Valdés, who was later to be head of Castro's G-2.[1]

After the raid, Castro was released almost immediately. Gutierrez Barrios, the Mexican police officer, helped Castro flee from Mexico in 1956 on the yacht *Granma* from the Port of Tuxpan. He landed with the loss of many of his companions, but with the remnant he made his way to the Sierra Maestra.

In the mountains, Castro was ill-prepared to take on the Batista government. He suffered from a poor supply base and an indifferent population support base. The interview with Herbert Matthews was of critical importance. Castro was able to convey the impression of the existence of a far larger army than he in fact had. Herbert Matthews was also critically important to Castro's image. In the three articles he published in February 1957 for the *New York Times*, Castro emerged as a self-effacing democrat, committed to constitutional democracy and economic and social reform.

Castro's rise to power was violent, undemocratic, and yet popular. He appealed to mass issues, especially through Cuban nationalism and his own brand of Marxism-Leninism. Throughout his struggle he was abetted by interests both at home and abroad in Mexico, and he was helped in the United States by the favorable impressions created by the articles of Herbert Matthews. With the fall of Batista, Castro came to power on a wave of popular domestic and international acclaim, despite the fact that neither his orientation, politics, nor core support groups were well understood at all.

Understanding Castro

From this brief sketch of Castro's life prior to his access to power, it is obvious that violence played a fundamental role in his personal development and his conception of politics. Whether because of or in combination with the martial inheritance of his father, and the illegitimacy of his birth Castro's attitude toward Cuba was ambivalent and antagonistic. Temperamentally he was far more of an outsider and hater than an establishmentarian and coopter. He felt driven by an intense desire to remake Cuba, unchecked by any sense of his own fallibility.

Castro developed into a violent leader, a charismatic leader, an autocrat. He was installed in power, never elected, nor is his temperament suited for compromise. Like many other Latin caudillos, Castro has never learned how to be conciliatory or how to compromise. Unlike many of these other autocrats however, Castro found an ideology which could legitimate his personalistic rule. He could assume a progressive mantle, even as he harshly reordered Cuba to his tastes. In this way he has been able to treat an entire country as his father had his latifundia and the Cuban people, as a patron does his peons.

At one level, some beliefs must be understood to be inaccessible to rational argument or the blandishments of good will. When one looks at the core of Castro, what one sees is a deep social resentment and a fundamental schizophrenia with respect to belonging to Cuba that has been translated into an ideological justification for combatting every symbol of authority, social and economic prestige, and conventional acceptability.

Castro has had to find a means to justify his overweening drive for power. He needed an ideological justification which could permit him to strike out and bring down those whom he felt conceived of themselves to be his betters. This ruling passion has allowed him to forge psychological alliances with all those who have shared his resentments. Thus his best friends around the world share his resentments or have been able to play upon them.

Castro saw Cuban society as being fundamentally unjust because he thought it was an environment created by the rich, the powerful and the self-satisfied. For these reasons, Marxism-Leninism was a useful value structure for changing this state of affairs. Marxism-Leninism justified the use of any expedient in Castro's revolutionary endeavor.

On this basis, Castro was inevitably attracted to Lenin because, as he himself says, Lenin argued that morality served the purposes of the revolution. Consequently, Castro rejected all normative standards which subordinate ends to means and embraced the revolutionary dictum that only the ends can justify the means. The profound paradox in Castro's revolutionary thought lay precisely in this commitment to two sets of norms. One permitted absolute amorality, immorality, and flexibility with respect to gaining power, the other required rigidity and regularity with respect to the revolution in power. When asked about his views on leadership,

56

Castro found Lenin as the highest type because of this intellectual apparatus undergirding Leninist leadership.

This psychological ambiguity or antinomian mentality in Castro demonstrates that his idea of power is not personalistic in the ordinary sense. He is able to frequently debunk the charges of personalistic drives for glory in his interviews by pointing out that there are no streets, roads, schools, or plazas named after him in Cuba. In this sense, he can repeatedly say that he is no Stalinist.

But this is due to the fact that his idea of power is historical and semi-religious. The other types of great leaders whom he discusses most frequently are Muhammed, Christ, Gandhi; leaders who had followings in the millions and who marked epochal changes in the history of peoples. No naming of a square or street or school could add one iota of significance to the importance of these leaders. They are historical figures which all the world must take into account through the centuries. Castro clearly has the appetite to be identified with this type of leader and this type of glory. In one interview he gave when asked about whether he had the qualities of a great leader, Castro replied in part:

> I think I have the qualities to do what I'm doing. Now, what makes a great leader? What does the conception of a great leader imply? Moses was a great leader; Christ was a great leader—here, I'm referring to spiritual leaders. I think Mohammed was a great leader. They were personalities in history who are known as leaders, because each had a doctrine, founded a doctrine, and was followed by multitudes. Even when they started out, they were backed by a few. Christ, it's said, was followed by twelve apostles at first, then by millions of believers. He was a spiritual leader, as was Mohammed. They were religious leaders—but leaders, nonetheless.
>
> I have an idea of what a leader is. Ho Chi Minh was a great leader. And, for me of course, the one with the most extraordinary qualities as a political and revolutionary leader was Lenin . . .
>
> There have been many religious and political leaders. History is full of leaders. Wherever a human

community has existed, a leader has emerged. The times determine what is required of them. Certain qualities are needed at one time, others at another . . .

The qualities required at one moment are not necessarily the ones needed at another. We're talking about serious leaders, aren't we. We're not talking about demagogues or electioneering politicians, because sometimes they have to be good demagogues, have good publicity, a good public image, and even be good looking, to get votes—a lot of votes . . .

If you ask, 'What about the qualities of a revolutionary leader?' I could go into it a little deeper. I might have a little more to say about that. I think a revolutionary leader needs to have a lot of conviction, passion, for what he's doing. He also needs to have a great confidence in the people. He must be tenacious and cool-headed and have a sense of responsibility and of identification with what he is doing and with the people. He also needs some training, some clear ideas. Well, there you have a few elements.

I'd like to add one more qualification to the concept of a revolutionary leader. He should also have a great sense of human solidarity, great respect for the people. He should view the people not as an instrument, but as a protagonist—a real protagonist—the subject and hero of the struggle.[2]

Castro has already created his own mythology. The Moncada Barracks, the Sierra Maestra, "Che" Guevara . . . Like the USSR or China, the Castro regime has felt the need to create its own symbolism and hagiography. A new civic religion has been substituted for older, spiritual aspirations. Priests have been substituted with ideologues, and the high priest and deity have been conflated in the person of Fidel Castro. Other Latin American leaders like Haya de la Torre and Juan Domingo Perón have known the importance of creating personal mythologies as political tools, but none has been as thoroughgoing as Castro. In his drive to see the spirit of his regime internalized by the people, Castro has himself up as a mystic apotheosis. There is an inherent dynamic to Castro's actions, an ever greater escalation of the arena, an ever greater exaltation of his power. To admit defeat, to retrench, to step down from power short of death would be to deny his mythic destiny. Unless, on the other hand, he is able—as so many Latin caudillos have done—to remake himself in an entirely new, more humble, and more human, image, but this would be to deny his role in history. The problem Castro has faced, then, since the success of his revolution in Cuba, was how to expand his arena of action.

ENDNOTES

1.   Ruiz, op. cit. p. 122.

2.   *Fidel Castro: Nothing Can Stop the Course of History* Interview by Jeffrey M. Elliot and Mervyn M. Dymally. (New York: Pathfinder Press, 1986) pp. 30-33.

CHAPTER VII

The Economy and the Castro Government

The fact that the people do not fully participate in the selection of their leaders means that the Castro government does not possess genuine legitimacy nor genuine security. The lack of such security manifests itself in two ways. The government either tries to keep the people happy by manipulating public opinion, or the government represses the people when it does not follow public opinion. In an elitist, dirigiste government like that of the Castro regime, the second alternative is almost inevitable.

As such the state with its supporting elite and the rest of the society become alienated from each other. Repressive measures feed themselves. A police state is created, and the state security apparatus spreads throughout the society. Rather than the bureaucracies or the party machinery feeling accountable to the people, sentiment develops that they have to perform actions for the people, administer for them, because the people are not capable of looking after their own welfare.

Rather than providing incentives for Cuba to grow towards more balanced economic relations with its foreign trading powers, Castro pursued the statism which had always been part of Cuba's economic policies to its logical extreme. He destroyed economic mobility and created a monopoly situation in which the government controlled all forms of economic advancement within the country. Because of the inability of the system to generate growth, he in turn had to rely on the Soviet Union for subsidies, and increasingly, on foreign business interests to provide him with foreign exchange.

Castro consolidated most Cuban industries in the hands of the state, enacted several measures of land reform, and expropriated all foreign property. He then developed and maintained an extensive internal security system, which has had the same effect in Cuba as it has had in the other countries where such regimes have been established.

At the outset of Castro's regime, this process of collectivization was accomplished as much through parastatal as state mechanisms. In 1959 mass movements were organized to mobilize the people according to social and labor affiliations. Examples of this were the Organization of Small Peasants (ANAP) and the Federation of Cuban Women (FMC), but these organizations often had a militarized character. The militia was organized during this period, as were the Committees for the Defense of the Revolution (CDRs), and the Association of Young Rebels (AJR), to serve as a revolutionary youth group.

Castro sought, at least nominally, to create a total revolution in Cuba. This revolution was based on a collectivization of Cuban life on every level: economic, political, and social. This collectivization was based on a new rationalism with the goal of establishing a "new Cuban man." Industry was to be organized by sector, and society by race, age, and gender, with the government and the Communist party serving as elite managers for the whole.

Yet in many ways, this new collectivization was anything but rational. It tried to impose new, artificial incentives, destroyed family structures, and limited the rights and freedoms of the people. The result has been economic and social disaster. Hence, the Castro regime has had to compensate by creating the police state and militarizing the society in order to maintain its power.

The Economy Under Castro

On the eve of Batista's overthrow, Cuba manufactured over 10,000 different items. The production of sugar as a share of her exports had declined, and her capital infrastructure had developed impressively. Although the United States was still the biggest investor in Cuba, the U.S. share of the capitalization of the Cuban economy had declined significantly over the past thirty years. Increasingly, capital was coming from within the society and from other international sources.

Castro effectively reversed this process. He reduced Cuba to an ever-greater reliance on sugar, and made Cuba increasingly dependent on the Soviet Union for trade and direct aid. Far from making Cuba economically prosperous or spurring her growth to annual levels of 10 percent as Che Guevara once claimed, Castro reduced the population to an ever more dramatic and singular dependence on the state.

Upon his accession to power in 1959, Castro redirected the economy in two fundamental ways. First, he moved to eliminate all ties to the United States and channelled his foreign trade toward the Soviet Union. Second, Castro moved to annex all private property and bring all of the means of production into the hands of the state. The increasing centralization of the economy in Castro's hands, meant that the process of statism reached its fulfillment. Instead of the elite maintaining a quasi-independent status from the state however, the new system meant that the upper classes derived their status as well as their authority from their position within the state. Instead of owners, they became managers, dependent on the over-all system to sustain them, but no longer accountable to consumers or larger economic forces.

During the early sixties, Castro tried to rapidly industrialize the economy. He channeled resources into heavy industry and sectors where Cuba had not enjoyed much development such as steel and other manufactures. This experiment led to serious economic disjunctions. While the rest of the world was enjoying a period of growth, the Cuban GDP fell an average 0.4 percent over the 1962-1969 period.[1]

In a severe oscillation, Castro decided instead to concentrate all of his endeavors in the sugar crop as a means for gaining foreign exchange. The first three years of his government were marked by declining sugar production. In fact, the cut-off of the U.S. quota was welcomed by the Cubans because it was seen as forcing the industrialization of the country. The decline in sugar production was directly correlated to the Cuban buying spree in Eastern Europe.

These policies substantially backfired. While the Cubans tried to buy industries and establish them in Cuba, they did not have the raw materials to sustain them. Nor did they have alternative cash flows to pay for these expensive acquisitions without continuing subsidies by the Soviet Union.

By 1964, the price of sugar was at unprecedented levels. Castro, in a dramatic switch, decided to "embrace the monoculture." He set as his goal, the famous mark of ten million tons of sugar by 1971. The Cubans put forward a prodigious effort and harvested 8.5 million tons of sugar that year, but with disastrous results for the rest of the economy. Land use had been disastrously mismanaged. Resources had been channeled at the expense of other industries. To compound matters, sugar went through a price bust at the same time.

Graph I
Percent of Collectivization, 1961-1977

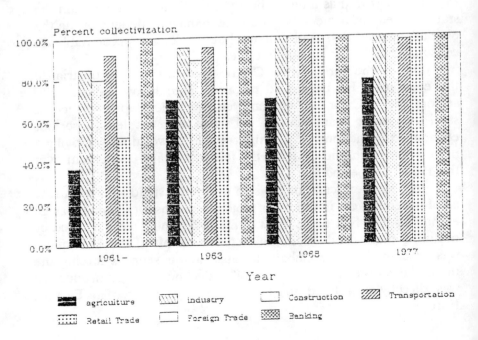

The misallocation of resources, the ballooning state bureaucracies, and increasing worker malaise led to an ever increasing dependency on state borrowing and Soviet dependency.

Indeed, it was the destruction of the economy in the late 1960s which gave the Soviets the leverage they needed to bring Castro more securely into their alignment. Where Cuba had a relatively free economy prior to 1959, she was slowly reduced to an ever more extensive dependency both economically and politically on the Soviet Union in the aftermath of Castro's revolution.

By the 1980s, the Soviet Union absorbed approximately two-thirds of Cuba's exports, and, in turn, was by far the largest exporter to Cuba.[2] Some critics like to say that this is still a smaller percentage of Cuba's over-all trade than the U.S. occupied during the 1950s.[3] These figures fail to take into account the structure of Cuba's trade with the Soviets, nor Cuba's trade with the rest of the Soviet Union's external empire. Combined, the CMEA countries accounted for over 80 percent of Cuba's trade.

Graphs II-IV
U.S. and Soviet Export Dependency[4]

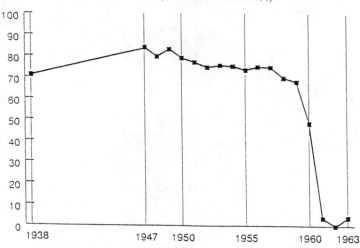

Cuban Imports From U.S.
(% of all imports from all countries)

Source: United Nations Yearbook of International Trade Statistics, 1951-1964 (various years)

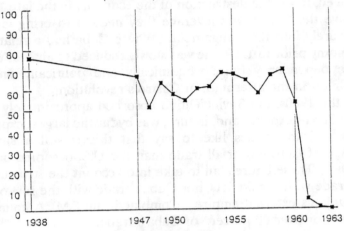

Cuban Exports to U.S.
(% of all exports from all countries)

Source: United Nations Yearbook of International Trade Statistics, 1951-1964 (various years)

Cuban Exports to CMEA Countries
(% of total exports to all countries)

Source: United Nations Yearbook of International Trade Statistics, 1951-1991 (various years)

Within this milieu, economic innovation and productivity have declined steadily. Castro has been reduced lately to exhorting the people to use bicycles instead of cars, oxen instead of tractors. At the same time, Castro has claimed that he has eliminated poverty, provided health care for all, and created a new climate of egalitarianism.

Castro has followed two basic methods of economic management. The first would be the basic model of central planning. State bureaucracies analyze the needs and resources of the country and allocate them accordingly, with the attendant delays, inefficiencies, and shortages and excesses. The second form represents a relaxation of the first. It involves the use of material incentives over moral incentives, some private property, and foreign concessions, while the state still maintains control over the central forces of the economy. Paradoxically, it is the capitalist measures which the Cuban government implements from time to time, which allow it to maintain its central planning system.

Given the experience of the 1959-1990 period, a reexamination of dependency is in order. Rather than economic dependency being a capitalist phenomena, it is becoming clear that it is a phenomena of proto-capitalist or Marxist-Leninist regimes.

Castro's Institutional Support

The state propaganda machine, internal security service and the sporadic emigrations have been the chief means Castro has used domestically to contain unrest. In the international arena there are two Cuban intelligence services involved in state-sponsored terrorism and narcotics trafficking. These are the Dirección General de Inteligencia (DGI) and the Americas Department (AD). The DGI was organized in 1961, and is the most famous of Castro's intelligence agencies. It came under the control of the Soviets in the 1968-1970 period, so Castro created another agency to be directly under his control, the Americas Department.

The DGI is located within the Ministry of the Interior. AD comes under the Cuban Communist Party Central Committee, but in reality is personally directed by Castro. The principal director of the Americas Department is Manuel Piñeiro Losada, "Red Beard," who has long been close to Castro. This intelligence agency works primarily within the western hemisphere. It is, according to one authority, the principal agency to facilitate military and sabotage training for clandestine guerrilla groups throughout the hemisphere.[5] Credit has been given to AD agents for forging the alliance between the principal terrorist groups in Nicaragua and for melding the insurgency factions in El Salvador, Guatemala, and Honduras.

The Armed Services

Castro's first action upon the flight of Batista, was to purge the armed forces. Even though many Cubans flocked to join the rebel forces in the last period of the guerrilla campaign, the rebel army was still far outnumbered by the armed forces. Castro realized that the regular army was a key obstacle to his gaining control of the country. Castro had General Cantillo, the head of the armed forces, arrested, simultaneously purging many of the Batista elements. Not content with these measures, Castro purged anti-Batista military officers like Colonel Ramón Barquin. Castro's justification was that viable military alternatives to his government had the potential of receiving U.S. aid to overthrow his regime.

Castro's second problem was coopting or destroying the other revolutionary cadres. The 26 of July Movement was by no means the only group in armed revolt. While Castro's forces were concentrated in the eastern mountains, other revolutionary groups took the battle to the streets. Castro warily began the process of unifying them because he understood how unwieldy and fractious these groups could become, and he also realized that they had the same legitimacy as his own group did.

Castro fought first against the emergence of any alternative leader within his own movement, and this process began even before the revolution was completed. Charismatic commanders within his own movement, such as Frank Pais or Huber Matos were either set up or imprisoned. Pais was killed by the Batistianos, and G. A. Geyer alleges that the tip-off might have come from within Castro's organization. Huber Matos was prosecuted and imprisoned by Castro. The forces of the Student Revolutionary Directorate and other rival military groups were also absorbed in this way.

Castro thus implemented a double purge of the armed forces during 1959. The spectacular public trials were only part of a strategy designed to give him control of both the regular army and the irregulars which had opposed it. The purpose however, was not to remove the military threat to democracy, but to make militarism an inherent part of his regime.

Castro began to reconstruct the army and swell its numbers. Following the classic model of the anti-economic state (a tradition which dates back to Sparta), Castro began to use the armed forces to export revolution abroad, either on his own account or as a Soviet proxy. While his efforts failed in the Dominican Republic and in Venezuela, Castro was able to effectively expand his operations to Africa.

TABLE I:
GROWTH IN THE CUBAN ARMY

Year	Military Expenditures Current	Constant	Armed Forces 1000s	Armed Forces per 1000
1963	213.0	306.0	80	10.66
1964	221	289	110	14.31
1965	213	272	110	13.97
1970	240	338	140	16.41
1975	-	-	120	12.9
1976	-	-	125	13.2
1977	-	-	200	20.8
1978	-	-	210	21.6
1979	1160	1865	210	21.6
1980	1140	1680	220	22.8
1985	1335	1520	297	29.4
1989	1377	1377	297	28.3

Source: U.S. Arms Control and Disarmament Agency

Before 1961, the Cuban army was almost non-existent. By 1989, a Cuban population of 10.5 million was supporting an army of 297,000 soldiers, easily the largest in Latin America. Castro, in militarizing the society, followed in miniature, the same process that had occurred in the Soviet Union and China. By creating such an extensive military force, Castro was able to create a power projection posture. In this way he compensated for Cuba's economic weakness and the formal ideological antipathy of his neighbors. But while Castro may have used the external threats to his regime as a rationale for its militarization, the real reasons were indigenous.

The military's discipline, political culture of obedience to authority, and revolutionary heritage, made it the greatest single base for the consolidation and maintenance of the Castroite political order. Its special status gave it an *esprit de corps* and a priority value within the Cuban political economic system. Its highest commanders have been and continue to be *raulistas*.

While there may be some opposition to Castro within the armed forces (as reflected by the Ochoa trials of 1989), they, along with the Ministry of Interior, are the key institutions for maintaining the Castro regime.

However, mandatory military service time has declined. The military is much more of a reflection of the people than the Ministry of Interior with its elite troops and institutional interest. For these reasons, the military probably cannot be relied upon to be as loyal to Castro as the Ministry of Interior if a general uprising were to take place.[6]

The Cuban Communist Party

The Cuban Communist party has played an ambiguous role in the development of the Castroite state. It lives in an uneasy alliance with the *fidelistas* and *raulistas*, having absorbed them and been absorbed by them. Castro has purged it repeatedly, and yet it is still unclear where the party's ultimate loyalties lie. It has too much of an institutional dynamic ever to be simply a supine organ of Castro's power.

The PSP's accommodationist past under Batista and its criticism of the July 26 movement created friction between its professional leadership and the Castro elite. Nevertheless, it quickly became a staunch supporter of the regime and was coopted by the middle of 1959. Carlos Rafael Rodriguez, its leader was incorporated into the Castroite command structure, even as many of its members were purged.

Like the CPSU in the Soviet Union, the CCP quickly expanded its base in Cuba. In the process, it became the chief civilian mechanism for advancement. Rather than suppressing ambition and creating a new Cuban man, the communist party became the focus of ambition and social advancement. The committed ideologues of the first generation began to give way to careerists and technocrats, and the Party lost its ideological fervor as it gained in elite adherence.[7]

However, unlike the CPSU, the CCP did not establish the same kind of relationship with the government. Rather it played a subordinate role, independent from Castro's direct control. Castro realized that he needed the CCP in order to give an institutional base to his government, but he did not see the party as necessarily loyal to him. The result was a government almost of coalition between two distinct leftist currents. One, characterized by the *fidelistas* and *raulistas* was directly beholden to Castro. The other, represented by the Communist Party was beholden to itself, and with separate, distinct ties to the Soviet Union. Castro's suspicions continued throughout the 1960s, and he purged the party in 1962, 1964, and 1968.

The Ministry of Interior, the armed forces, and the communist party form the institutional base of the Castroite regime. In order to ensure their loyalty, Castro has grafted onto their leadership supporters who are only loyal to him, and repeatedly purged their membership. Raúl Castro controls both the military and the armed services; Fidel Castro controls the party directly as its First Secretary. As the revolution ages and the generation which had actual experience in the fighting is attrited, a new generation develops with a different set of experiences and motivations. Its loyalty, while superficially accorded to Castro, is more directed toward the perpetuation of the corporate institutions of the regime.

The lack of individual rights and liberties and the destruction of the economy have led to a situation in which the Castro government has been forced to rely on its state institutions in opposition to the will of the society. Such is Castro's dilemma however, that he is caught between two alternatives. In order to continue his control over the country, Castro has channeled resources which would otherwise go toward institution building into maintaining his regime. At the same time however, as he and his generation age, the next generation is developing with a desire to maintain its power within an institutional framework. As such the Castroites are engaged in a dual task: maintain Castro's power, but also ensure their own concomitant perpetuation.

ENDNOTES

1. Carmelo Mesa-Lago, "The Economy and International Economic Relations," in *Cuba in the World* ed. by Cole Blasier and Carmelo Mesa-Lago (Pittsburgh, 1971).

2. Trade Policy Director Felix Luaces noted that the Soviet state export-import company, Prodingtor "exports to Cuba most of the food we receive from the Soviet Union, basically butterfat, milk by-products, canned meat, different types of canned goods, vegetable oils, and other essential items. At the same time, this company is the only importer of Cuban sugar; in other words, it monopolizes 100 percent of the Cuban sugar imported." FBIS-LAT-91-121, 24 June 1991, p. 2.

3. Cf. Louis Perez, p. 355.

4. Various observers have commented that Cuba demonstrates less "dependency" after the 1959 revolution than before. Most notable is the work of William Leogrande, who measures trade dependency, reliance on single trading partners, monocultural export patterns, debt accumulation, etc., to conclude that Cuba

has been less dependent on the Soviet Union than it had been on the U.S. before the Castro revolution (William M. Leogrande, "Cuban Dependency: A Comparison of Pre-Revolutionary and Post-Revolutionary International Economic Relations," *Cuban Studies* 9 (July 1979): 1-28). Several criticisms are in order.

First, Leogrande's definition of "trade dependency" is "the extent to which the economy of a nation is geared to production for an external market" (Ibid. p. 5). The implications are twofold: that participation in the international economy is *prima facie* evidence of "dependency"; and that only autarkism represents complete "independence" and is therefore the ultimate goal. Such a case will probably not be accepted by most observers as very compelling.

Second, Leogrande measures Cuban trade with the United States before 1959 as a percentage of total Cuban GNP. With Cuban-Soviet trade, though, he uses Cuban "GMP," or Gross Material Product. GMP is a uniquely Cuban gauge that has no meaningful equivalent in the West; it includes not just GNP but also valuates domestic services, the number of physicians graduated, the number of university students, etc. (Carmelo Mesa-Lago, *The Economy of Socialist Cuba: A Two-Decade Appraisal* (Albuquerque: University of New Mexico Press, 1981): 199-201). GMP thus artificially inflates the size of the Cuban economy and distorts pre- and post-revolutionary comparisons, since pre-revolutionary statistics use GNP as a baseline while post-revolutionary figures rely on the inflated "GMP" as the gauge. As Robert Packenham explains, if *GNP* is used as a consistent denominator, then by most measures Cuban dependency on the Soviet Union is greater than previous Cuban dependency on the United States (Robert A. Packenham, "Cuba and the USSR since 1959: What Kind of Dependency?" in *Cuban Communism*, sixth ed., ed. Irving Louis Horowitz (New Brunswick: Transaction Books, 1987): 112).

Third, Leogrande compares Cuban-U.S. trade with Cuban-Soviet trade because he is unconvinced that the Soviets actually influence the trade patterns of their allies (Leogrande, *op. cit.*, p. 13). Yet as Mesa-Lago shows, if CMEA countries are included, Cuban dependency on the Soviet bloc is greater than pre-revolutionary dependency on the United States, and if GNP rather than GMP is consistently used, there is an even further increase in overall Cuban dependence (Mesa-Lago, *op. cit.*, pp. 79-82, 92-93).

The methodology used in our accompanying charts is different from Leogrande's and merits a brief explanation. Cuban trade with the United States in the pre-revolutionary period is measured by dividing Cuban exports to the United States by total Cuban exports worldwide. This method has the advantage of providing us with a consistent gauge measured *as a percentage of total trade*, thereby accounting for periodic variables such as commodity price fluctuations, inflationary tendencies, and exchange rate differences.

Our methodology also measures Cuban trade with the CMEA countries rather than trade with the Soviet Union alone. Leogrande rejects this approach because he is uncertain that the Soviet Union influenced its partners' trading habits. Irrespective of this view, it is undeniable, however, that Cuban trade with the CMEA countries represents a much greater degree of dependency and concentration than Cuban trade with pre-revolutionary Cuban-U.S. trade. Our methodology also relies exclusively on internationally accepted United Nations statistics; Leogrande relies in part on U.N. figures, but also on data from the Cuban Central Bank and National Planning Commission, which some observers consider unreliable sources. I am grateful to Bill Prillaman for researching this topic for me.

5. Roger W. Fontaine, *Terrorism: The Cuban Connection* (New York: Crane Russak and Company, 1988) p. 13. The Americas Department was abolished in the early 1990s because Castro could no longer afford to support guerrilla groups abroad.

6.   Signs of disloyalty in the armed forces have been widespread. They have ranged from the defection of General del Pino to the flight of Major Lorenzo in a Mig-26. Military experts have been voicing the perception that there may be even greater subterranean discontent within the army than is already apparent. Manuel A. Granado, a retired colonel in the U.S. Green Berets summed up the difference in loyalty between the Ministry of Interior (Minint) and the armed forces in this way: "of the three structures which control power (the armed services, the Party and the Police), the only one which has a popular base is the army, and although they are very well equipped and managed, their popular base is important to bear in mind in any confrontation with the people because of their identification with them." translated by the author from *Diario Las Americas* October 15, 1991.

7.   Jorge Dominguez noted in *Socialist Cuba* (New York, 1987) that by 1986 "nearly three-quarters of party members had a ninth grade education or higher but 48 percent of the members of the Third Party Congress and 78 percent of the Central Committee's full and alternate members had a university education. In short, the party...has become more of an elite party, more capable of governing, but also less representative." p.7.

CHAPTER VIII

Cuba's Political Culture

Cuba, prior to Castro, was at a point where it was prospering economically in historical terms, and was beginning to come to grips with its political apparatus. In the latter half of the 1950s, there was an extraordinary explosion of political activity, but the violent left was only one factor among many. There were significant hopes that the broad-based opposition to Batista could be harnessed to produce the conditions necessary for a competitive democracy. However, with the accession of Castro to power that dynamism disappeared.

In its place, arose three phenomena. The first was the development of official political culture, which superimposed an ideal society over the reality which was Cuba. The second was the development of silent protest in those who opposed Castro's regime within the island. The third phenomena was the reemergence of that vibrant political discourse in the Cuban diaspora.

U. S. policy makers did not understand the lack of political resistance to Castro's determined following, nor did they understand the fragile nature of the nascent political culture in Cuba. Ambassador Bonsal wrote about his view of the consolidation of the Revolution as it happened. He said:

> The real failure of judgment at this particular juncture was not in the determination of what Castro had been, was, or would be. The primary error—one in which I participated was the belief that the nature, the will for democracy, and the strength of a Cuban society released by its own efforts from the dictatorship if Batista would

be the dominant factors in determining the character and the measures of the new Cuban government rather than the notions of a power-mad Fidel Castro.[1]

As we have seen, the forms of Cuban government had never been sufficiently broad-based or diffused throughout society in order to prevent the rise of a determined minority. The Cuban population was not ready for democracy not because they did not fight for it, as the Ambassador seems to indicate, but because of Castro's political ability, and the lack of development of formal political institutions which could counter-balance Castro's charismatic personalism.

There was widespread uncertainty about the direction of the government, and the Batista dictatorship had debilitated the ability of the population to coalesce as a democratic unity. Nor did it help of course, that the United States was largely passive and did not display very much leadership during this period.

A combination of a limited experience with democratic politics, a highly politicized elite, and a conscious deception on the part of the Castro partisans may contribute to an understanding of this phenomena. There was no well-organized and popular political movement that fundamentally articulated the traditional values of a socially conscious, conservative party. Instead, dating from the fall of the Machado government in 1933, the university tradition produced a leftist leadership class that was disposed to use violence in order to implement its social, economic, and political agendas. Grau San Martin, Prío Socarrás and Eduardo Chibás to the contrary, Cuba really did not have a tradition of leaders truly dedicated to democracy, and democracy, at least in the eyes of the militant left, had been discredited as a structure for taking effective political action. For these reasons, the turn toward communism or socialism was not as effectively opposed as it might have been domestically.

Once Castro managed to consolidate his regime, he set about trying to construct the "New Cuban Man." The New Cuban Man was supposed to be an honest, hard worker, altruistic, and selfless in his devotion to his fellow workers, and steadfast in his identification of his needs and values with those of Castro's, and by extension, the Cuban state.

However, communism and the promotion of a democratic, self-governing polity are mutually antithetical. Contrary to utopian expectations, the basic nature of the Cuban people did not change under communism, but the structure of their values and incentives did. In a self-governing polity, the primary political motivations should be moral freedom and moral autonomy. Under a dictatorship, all virtues are subsumed under the overarching search for security.

What has been produced in Cuba, is a seemingly docile population caught up in what Vaclav Havel, the playwright and president of Czechoslovakia, has called "the culture of the lie." Both the state and society interact falsely, communicating in subtle codes rather than straightforwardly. Propaganda becomes a major political support in terms of boosting the regime, distrust and silence become the defenses for the majority of the population.

Given the insecurities of the Castro regime, rapprochement between the state and the people has become increasingly difficult. It has manifested itself in two ways: negative integration and bread and circuses. On the one hand, the Cuban government has been forced to manufacture external enemies or play up on Cuban anti-Americanism to create a sense of common danger and national unity against the threatening external world. On the other hand, it has created extravagant national festivals and celebrations like the Pan Am games of August 1991.

While the governing structures and the repressive apparatus of the state are Castro's real center of power inside Cuba, what elevates his regime is that it provides the illusion of sovereignty. It pretends to be mass-based, and responsive to the needs of the people. In this sense, rhetoric and personality are of profound importance.

Castro's regime becomes palatable, not because it satisfies material desires, but because it speaks to the aspirations of the Cuban people. The Cuban government learned early and well the principle that something said long and well enough becomes its own reality. Positive perceptions of egalitarianism, independence, and social welfare—the central tenets of Castro's regime—are products of a collective state of mind, rather than concrete actualities.

At the same time, the cult of personality around Castro is also of vital importance. His ability to connect with the Cuban people on a fundamental, subterranean level, creates a feeling of empowerment, even when it does not exist in reality. Demagoguery becomes a substitute for democracy.

Castro has created his own mythology. The Moncada Barracks, the Sierra Maestra, "Che" Guevara . . . Like the USSR or China, the Castro regime has felt the need to create its own symbolism and hagiography. A new civic religion has been substituted for older, spiritual aspirations. Priests have been substituted with ideologues, and the high priest and deity have been conflated in the person of Fidel Castro. Other Latin American leaders like Haya de la Torre and Juan Domingo Peron have known the importance of creating personal mythologies as political tools, but none has been as thoroughgoing as Castro. In his drive to see the spirit of his regime internalized by the people, Castro has set himself up as a mystic apotheosis.

The Cuban system cannot tolerate mass criticism, for fear that it would lose the grounds of its nominal legitimacy. For this key reason, Cuban discontent has been forced underground. This process has led to the development of codes and nicknames in songs, radio broadcasts, and popular art. Absenteeism, alcoholism, and malingering on the job are well-noted phenomena in Cuba. Safety records are atrocious, though hushed up, production schedules are more fiction than fact, and emigration is a frequent consideration. The lack of active resistance does not mean that the Cuban people have not resented Castro's rule. They have manifested that discontent through their passive resistance, and through their skirting of the political system.

The Diasporan Population

Perhaps, the factor that has most greatly impeded the overthrow of Castro has been the near proximity of the United States, and the ability of Cubans to leave the island. The United States has acted like a vacuum cleaner in the sense that it has sucked out of Cuba, precisely those people with the most initiative and greatest aspirations for freedom. Free in the United States, the pluralism and dynamism of the Cuban community is clear, and it shows what a repressive and heavy handed government Castro has had to employ in Cuba in order to keep the Cubans subordinate to his authority.

From the outset of the Castro regime, there has been emigration from Cuba, though it has tended to come in several distinct waves, reflecting the growing realization of Cuban society of the injustice of the Castro system. The first wave began with Castro's accession to power and continued through the early sixties. It was characterized as being wealthy, professional, and white collar workers. The second wave of the mid-seventies was more middle class and blue collar.

The last, grouped around the Mariel boatlift of 1981, introduced some of the lowest elements of Cuban society into Florida and the southern United States. Castro boasted that he emptied his jails and his mental hospitals, but ignored in the boatlift was the sheer quantity of Cubans desperate to leave Cuba. By 1981, it was clear that Cuban dissatisfaction with the Castro regime had reached all levels of society, and that Castro was using emigration as an escape valve to reduce pressure against his government.

The Cuban population overseas, has tended to concentrate in Miami and southern Florida, but there are significant Cuban populations scattered throughout the rest of the United States, Spain, and Latin America. In the diaspora, the opposition to Fidel Castro has ranged from paramilitary groups like Alfa 66 to the Cuban American National Foundation led by Jorge Mas Canosa, to other political groupings around personalities like Carlos Alberto Montaner and Ricardo Bofill. The ideological composition of the diasporan Cuban community is hardly monolithic. From Catholic conservatives to social democrats to quasi-apologists for the Castro regime, vie within the Cuban community, and the result is internal conflict among the diasporans. Nevertheless, despite this variety, the Cubans have been able to generate significant support for their community within the United States, though this may not manifest itself as overtly as the diasporans would like.

The secret historically, of diasporan power, has been the influence a diasporan people may exercise in the leading power with regard to their former homeland. It has never been possible for a diasporan people to directly retake their homeland if the forces in that homeland are backed by a power superior to the capability of the diasporan people. Diasporans affect the politics of their host countries by agitating for activist foreign policies with regard to their former homeland. The diasporan people often see their main political agenda as shaping the agenda of the principal power that will oppose the powers backing the controllers of their former state. To the degree that the Cubans in the Diaspora never received the full support of the United States in their direct efforts to oust Castro, they have been frustrated. However, in the context of the collapse of Soviet central power, and the need of the new republic-dominated union for foreign assistance, the opportunity for using the major regional power of the United States to accelerate the collapse of the Castro regime is more feasible.

In this regard, diasporan power has manifested itself in lobbying for an extension of the embargo against Cuba, the establishment of Radio and TV Martí, and a high acceptance of Cuban emigrants by the United States. The departure of the diasporans from their homeland may have been wrenching, but after thirty years of Castro's government, the diasporan community now finds itself a part of two political worlds, and there may be some difficulties for the diasporans in reconciling these two worlds.

A Semi-Sovereign State for a Semi-Sovereign People

Cuba, prior to the Castro revolution was a country struggling to be free. The people most ardently desired a return to democratic self-government, not economic expropriations or realignment with the Soviet Union. Their problem was that they had a state tradition which did not feel accountable to them, and an intellectual disenfranchised element which created a powerful analytical apparatus obscuring the real sources of their dependence, and placing the blame for their problems on the United States instead of on the statist tendencies of the government.

The result was a country which possessed some elements of economic independence and some elements of democratic self-awareness, but not enough to resist a ruthless seizure of power or the magnetic attraction of a demagogue like Fidel Castro, who instead of liberating his people to exercise their sovereignty would rob his countrymen of all of their political and economic freedom, while providing them with a myth of their own empowerment.

ENDNOTES

1. Philip W. Bonsal. *Cuba, Castro, and the United States* (Pittsburgh, 1971) p. 6.

PART II

CUBA AND THE COLD WAR

The purpose of this section is to show how the Cold War created an anomalous situation for Cuba, and how the evolution of the Soviet system has created patterns of opportunity and problems for the Cuban regime. Furthermore, it seeks to show that rather than allowing Cuba to throw off her mantle of dependency and semi-statehood, her affinity with the Soviet Union has led to a further reduction of her dignity and welfare.

In comparison to the long relationship with the United States, Cuba's relationship with the Soviet Union was an improvised affair. In the space of four years, the Soviet Union supplanted the United States as Cuba's principal trading partner, and with all of the shock that the economic conversion generated, also assumed a significant debt burden in short order. However, Cuba's economic weakness was more than made up for by her strategic value to the Soviets, and Cuba's importance to the overall strategic requirements of the two superpowers was enough to guarantee a significant role for her in the ensuing thirty years after Castro's ascent to power in 1959.

In this long and titanic struggle, Cuba's position often reflected the relative power of the two countries, and the different strategies the two countries employed in their attempts to defeat the other politically. What emerged during the decades of the 1960s and 1970s was a Cuban-Soviet strategy which seemed at the point of checkmating U.S. initiatives. Despite Castro's independent action in the Americas, and his policy differences with the Soviet Union, the key to the ascendancy of Cuban power during this period, was

Castro's willingness to serve as the forward launching point for Soviet power projection.

At the same time, the nature, effectiveness, and seriousness of this strategy was obscured in American domestic political discourse. Dating from President Kennedy to President Carter, U.S. presidents had, at least rhetorically, called for the overthrow of Castro, and yet had not understood the nature of Castro's power, nor had they taken steps to grapple with his hold on power directly. Castro was able to break out of his initial posture of defensiveness vis-a-vis the United States, and was increasingly able to promote revolution and armed struggle abroad. By the end of the Carter administration, not only was the Cuban government directly or indirectly involved in promoting violence and destabilization in Nicaragua, El Salvador, Grenada, and throughout the hemisphere, but was also involved in conflicts as far away as Angola and Ethiopia.

By 1980, Castro was at the height of his power and international influence. He had taken Cuba from its place as a backwater in the international arena, to being one of the most proactive agents in setting the world agenda. In gaining this world presence however, he had also converted Cuba into a police state, destroyed her economy, and made her dependent on the Soviet Union for her power, prestige, and economic sustenance.

CHAPTER IX

Castro in Power and the U.S. Attitude

Cuban experience since at least the past Platt Amendment seemed to indicate that Castro's tenure would not endure unless he reached an accommodation with the United States. For this reason, his roots in the Ortodoxo party and his stated commitment to democracy, at first seemed to presage a good U.S.-Cuban relationship. But as Huber Matos shrewdly pointed out, democracy did not seem to offer the same opportunities for Castro that communism did, but communism would prove to be totally unacceptable to the United States. Castro's dilemma therefore, upon his accession to power was how to posture his country so that he would be able to protect himself from the United States, and yet maintain total control over the population. An alliance with the Soviet Union seemed to be the natural solution to this problem.

Castro was well aware of the importance of the Soviet Union, and the fact that his power was only partially rooted within his own country. He is quoted as saying:

I think that if we had liquidated Batista in 1953, imperialism would have crushed us; because between 1953 and 1959, the world witnessed a change in the "correlation of forces" that was very important. The Soviet state was still relatively weak in this epoch. For us, the Soviet state that helped us so decisively later, in 1953 could not have done it.[1]

In this sense, domestic factors and foreign conditions represented two halves to the whole of Castro's power. The domestic political situation of the United States, with a liberal, reactive mind-set in the State Department, combined with an assertive, rising Soviet Union, created an external environment which was very favorable to Castro. The Soviets had much to gain from the relationship and were in a position to facilitate it, while the Americans did not know how much they had to lose, nor did they understand how to stop the Cuban regime's embrace of communism. In this regard, Castro's diplomacy over the 1959-1960 period was masterful, and is a paradigm for the successful transfer of client state allegiance.

During 1958, a profound sea change occurred in U.S. attitudes toward the Cuban revolution. Under the terms of mutual defense assistance agreements signed with Prío Socarrás in 1952, the United States had given the Batista government over $11 million between 1954 and 1958.[2]

Castro came to power after Batista resigned January 1, 1959. At first the United States did not know how to deal with Castro, and there was a serious policy split within the Eisenhower administration. Castro was able to exploit these differences and forge an alliance with the Soviet Union which allowed him to gain complete control.

The United States imposed a military embargo on Batista in March 1958, and searched for a viable political alternative to his regime. The group inside the U.S. government that felt Castro was more liberal than nationalist, and more democratic than Marxist, prevailed, but they were opposed by a significant group within the State Department. This group included the American ambassador in Cuba, Earl. E. T. Smith, and Ambassador William B. Pawley who had been in Colombia at the time of the "Bogotazo" as a member of the delegation to the OAS. Ambassador Robert C. Hill, who had arrived in Mexico shortly after the Santa Rosa raid, was also opposed to Castro's rise to power. The testimony of these three ambassadors and that of Ambassador Arthur Gardner, provide extraordinary evidence of the degree elements in the US government warned about Castro's pro-communist activities.[3]

It is clear from the sequence of events following Castro's seizure of power, and his alignment with the Soviet Union in February 1960, that the United States had not recognized the full implications of his political hostility, and had not abandoned its historical attitude against extra-hemispheric powers aligning their systems with systems in this hemisphere hostile to the United States. The historic U.S. position against extra-hemispheric powers penetration of the Western Hemisphere remained a visceral part of U.S. strategic thinking, yet the United States was relatively unsophisticated about developments within Latin America which might lead to anti-U.S. alliances with extra-hemispheric powers.

Historically, the United States' Monroe Doctrine which articulated these foreign policy objectives was the result of practical experience with European power interests in the Western Hemisphere. This experience extended from Washington's reluctance to liberate Canada with French troops and the Ntooka Sound Controversy where a Spanish frigate fired on a British merchant vessel. The policy which was formulated, reflected a wariness of European power which extended from Washington's Farewell Address to the Congressional No-Transfer Declaration of 1811 and the Monroe Doctrine. The United States in every case sought to create as favorable circumstances as it could for its own security. It sought to prevent territory in this hemisphere from being transferred from a weaker to a stronger European power, and aimed to prevent the subservience of the recently independent Latin American states to the hegemonic drives of expanding European powers.

This anti-European security posture continued throughout the nineteenth century. European power projection into this hemisphere through alliances with Latin American states continually reinforced U.S. sensitivity. The British supported Santa Anna in Mexico, against U.S. efforts to incorporate Texas into the American union, and it seemed that the British backed Mexico in order to keep the United States from becoming a transcontinental republic. This anti-European attitude was further reinforced by the French effort to extend their influence into this hemisphere during the Civil War by backing the Maximilian monarchy. Again, before the end of the nineteenth century, policy makers in the U.S. argued in part, that it had to gain dominance over an isthmian canal route, and base itself in both the Caribbean and the Pacific in order to resist the new imperial ambitions of an expansive Germany.

When Germany offered an alliance to Mexico even before World War I broke out, it gave the Mexicans the enticement of regaining the lands lost in the war with the United States. Naturally, U.S. sensitivity to extra-hemispheric exploitation of alliance opportunities in this hemisphere was activated. This sense of European expansionism was kindled again prior to and during World War II, when Hitler was seen as attempting to gain territories in the Caribbean as a result of Germany's conquest of France, the Netherlands, and Denmark, and also in the fact that Germany sought alliance relationships with military governments in Argentina and authoritarian ones in Brazil. Indeed, when the United States discovered Luftwaffe pilots flying small private commercial airline services in Colombia, the sense that the European power projection was aimed at the United States was further underlined.

In this regard, the Monroe Doctrine was a posture of U.S. national interest and was not enunciated as a doctrine of regional international law, let alone of international law. When the Argentines sought to invoke it in 1832 in order to gain U.S. assistance in ejecting the British from the Malvinas/Falkland Islands, the U.S. government made it abundantly clear that only the United States could invoke the Monroe Doctrine, and that it was unavailable in a multilateral sense. Clearly, the OAS structure set up in Bogota in 1948 was designed to alleviate Latin American fears that the Doctrine might be used in a unilateral way against their interests, and it showed that U.S. foreign policy makers felt sufficiently secure that they began to discard the security mind-set behind the Monroe Doctrine.

Nevertheless, this long historical understanding made it rather surprising that the United States was so insensitive to the potentially radically anti-American ideology and posture of the leaders of the July 26 Movement. The best explanation for this relative insensitivity to the potential of radical nationalism in Cuba and in Latin America generally, can probably be accounted for by the fact that post-World War II geopolitical realities had fundamentally changed, and the ruling mind-set within the United States had changed as well.

Instead of having a populace which supported interventions as it had done at the turn of the century, the U.S. had increasingly lost its sense of being the "policeman of the Americas." There were significant elements within the society which provided a revisionist, critical view of U.S. foreign policy. One of the legacies of past interventions[4] was that leading liberal newspaper writers identified with the anti-imperialist criticisms of Latin radicals, and there was a fairly widespread sense of guilt among leading elements in the U.S. establishment. For these reasons, the United States was a silent actor at the outset of the Cuban revolution, and then when it did intervene, it did so half-heartedly, in part because of the splits in its domestic public opinion.

Castro initially ran the Cuban government as an outsider of the formal government administration, but he soon abandoned this role. Political considerations forced him to be more orthodox. His rule from outside the formal institution was being used against him because it was allowing his opposition to label his government as part of a standard communist operation called the Yenan Way. This was a method of creating a government in guerrilla territory and enacting agrarian reform and passing revolutionary laws while the formal government was apparently in charge.

Castro did not want to expose his true inclinations too quickly. The mass executions in early 1959 generated enormous outcry, as did the destruction of Batista's anti-communist investigation agency's files. So despite the official communist party support of the new regime, and the exclusive legalization of the Communist party paper, Castro moved to forestall a premature identification of his regime with the Communist revolution.

During this period, Castro realized that his principal target audience was the U.S. since it was the main center of his opposition. While he could move ruthlessly against his domestic opposition, he was forced to use persuasive tactics for foreign consumption. In this way, he hoped to divide foreign opposition to the consolidation of his power, and he astutely endeavored to create doubt within the U.S. government as to his true intentions.

In keeping with this strategy, Castro moved to keep the United States off balance by his visit in the spring of 1959. This move counteracted the growing concern in the United States over the execution of army officers, the repression of the free press except for the communist newspaper, and the increasing trends towards state control over the economy. Consequently, two schools of thought developed within the United States. The optimistic school argued that Castro was forced to take his domestic postures due to political pressures, and that he was at heart a committed democrat who could be coopted by the United States if the government sanctioned his power and authority. A more pessimistic school of thought however, held that Castro's practice indicated his anti-democratic tendencies, and they pointed to the consolidation of power which he was already in the process of implementing.

Nevertheless, Castro's charisma and democratic gestures were convincing enough that, despite these concerns, the U.S. sent as its ambassador, Philip Bonsal, who had been among the leading group within the State Department advocating Castro's accession to power. Ambassador Hill reported that Ambassador Bonsal was of the opinion that "we must be patient; that eventually Castro would return to the family of good neighbors in Latin America." Furthermore, Hill added, Bonsal "maintained this position during his tenure of office as ambassador of the United States to Cuba."[5]

It seems abundantly clear that there were significant sectors within the U.S. government which tried to abet the democratic conversion of Castro. Despite the efforts of the optimists within the State Department however, Cuba continued to slip into the grasp of the Soviet Union.

Bonsal's attitude was prototypical of a great many people however. He did not want to be "on the wrong side of history." Castro seemed to be genuinely popular with his people and popular among the progressive elements of this country. There may have also been a certain amount of cynicism mixed in as well. Latin America is full of examples of leaders mouthing anti-American slogans and then making covert deals with the U.S., and Ambassador Bonsal may have shared a widespread attitude that Castro could be managed.

CHAPTER X

Forging the Soviet Connection

Traditional Soviet Strategy

Until the Gorbachev era, the Soviets were seen as clearly having an interrelated security doctrine that combined military alliance and strategic concepts. Soviet military policy was designed to divide the West—Europe, the United States, and Japan—into three different military spheres. The Soviets were to have superior conventional forces over NATO, superior naval interdiction forces over Japan, and a strategic intercontinental nuclear counterforce first-strike superiority over the United States. The Soviet Union had clearly adopted a "land power" posture vis-a-vis the United States.

In the contemporary development of land and sea power relations, the United States has inherited the British position of being the predominant maritime power versus the predominant land power of Europe and Asia, the Soviet Union. A land power in this sense, is that power which can dominate its region or continent on the basis of its ground forces. In conflict with a land power, the sea power tries to prevent it from dominating its region or continent. This strategy is designed to preserve the freedom of the sea power against the threat of the larger land forces of its principal rival.

The historic understanding of how a land power should seek to defeat a sea power has its roots in the understanding Thucydides had of the Peloponnesian War. The Spartans not only understood the way Athenian sea power had prevailed against the Persians in their historic invasion of the Greek peninsula, but also learned to appreciate the advice of their great king, Archidamus. Archidamus made it clear at the outset of the war that a frontal attack on Athens would not succeed. Out of his counsellings, and those of Alcibiades, the Athenian traitor, the classic model for defeating the maritime power emerged over the course of the protracted conflict and the understandings that it solidified.

For the land power to defeat the sea power, it needed to develop its own sea power and employ it in an indirect manner against the alliance position of the sea power. The Spartans learned to develop their sea power so that they come to the assistance of those forces inside the maritime alliance system of Athens which sought to break from that alliance. What this was designed to do was to transform the alliance from a base of support of the central power to an area of absorption of its resources and manpower.

The financial system which maintained the alliance system of the sea power also needed to be attacked. In this regard it was important to attack the liquidity of the commercial system by which the metropolitan power was able to finance its relationships with its alliance system. In the Spartan case, this aspect of their strategic necessity against Athens was not understood until after Alcibiades defected to them. As a result of this intelligence, the Spartans were able to occupy the mining areas of the Athenian empire, and thereby deprived it of the metallic backing of its currency.

The fact that the Soviets began to employ an aggressive, forward deployed strategy marked a departure from traditional Russian imperial strategies. Under the Tsars, territorial acquisition had come through a process of sparking conflicts with contiguous neighbors and manipulating balance of power politics vis-a-vis the Prussian and Austro-Hungarian empires.

When an external threat had emerged such as Napoleon or Hitler, Russian and Soviet strategy had been to employ an aggressive defensive strategy, involving retreat and counter-attack and a reliance on superior resources. In the postwar era, the Soviets were confronted with a much different scenario. Where previously expansion had been on the basis of continental or European ambitions, the postwar reality thrust the Soviets toward a global agenda.

There were three engines for Soviet expansion. The first was the church militant of international marxism. Within the Soviet

Union it fed an imperialist fire, already well-known to Russian nationalists. Paranoia about capitalist subversion.

The second was the structural nature of the Soviet regime. Unable to sustain itself economically, a policy of acquisition justified the maintenance of a military economy.

The third was that the opportunity was there. The western democracies were perceived to be weak, uncertain in their relations to the Third World, and divided in their political aims.

The problem was that in straying from its traditional geopolitical role, the Soviet Union also surrendered some of its natural advantages. For the first time it was matched against an opponent which had even greater resources than itself in the United States. Also, by becoming an aggressor and protagonist in foreign affairs, it was forced to export resources abroad rather than maintain itself at home, and suffered the risk of overreaching itself just as Napoleon and Hitler had done against it.

Just as Sparta had begun to develop a navy, challenge the Athenian alliance system and undermine its liquidity, so now the Soviets began to work toward strategically defeating the United States. They looked forward to using the Cubans to engage the United States as a naval threat with its strategic access to the Gulf of Mexico and Florida, and as a base for operations into Latin America. Cuba would form an integral component of this strategy, but it took some time for the Soviets to adapt to the exigencies of the developing alliance.

Despite the potential pitfalls of this strategy, the same forces motivating the Soviets to expand also played a substantial role in bringing the Cubans into their sphere of power. Ideological coincidence, if not identity, structural weakness, and fundamental regime antagonism to the United States were all impelling factors.

There is a substantial literature that discusses the Soviet relationship with Castro and Latin America during the Cold War.[1] What this literature notes is the ups and downs in Soviet-Cuban relations, but underlines the Soviet unwillingness to forego the alliance with Castro's Cuba, despite its periods of disagreement, friction, and diverging interests.

The forging of the Soviet tie began in July 1959, when Ramiro Valdés made contact with the Soviet Ambassador in Mexico.

Again, the Cubans made contact in November 1959 with the Soviet Vice Premier Anastas I. Mikoyan, who was allegedly in Mexico to open a Soviet industrial exposition.

In November, Ernesto "Che" Guevara was named the head of Cuba's National Bank. This move purged Felipe Pazos, the previous director, from the government. Pazos was a key figure who had entered the Castro government to keep its radical secular and pro-Marxist tendencies in check. With Guevara in charge however, it should not have come as a surprise that on February 15, 1960, the Soviet Union and Cuba signed an official trade agreement during the Mikoyan visit to Cuba.

The pact between the Soviet Union and Cuba involved a one hundred million dollar credit granted over a twelve year period for which the Cubans only had to pay 2.5 percent interest. These credits were to be used to purchase goods from the Soviet bloc for which in turn, the Soviets pledged to buy five million tons of Cuban sugar at the rate of one million tons a year. That this was as much a political as an economic deal, came from the fact that the Soviets paid twelve cents below world market prices, and were paying one half of what the US had previously been paying to Cuba.[2]

(It should be noted in passing at least, that during Castro's visit to the United States in April 1959, then-National Bank President Felipe Pazos and Minister of Finance Dr. Lopez Fresquet, reported that Castro *was* offered assistance by the United States.)

By May 1960, the process of forging the alliance with the Soviets was completed with the renewal of diplomatic relations between the Soviet Union and Cuba. The new Soviet ambassador, Sergei M. Kudryevtsev was the alleged head of a spy network that had operated in Canada according to the Canadian Royal Commission on Espionage. "Che" Guevara was euphoric over the new relationship, and proclaimed that Cuba was now defended by the greatest military power in history.

The Soviet-Cuban economic relationship moved ahead apace. A second Soviet-Cuban agreement was negotiated in December 1960 which forged more technical arrangements, The Soviets sent several groups of advisors to help the transformation of the Cuban economy. By March 1961, three thousand technicians had arrived in Cuba. The communique of the December 1960 agreements noted the mutuality in foreign policy of the two states, and said "during the talks, the two parties discussed problems relating to the present international situation, and they reaffirmed their agreement on mankind's problems today."[3]

A confirmation of the Soviet view of Cuba as their protectorate came with Mikoyan's statement on February 7, 1960 when he stated "those who threaten war now know that we have sent a rocket to the moon . . . and that we can send it with the same precision to any part of the world."[4] and Khrushchev on July 9, 1960 said, "we shall do everything to support Cuba in her struggle . . . We shall help our Cuban brothers fight a blockade, and the blockade will be a failure . . . Speaking figuratively, in case of necessity Soviet artillery men can support the Cuban people with rocket fire if aggressive forces in the Pentagon dare to start intervention against Cuba."[5] While visiting Moscow in July of this same year, Raul Castro said that he was delighted "that the Soviet Union would use every means to prevent any United States armed intervention against the Cuban republic."[6]

Between August 1 and October 27, 1960 the Communist Bloc sent Cuba 22,000 tons of armaments, and on September 2, 1960 China recognized the Castro regime. Finally, on October 27, 1960 in a harbinger of the Cuban Missile Crisis, Khrushchev declared "Soviet rockets are ready in case the United States attacks Cuba."[7]

Clearly, the Soviet alliance was initiated before the first six months of 1959 was over and was solidified in the first half of 1960. The United States Ambassador to Castro, Philip Bonsal was recalled in January 1960. This action signalled U.S. recognition that Cuba had moved into the Soviet camp. Additional evidence of the Cuban-Soviet embrace is that the Castro seizure of U.S. owned property reached its apex between March and October of 1960, when more than $1.5 billion worth of US assets were expropriated.[8]

The Bay of Pigs. Castro had intelligence of the training of a guerrilla invasion force in Guatemala. He suspected however, that it would take place some time before the inauguration of Kennedy as president. When that did not occur, he continued to expect hostility from the Kennedy administration. Reports from people who were on the island prior to the invasion, give the sense that most of them thought that the invasion would be successful. People who were held in detention centers report that their guards were currying favor with them until the invasion collapsed. The subsequent euphoria of Castro has never abated. Now some thirty years later, he still uses in his speeches to the Cuban people this failure as a tribute to the triumph of Cuban arms, Cuban patriotism, and Cuban righteousness. For Castro, the Bay of Pigs has helped raise him in his own eyes to the pantheon occupied by José Martí. In effect, Martí has moved from being an apostle of Cuban nationalism to a prophet for Castro's first coming. Castro in the new mythology, is the secular redeemer of Cuba after its failed effort to achieve independence following the Spanish War, when Cuba fell under the protectorate of the United States. Castro, with the Bay of Pigs, sees himself as having fulfilled the promise of Cuban nationalism.

Perhaps the importance of the Bay of Pigs does not lie in the fact that it was what pushed Castro into the arms of the Soviet Union as apologists for Castro would like one to believe. Rather it is important for what it reveals about the attitudes of the United States at the outset of the Kennedy administration. The fiasco of the Bay of Pigs had profound consequences for future U.S. policy, and it made an indelible impression on Castro with respect to what he could and could not do in the international arena.

Regrettably for U.S. interests, President Kennedy probably chose the worst of all possible options for a great power. He intervened in a smaller country that he knew was aligned with a power that was challenging the United States throughout the globe, and he did so unsuccessfully. Despite the characterization that this may have been a model of self-restraint, it might more fittingly be seen as a textbook example of great power ineptitude. It would have been far better to have done nothing as opposed to being unsuccessful. While doing nothing would have allowed Castro to continue in power, inaction would have at least left open the possibility for future action, and would have given the U.S. some continuing leverage. A successful invasion of course, would have defeated the Soviet geopolitical strategy, and perhaps brought about a genuine democratic transition.

To fall between the two, meant that both Khrushchev and Castro held Kennedy in utter contempt. Khrushchev later verbalized this attitude at Vienna in his browbeating of the young president, and added on it by building the Berlin Wall. These actions in turn, provoked the chastened and electorally threatened Kennedy, to embark on a mobilization and an extraordinarily imprudent intervention in Vietnam.

Another consequence of Kennedy's image problem however, was the decision made by Khrushchev and Castro to bring missiles to Cuba. Neither Khrushchev nor Castro felt that Kennedy knew how to effectively use his power, and that he was more obsessed with public opinion at home than political positions abroad. They dramatically underestimated Kennedy's firmness in dealing with the crisis. Their belief that the United States would not react to the installation of nuclear missiles in Cuba almost brought about a nuclear exchange.

The fact that the Bay of Pigs was a fiasco had other repercussions as well. Castro came to be held in extraordinary esteem as the first Latin leader to repel an attempted American intervention. In this regard, he redeemed all of the frustrated nationalist wounds that not only the Cubans, but all of the Latin peoples, had felt that they had received at the hands of the "yankee imperialists."

In addition, the Bay of Pigs broke the belief that the pro-American Cubans had held since the Platt Amendment that they could rely on the United States to correct the gross aberrations of the Cuban political system. Many Cubans until then, had never developed a sense of responsibility in their struggle against revolutionary elements or foreign machinations. The failure of the Bay of Pigs found them unprepared for the new reality of Cuba, but it may have had the effect of making them realize that the government of their country was their own affair, and would not be brought about to their own satisfaction except by themselves.

As such, the Bay of Pigs, far from marking the definitive break with the United States, should probably be seen as the confirming event of the new Cuban-Soviet alignment. While the limits of that relationship remained to be developed, the failure of the Bay of Pigs meant that the Soviets had a long-term ally consolidated off the coast of Florida. Not only had the Soviets turned a former member of the U.S. alliance system, but Cuba represented a launching pad for further undermining U.S. alliances in Latin America. At the same time, the Castro regime had found a reliable partner capable of sustaining it despite its structural weakness and the various regime threats that the United States posed. While this relationship would fluctuate in intensity over the next twenty years, it would prove very profitable for both Cuba and the Soviet Union, and pose a serious threat to U.S. security.

ENDNOTES

1. Some useful studies on this subject are Cole Blazier, *The Giant's Rival*; Stephen Clissold, *Soviet Relations with Latin America 1918-1968*; Herbert S. Dinerstein "Soviet Policy in Latin America" *The American Political Science Review* (1967); Jacques Levesque *The USSR in the Cuban Revolution: Soviet Ideological and Strategic Perspectives 1959-1977* (1978); Ilya Prizel *Latin America through Soviet Eyes: The Evolution of Soviet Perspectives during the Brezhnev Era* (1964-1982).

2. Daniel James, *Cuba: The First Soviet Satellite in the Americas* (New York: Avon Book Division, 1961) p. 252; also Cole Blazier, *The Hovering Giant* (Pittsburgh, 1976) p. 189; Bonsal, op. cit. pp. 130-131, and Andres Suarez, *Cuba: Castro and Communism, 1959-1966* (Cambridge; MIT Press, 1967) pp. 84-85.

3. James, op. cit., p. 262.

4. Ibid., p. 257.

5. Ibid.

6. Ibid., p. 258.

7. Ibid., p. 257.

8. On March 11 $10 million of US sugar mills were seized. On April 5, US-owned telephone companies worth $50 million were seized. On April 6, some 272,000 acres of United Fruit Lands worth $32 million were seized. On June 11, most of the large US-owned hotels were nationalized. On June 29, the large Texaco refinery was nationalized. And in October, the US-owned banks were nationalized and some 166 US-owned companies were seized.

CHAPTER XI

From the Cuban Missile Crisis to Carter

The next period in Cuban-Soviet relations went from the nadir after the Cuban Missile Crisis to a nearly complete rapprochement between 1968 and 1970. Castro in this period, perceived the Soviets as having backed down in the face of U.S. threats, and attempted therefore to strike out on his own to promote revolution throughout Latin America. He supported various guerrilla groups in the Andean, Caribbean, and Central American region. The Soviets, after the Crisis, went through a period of supporting revolutionary movements while seeking to maintain normal relations with established governments.

Castro's reaction to the Cuban Missile Crisis was the event that plunged Cuban-Soviet relations into their most difficult period. Castro was distressed that an agreement to withdraw the missiles was forged above his head by Washington and Moscow. His unhappiness was apparent, and the Soviets moved to ease it.

For our purposes, this period is particularly instructive. It covers Khrushchev's fall, the early Brezhnev years, the attempt to placate the US, Castro's desire to manage the Sino-Soviet rivalry, and the wish not to abandon the revolutionary agenda. In addition, the Nixon era provides an insight into how the Soviets and the Cubans behaved when the Soviets attempted detente with the US without abandoning Cuba as a revolutionary client.

The immediate ending of the Cuban Missile Crisis enraged Fidel Castro. It also provided an opportunity for the Chinese to ingratiate themselves with Cuba at the expense of Moscow. Anastas

Mikoyan had been sent to Havana in an attempt to restore tranquility in Soviet-Cuban relations, but Mikoyan also ruffled Castro's feathers. He had to inform Castro that the IL-28 bombers which Moscow had given to Cuba were also part of the Washington-Moscow accord ending the crisis. Because of their capacity to carry nuclear weapons, Washington had considered them part of the offensive weapons agreement, and they had to be removed.

The Soviets sought to woo Castro in the aftermath of these disagreements. He visited Moscow for the first time from April 27 to June 5, 1963. It was after this stay, that signs of a reconciliation between the two countries began to emerge. Khrushchev was clearly trying to calm troubled waters with the United States, and to isolate China. The Soviets opposed the armed struggle in Latin America, but Castro was anxious to support it. All that the joint declaration at the end of Castro's visit said on this matter, was "the practical forms and methods to be used in the fight for socialism in each country should be established by the people of that country."[1]

Khrushchev desired Cuba to endorse peaceful coexistence and peaceful competition and to refrain from the armed struggle. Castro however, was particularly supportive of the armed struggle in Venezuela. At best, his position was a disguised breach with the Soviet point of view. The official communist parties of Latin America backed Khrushchev's position, but the Cuban press at the same time was openly declaring that Latin America was ripe for the armed struggle.

In January 1964, Fidel again visited the Soviet Union and again signed another non-committal communique. After Khrushchev's fall in late 1964, the Soviets moved to a more conciliatory position regarding the armed struggle.

The Soviets were obviously trying to heal the differences between the two countries. They were alarmed by the US intervention in Santo Domingo, the downfall of the Goulart government in Brazil, and "the Johnson Doctrine" in which the U.S. president stated "the American nations cannot, must not, and will not permit the establishment of another communist government in the Western Hemisphere."[2]

The changing attitude in the USSR was demonstrated in several ways. In early 1965, the anti-Castro Director of the Latin

106

American Institute of the Academy of Sciences, S. S. Mikhailov was replaced. Radio Moscow also began broadcasting favorable comments in Quechua about the popular struggles in Peru. The Soviets were both skeptical of the success of armed insurgency in the light of the backlash it saw in US policy. At the same time they were desirous of bringing Castro's insurgency activities under control. The Soviets began to gain the upper hand in their relationship with Castro at the first Tri-Continental Conference held in Havana in 1966. Under the supervision of KGB colonel Vadim Kopshergin, Moscow established its first ten terrorist training camps in Cuba. The aim was to gain control over Castro's free lance terrorist operations and operational direction over the world wide campaign against the US involvement in Vietnam.

The Tri-Continental Conference was also designed to wrest influence from China in the Afro-Asian Peoples Solidarity Organization (AAPSO). The Soviets were seeking to dilute Chinese influence by including the Latin Americans within AAPSO, and then fusing it in the Tri-Continental structure to bring about AAPSO's dissolution. Although the Cubans were not unwilling to work to neutralize Chinese influence, they finally moved to create a separate, parallel organization to AAPSO, the Latin American Solidarity Organization (OLAS).

The first meeting for OLAS was in July 1967. A giant portrait of Simon Bolivar provided the backdrop to the conference, and it gave more than a symbolic identification of the Cuban Revolutionary movement with that of the great Liberator. This key to the strategic thesis of the revolutionary struggle in Latin America was that if Bolivar did not consider Colombia free as long as Spanish power remained secure in Peru, then the same principle was applicable to Cuba's security. Cuba would not remain free until all of Latin America was revolutionized. At the conference both the armed and pacific routes to power were endorsed. Backing was provided for the Salvador Allende drive to power in Chile by the electoral box and the "Che" Guevara assault on power through guerrilla warfare in Bolivia.

A secret agreement was concluded at the end of 1968 which obligated the DGI to operate under the control of the KGB. A firmer set of rules were elaborated in May 1970 when Raúl Castro visited Moscow. In this accord, Cuba agreed to cut its armed forces and received a $4.6 billion loan, for which repayments began in 1986, and were to run for twenty-five years at no interest. By July 1972, Cuba was admitted to the socialist economic camp (Comecon) as a full member, and it was agreed in 1974 that Cuban and Soviet five year plans for the 1976-1980 period were to be coordinated by Juceplan and Gosplan. Between 60 and 70 percent of Cuban trade was within Comecon.

By 1972 Cuba's total debt to the Soviet Union was $4 billion. Annual repayment on these loans was estimated to be between $130 and $150 million. The Soviets accounted for nearly 50 percent of the total Cuban imports. This process of rapprochement salvaged Cuba's economic disintegration and provided the Soviets with strategic and foreign policy advantages. The Soviets received docking facilities at the Cienfuegos Submarine tendering complex, a satellite tracking station, and a refueling base for its reconnaissance flights. The Soviets also received political support for the Brezhnev doctrine during the 1968 Czechoslovakian invasion and political help against China in their Third World competition with the Peking government. These deals completed the process from extreme tension and competition to one of close cooperation and mutual assistance between the Soviets and Cubans. The Soviets were finally able to bring the Cubans into line because of the disastrous economic policies that Castro's government had undertaken. Castro had ambitions of becoming a new Bolivar; the logic of his revolution and his sense of history demanded a trans-American enterprise. To the extent that he seemed to succeed without Soviet help, the less he was inclined to accept Soviet tutelage. If Castro could have developed an independent power base in Latin America, Cuban dependence on the Soviet Union might not have evolved to the degree it did. The thwarting of both his political objectives abroad and his economic policy at home led Castro pragmatically to seek to carry on his agenda through the Soviet Union.

Once the conciliation between the two countries had been effected, the Soviet-Cuban relationship came to be marked by both maximalist and minimalist approaches to foreign policy goals. The minimalist agenda for Castro, was to preserve his regime's security, increase his international autonomy vis-a-vis Latin America and the United States, develop his power base in Cuba, and gain economic assistance. These core minimal or defensive interests, were essentially achieved with the forging of the Soviet alliance in the early 1960s, but became increasingly evident by 1970.

Castro's maximalist agenda was aimed at extending Cuban influence within the Third World and leading the Third World struggle against the United States. Castro's effort was particularly focussed on the Caribbean, Central America, and Africa. By promoting successful armed insurgencies in the Caribbean Basin and around the world, Castro sought to raise Cuba to the front ranks of Third World powers.[3]

U.S.-Cuban Relations

Despite the Cuban regime's antipathy to the United States and to democracy, prior to the Reagan Administration, US-Cuban relations were based on several tacit assumptions. The first was that however uneasily and unofficially, the United States would respect the validity of the Castro regime's claim to govern Cuba.[4] For this reason, the United States was obliged to respond to Cuban provocations by directing itself toward their international manifestations, rather than directly attacking the source. In other ways, the U.S. attitude oscillated between viewing Cuba as an irritating sore spot during the Johnson and Nixon Administrations to conciliation during the Carter Administration.

Nevertheless, ever since Kennedy imposed the economic blockade in 1960, the Cuban regime was able to generate enormous anti-American hysteria. Domestically, there have been claims of eminent war. The United States has proved a convenient scapegoat for the deteriorating economic conditions that the island faces.

A complicating feature of these relations has been the substantial pro-Cuban support network in the United States, and also the enormous difficulty in getting information out to the American public on the true nature and intentions of the Castro regime. One of the most interesting students of communist regime propaganda and influence on western societies, Paul Hollander, studied this area in *Political Pilgrims*, and focussed particularly on the Cuban and Nicaraguan phenomenon in his monograph, *Political Hospitality and Tourism: Cuba and Nicaragua.* Hollander notes that Cuban and Nicaraguan political hospitality were aimed at strengthening favorable attitudes among visitors by providing them with a selective display of the country's activities and catering to their images and inclinations.

For example, Castro wants to project a sanitized vision of his prison, the testimony of people like Armando Valladares to the contrary. So there are cases of obliging U.S. journalists returning from Cuba, showing pictures of Castro holding "an impromptu discussion with prisoners undergoing rehabilitation in their Isle of Pines Barracks" and pictures of other prisoners who look as if they have just finished working out at a health club.[5]

According to Hollander the key to this sort of operation has been "the importance of favorable predisposition on the part of political tourists as a major determinant of the success of political hospitality." He concludes that this hospitality plays "an important part in confirming such predispositions and [provides] experiential support for hopes and longings which—as contemporary history has shown—can be projected upon a number of different societies at different times."[6]

These benevolent attitudes toward the Cuban revolution and Castro were displayed from the beginning. Scott Nearing, Waldo Frank, C. Wright Mills, Susan Sontag, and Norman Mailer were some of the pro-Castro American writers. Nearing, for example, praised "Castro's spectacular success in challenging Washington's power monopoly in the Western Hemisphere."[7] Frank found it unreal to call Castro a dictator, "perhaps the name needs redefining."[8] Mills discovered in Castro the beginnings of Third World liberation, "the people behind this voice are becoming strong in a kind of fury they've never known before."[9] Sontag saw liberation of human energy in Cuba's collective redemption and a future the U.S. should aspire to.[10] Mailer found Castro leading a third way, a Cortés riding Zapata's white horse belonging "neither to the United States nor to the Russians but to We of the Third Force."[11] These were not isolated voices, but representative of a new left ideology which was starting to take root among U.S. intellectual elites.

During the early seventies, certain sectors of the U.S. government were at odds with official government policy. As a result, Castro was lionized by some Americans at the same time that regime to regime relations continued at a very frosty level. The attitudes that intellectuals reflected towards Castro had their benign counterpart in a section of the policy community, prior to Carter's arrival to office in 1977. The commission on U.S.-Latin American relations chaired by Sol Linowitz, issued its report in December 1976. The Commission report called for a basic change in the U.S. approach to Latin America and the Caribbean, arguing that military security need not be the overriding goal and ordering principle for U.S. policy in Latin America, that the United States should not continue the policy of the isolation of Cuba, that "Cuba's material support of subversive movements in other Latin American countries has diminished in recent years," that the United States should seek to end the Cuban trade embargo, and that "an equitable new agreement with Panama regarding the Canal would serve U.S. interests not only in Panama but throughout Latin America."[12] The Staff Director of the group, Robert A. Pastor, served as President Carter's National Security aide for Latin America in the National Security Council.

Carter carried these benevolent attitudes with him to the White House, and ushered in a new period of at least nominal U.S.-Cuban rapprochement.

ENDNOTES

1. Jacques Levesque, *The USSR and the Cuban Revolution* (New York; Praeger, 1978) p. 93.

2. Ibid., p. 109.

3. Edward Gonzalez, "The Cuban and Soviet Challenge in the Caribbean Basin" *Orbis* vol. 22, no. 1. Spring 1985, pp. 73-94.

This article provides an excellent analysis of Castro's strategies for the period.

4. This assumption was based on the Kennedy-Khrushchev accords in 1962. These accords apparently include the ten letters exchanged between the two heads of state (declassified in 1973), and at least six other formal and informal diplomatic exchanges. In June 1982, President Reagan suggested that the Soviets had violated the Kennedy-Khrushchev Accords, and on September 14, 1983, President Reagan said, "that agreement has been abrogated many times by the Soviet Union and Cuba, in the bringing of what can only be considered offensive weapons, not defensive, there." The offensive forces that have been introduced into Cuba include: the Soviet Bear 'D' Bombers which are superior to the I1-28 bombers discovered in 1969. The construction of submarine facilities in Cuba in 1970. The introduction of Soviet Mig 23s in March 1978. The discovery of a Soviet combat brigade in July 1979. The introduction of TU-95 Bear "F" bombers in 1982, and the Mig 29 in 1989.

5. Lee Lockwood, *Castro's Cuba, Cuba's Fidel* (Boulder, Westview Press, 1990) pp. 266-269.

6. Paul Hollander *Political Hospitality and Tourism: Cuba and Nicaragua* (Washington D.C.: The Cuban American National Foundation, 1986) p. 32.

7. Scott Nearing, *The Making of a Radical: A Political Autobiography* (New York: 1972) p. 240.

8. Waldo Frank, *Cuba, Prophetic Island* (New York, 1961) p. 163.

9. C. Wright Mills, *Listen Yankee: The Revolution in Cuba* (New York; 1960) p. 7.

10. Susan Sontag, "Some Thoughts on the Right Way (for us) to love the Cuban Revolution" *Ramparts*, April 1969, p. 7.

11.   Norman Mailer, *The Presidential Papers* (New York, 1963) p. 75.

12. Cf. *A Second Report of the Commission on United States-Latin American Relations, the United States and Latin America: Next Steps* (New York, 1976). For an additional discussion of this work read "The Pattern in Central America" by David C. Jordan in *Strategic Review* Fall 1979, pp. 5-6.

CHAPTER XII

Carter's Peace Initiatives

The Rhetoric of Rapprochement

When the Carter Administration came to power in 1976, there was an effort to see if a concessionary foreign policy attitude toward the Soviet Union and Latin America—Cuba in particular—might reverse the trends in the increasingly hostile international environment. The United States claimed it no longer had "an inordinate fear of communism" and rapidly concluded negotiations for turning over the Panama Canal to the Omar Torrijos dictatorship in Panama.

Robert A. Pastor points out that the most important source of influence on the Carter administration was the Sol Linowitz-chaired Commission on U.S.-Latin American Relations. According to Pastor, the reports of the Commission helped the new Administration define its relationship with Latin America, and led to the implementation of 27 of 28 specific recommendations. This influence was underlined when Cyrus Vance, the new Secretary of State, met with Sol Linowitz to discuss the report and asked him to be one of the two negotiators for the Panama Canal Treaties.[1]

The Carter government also moved to negotiate a more normal relationship with Cuba. Cyrus Vance, at his confirmation hearings stated that "if Cuba is willing to live within the international system, then we ought to seek ways to find whether we can eliminate the impediments which exist between us and try to move toward normalization."[2]

In June 1977, the US reached an agreement with Cuba to establish interest sections in Havana and Washington. These mini-negotiating posts were inaugurated on September 1, 1977. Each delegation contained eight to ten members and was headed by a Counselor. The U.S. delegation operated in Havana under the Swiss flag, and the Cuban delegation operated in Washington under the Czech flag.

In March 1977, the U.S. through Cyrus Vance, said it was ready to talk with Cuba concerning fishing agreements and athletics teams exchanges, and that the US was reviewing its ban on travel to Cuba. On March 5, 1977 the U.S. made its preconditions for the normalization of relations. The U.S. wanted Cuba to show a substantial commitment to the non-interference in the internal affairs of the Western Hemisphere nations, a decrease in its military involvement in Africa, and demonstrate its commitment to human rights by releasing political prisoners. As a show of good faith, between March 18 and April 1, regulations prohibiting the travel of US citizens to Cuba expired and the U.S. Treasury made it legal for US visitors to spend money in Cuba. Also in this period formal talks on fishing boundaries between the US and Cuba began.

A sign that the Cubans were pleased with these talks came when Raúl Castro stated on April 11, "the war [between Cuba and the US] has ended . . . we are reconstructing the bridge brick by brick . . . it will take time. When both sides reconstruct the bridge, we can at the end shake hands without having winners or losers."[3]

By the end of this month a US-Cuban fishing agreement was completed and followed by a delegation of Cubans who attended an international citrus conference in Orlando, Florida. The US Senate Foreign Relations Committee approved a proposal to lift the US trade embargo on Cuba on May 10. On June 1, Carter reported that his ultimate goal was full friendship of the United States with Cuba, but because of growing opposition in the US Congress, he withdrew his proposal to partially lift the embargo against Cuba.

The Reality of Aggression

Despite the signs that the initiatives of the Carter Administration were inducing favorable rhetorical responses from Castro, the actual substantive policies of Castro (with Soviet backing) were entering into a maximalist period. The Cuban military almost doubled between 1976 and 1980, from 125,000 to 220,000 men under arms. Cuba, as a proxy of the USSR, moved aggressively to install pro-Soviet regimes in Africa, the Caribbean, and Central America. Simultaneously, Castro stepped up his bids for leadership in Latin America and in the Group of Non-Aligned Nations.

Between 1975 and 1976, more than 36,000 Cuban combat troops were sent to Angola. While seemingly progressive changes were taking place in the rhetoric between the United States and Cuba, an additional 12,000 Cuban troops were dispatched to Ethiopia.

The Cuban troop figures of 12,000 were disclosed by Castro in his then-secret speech for the People's National Assembly of December 27, 1979. But the reports in the American press clearly indicated that Castro was continuing his activity in the summer and fall of 1977. During the summer of 1977, five Cuban transport convoys were believed to have sailed to Angola from Cuba with troops and both military and civilian advisors. Some members of the press were estimating even then, that Castro's Africa corps was close to 20,000.[4]

Consistent with the efforts to forge a rapprochement with Castro, the State Department minimized these reports. Assistant Secretary of State Richard Moose considered these services of Castro for the Soviet Union as "no burning issue." Some Cuban experts interpreted these actions as "shrouded efforts to reduce his commitment."[5] Yet by November 1977, the United States government was warning against 27,000 Cuban military personnel and civilian advisors in Africa, who could threaten the movement toward the resumption of normal U.S.-Cuban relations.

Hodding Carter III said that a new study by the Administration had detected a major build-up of the Cuban presence in Africa, including 23,000 Cubans, 19,000 of them military, in Angola. Referring to the Carter Administration's steps to improve ties with Cuba after a sixteen-year break, the State Department spokesman said that the situation in Africa "will have an impact on peace and even the possibility of normalizing relations." Hodding Carter noted the newly opened interest sections on September 1, 1977, but added, "in light of the military activity we have gone as far as we can go at this time."[6]

The expeditions to Southern Africa and the Horn were undertaken with the logistical support of the Soviet Union, and Castro attempted to achieve his maximalist position in Africa of eroding the US presence in the region.

In addition to Castro's objective of extending the Cuban influence into Africa and eroding the US presence there, Castro initiated a similar policy with respect to the Caribbean and Central America. In March 1979, the New Jewel Movement (NJM) led by Maurice Bishop seized power in Grenada. Bishop immediately received Cuban and Soviet Bloc backing in his effort to consolidate power in Grenada.

This was followed by the triumph of the Sandinistas in Nicaragua on July 19, 1979. According to the account of the then-National Security Advisor Robert A. Pastor, the Carter Administration foresaw a Sandinista victory in the mid-1980s. The Administration decided not to respond antagonistically however, because it did not want to behave like the US had after Castro's 1959 victory which it thought had been "an overreaction."[7] This attitude was held despite the Administration's "viewing the key Sandinista military leaders as Marxist-Leninists who admired Cuba and despised the United States. . . ."[8]

Moscow and Havana shared a willingness to not only back the new Sandinista regime, but to assist the Marxist insurgency, the FMLN in El Salvador. Rather than find that its policies had converted the USSR and Cuba into cooperative allies, the Carter administration found that it was being placed increasingly on the defensive. The aggressiveness of these countries and the success of their clients around the globe meant that not only had Carter not been able to improve relations through conciliation, but had actually allowed the spread of regimes ideologically inimical to U.S. interests.

In short, the period of a major American effort to open and improve relations with Havana, was interpreted as weakness without providing any pressure on Cuba to modify its behavior. Consequently, there was a major escalation in Castro-backed insurgencies in the Caribbean, Central America, and Africa. By the election of Ronald Reagan in 1980, the US position in the Central American-Caribbean Basin area was at an all time low.

The Cuban Paradigm

The functioning Cuban state was externally dynamic, internally static. Its internal structures which were its mainstay: its security system, military, and propaganda apparatus, were primarily status quo maintaining organizations; designed not so much to improve conditions, but to prevent people from organizing in protest of those conditions. This institutional organization meant that the Castro regime was externally directed rather than internally driven, and meant that the Cuban state was a tool for the export of Marxist-Leninist ideology and revolution, Soviet state interests, and Castro's private political ambitions. What gave the Castro regime its defining character as an externally directed state was its fundamental support by the Soviet Union, and the inability of the United States to formulate a strategy to sever those relations and undermine Castro's international position.

ENDNOTES

1.   It was pointed out at this time, by the Republican minority of the Senate Foreign Relations Committee, that Sol Linowitz might have a conflict of interest in the negotiation because he was a member of a bank which held part of the Panama public debt. "The Minority Views of Senator Robert P. Griffin" 95th Congress, 2nd session, Feb. 3, 1978. Griffin wrote as follows, "Since General Torrijos came to power in 1968, Panama's national debt has grown from $167 million to about $1.5 billion—an increase of nearly 900 percent—giving the country the dubious honor of having the highest per capita debt in Latin America. Between 1975 and 1977, under Gen. Torrijos' leadership, the interest on Panama's debt has increased from

$138 million to $243 million—a jump of more than 75 percent in just two years." p. 195.

Senator Griffin added that "Mr. Linowitz was appointed only on a temporary basis—for a six-month period. Under the law, an appointment on this basis does not require confirmation by the Senate. Such an appointment operates to bypass the usual scrutiny by a Senate committee of a nominee's qualifications and possible conflicts of interest. If hearings had been held, the Senate would have learned that Mr. Linowitz was serving as director of a New York bank that participated in making huge loans, still outstanding, to the Torrijos government of Panama. Furthermore, the Committee might have cleared the air with respect to allegations that Mr. Linowitz formerly represented the Marxist Allende government of Chile and was required in connection therewith to register as an agent of a foreign government." p. 199.

It should probably be added here, that the Carter administration was particularly proud of its human rights initiative. As Mr. Pastor wrote, "the Carter administration believed that dictators were the problem, and that human rights was the solution." Robert A. Pastor, "The Carter Administration and Latin America: A Test of Principle" in *United States Policy in Latin America: A Quarter Century of Crisis and Challenge*, 1961-1985 ed. by John D. Martz, (Lincoln and London: University of Nebraska Press, 1988) p. 92. It is interesting that Griffin writes in this regard, "last year the Torrijos government had the worst human rights record of any country in this hemisphere, except Cuba. Indeed, in this respect, Panama was rated by Freedom House as being at about par with the Soviet Union." p. 182.

2. Pastor, op. cit. p. 79.

3. *Cuban Studies* vol. 8, no. 1, Jan. 1978 pp. 39-40.

4. Rowland Evans and Robert Novak, "Castro's Quest For Partners in Angola" *Washington Post* Oct. 5, 1977, p. A13.

5. Ibid.

6. John M. Goshko, "Expanded Cuban Presence Decried by U.S." *Washington Post* November 18, 1977. p. A22.

7. Robert Pastor, *Condemned to Repetition* (Princeton: Princeton University Press, 1987), pp. 4-5.

8. Ibid.

PART III

THE INTERNATIONAL STRATEGIC TRANSITION

On Christmas Day, December 25, 1991, Mikhail S. Gorbachev resigned as the last leader of the Soviet Union. He marked this resignation with a decree relinquishing control of the Soviet strategic arsenal to Boris N. Yeltsin. In his resignation speech, Gorbachev noted that the USSR "was going nowhere and we couldn't possibly live in the way we did. We had to change everything radically."[1]

The year 1980 marked a dramatic transition in the "correlation of forces" and with it, the beginning of the crumbling of the Soviet side of the paradigm which had sustained Cuba and the attraction of the Cuban model for the Latin American states. As we have indicated before, Castro's regime had two centers of gravity: one domestic, the other, the Soviet Union. The policies which the Reagan Administration developed began to destabilize both of these centers of gravity, and profoundly altered the character of the Castroist regime.

Whereas the Marxist-Leninist political system had been able to sustain itself and flourish through a period of controlled aggression and controlled trade while the West was in a reactive mode to its initiatives, the adoption of a pro-active foreign policy forced the Marxist-Leninist regimes into new defensive and awkward positions to which they were unaccustomed. The two bases of support upon which Castro relied on, had given his regime a profile which would dramatically change during the decade. Prior to the 1980s, his regime had taken a revisionist stance vis-a-vis the Latin American state and social order, and had been characterized as aggressive, progressive, and charismatic. Increasingly as the eighties wore on however, his regime came to be seen as defensive, counter-progressive (anti-democratic), and an unappealing political alternative. Rather than vying for the leadership of Latin America as he had at the beginning of the 1980s, Castro came to be seen as increasingly isolated and marginalized from the real course of Latin American development. The 1980s can therefore be characterized as a period of American action and Marxist-Leninist reaction, and this tergiversation would have a profound impact on the nature of these regimes.

ENDNOTES

1. *New York Times* Dec. 26, 1991, p. A12.

CHAPTER XIII

Reagan and the Roll Back of Communism

The election of Ronald Reagan in November, 1980 was interpreted as the return of the most reactionary, militaristic, and imperialistic forces in the US government. There was a sense that the freedom of manoeuvre which the Marxist-Leninist regimes had enjoyed during the tenure of Carter would be constricted. Indeed, Castro found his actions increasingly opposed, his international support base undermined, and the legitimacy of his own government increasingly questioned. A wave of democratic revolution swept through the Americas, leaving Cuba as the only dictatorial regime in the Western Hemisphere.

In an attempt to establish itself before Reagan's inauguration in 1981, the Cuban-backed FMLN launched an effort to seize power at the end of 1980 in order to present the new Republican administration with a communist regime in El Salvador as a *fait accompli*. The insurgency initiative led the Carter Administration to send arms to the Salvadorean government in a successful effort to prevent this seizure of power. The failure of the FMLN guerrillas would prove a harbinger of events to come.

Ronald Reagan came to power in 1981 riding the crest of an intellectual movement in the United States that sought to prevail in the international struggle with the Soviet Union, both as a land power and as a revolutionary ideology. The gathering of strategic thinkers was drawn from American universities and think tanks, and they were both strategic and historic thinkers about international relations. William Casey, Constantine Menges, Frank Gaffney,

Jeane Kirkpatrick, Richard Allen, Richard Perle, Lt. Gen. Daniel Graham and others contributed to the formulation of the Reagan Doctrine.[1]

Normally, the Reagan Doctrine is seen to refer to the Reagan Administration's policy for dealing with regional conflicts where Third World regimes had the backing of the Soviet Union. In this narrow sense, the Reagan Doctrine was a name applied to the policy of supporting guerrilla movements in Third World countries governed by Soviet-backed client regimes. It was in this narrow sense, that journalists such as Charles Krauthammer used the title "Reagan Doctrine." As such, the policy was seen as being implemented in Afghanistan, Nicaragua, Angola, and Cambodia.

There was as a result, much discussion as to whether or not this was a continuation of the "containment doctrine" or the implementation of the older "Roll Back Doctrine" under a new label. In fact however, this narrow understanding of the Reagan Doctrine was part of a much broader effort to undermine the Soviet power projection and military build-up which had developed under the detente premises of the 1970s. In effect, there had developed a struggle within the foreign policy establishment elite as to how to deal with the Soviet gains of the 1970s. Reagan officials had noted that some ten new clients of the Soviet Union had emerged during the 1970s.[2] The Soviet military capability was no longer deterred by the U.S., and Moscow was in the process of gaining additional economic resources from the West. Reagan officials therefore adopted a prudential policy to reverse or check all these gains. The Reagan Doctrine is used in this essay to cover the broader agenda of the new administration.

A general awareness of the nature of the geopolitical, strategic, and ideological struggle developed which led to an effort to forge a strategy for the defeat of the Soviet Union. In the area of geopolitics, the strategy drew on the historic means by which a sea power successfully defeats a land power in the struggle for position and resources in the international arena. This meant that there would be a reversal of forces whereby the sea power would no longer accept the struggle exclusively in its own spheres of influence and among its own allies, but would seek to engage the Soviet forces and its clients in areas whereby those forces and those clients would have to expend their resources in costly efforts to maintain their positions, clients, and allies. This strategy in essence, was the concept behind the Reagan doctrine.

In addition, this strategy aimed at supporting nationalist forces within the Soviet imperium itself, whereby it would provoke strains in the very center of the Soviet imperial system. On the strategic front, the Reagan doctrine was designed not to match the Soviet system missile for missile or plane for plane, but to seek a strategic, technological innovative change which would make much of the Soviet strategic arsenal obsolete and thereby impose a massive cost on a political economic system that was not nearly as adaptable or as developed as that of the United States.

Finally, the Reagan doctrine sought to attack the principal mechanism of financial support for the land power, which paradoxically came from the West itself. Over the years, substantial financial and corporate interests had developed long-standing relationships with the Soviets whereby they helped to provide it with needed financing, technology, and investments. These investments had permitted the Soviets to maintain their highly competitive military posture vis-a-vis the United States.

On the basis of this three pronged attack at the Soviet's expansionary client system, principal intimidating capability, and at its external financial support network, those forces within the Soviet Union which understood the long-term implications of these policies for the continued viability of the Soviet regime, sought to alleviate these pressures by forging a profound detente relationship with the United States.

With regard to Latin America, many commentators have seen the blueprint for the Reagan policy in the 1980 Committee of Santa Fe report, "A New Inter-American Policy for the 80's." This report certainly fit into the larger trend of policy experts and academics who were attempting to seize the initiative from the Soviet Union and reverse the accommodation of Soviet gains in the strategic and geopolitical arenas. In this regard, the committee report laid out a plan to assist free market economies and promote regime development that would resist statist political programs and subversive Marxist insurgencies. The strong commitment to the protection of regimes under communist assault was labelled by some as a far right document, but it foreshadowed the successful shoring up of the leading democracies and the numerous successful transitions from authoritarianism to democracy in the 1980s.[3]

Perhaps the most important individual in articulating a forward strategy for the region in the Reagan Administration was Jeane Kirkpatrick. She wrote an article published in *Commentary* titled "Dictatorships and Double Standards" which deeply impressed then candidate Ronald Reagan. Her objective was to stem the declining U.S. geopolitical position in Central America and the Caribbean. In it, Kirkpatrick correctly noted the pro-Castro affinities of Panama's dictator Omar Torrijos, and censured Carter's policy. She wrote that Carter's "crowning achievement has been to lay the groundwork for a transfer of the Panama Canal from the United States to a swaggering Latin dictator of Castroite bent."[4]

The subsequent policies of the Reagan administration led to the freeing of Grenada from the grip of Maurice Bishop's successor communist regime. At the same time, the Reagan administration supported anti-communist and pro-democratic movements all over the region, with the most notable examples being the support of the Nicaraguan contras and the unqualified support for the consolidation of a democratic regime in El Salvador and the containment of the Salvadorean insurgency. In all, during the Reagan administration, the world witnessed the victory of pro-democracy forces in Peru (1980) just before Reagan's election, Bolivia (1982), Argentina (1983), Uruguay and El Salvador (1984), Brazil and Guatemala in (1985).

Cuba began to feel the strains of the global strategic conflict, as the Reagan administration began to develop a Latin American strategy designed to contain its influence and promote democracy within the hemisphere. A central piece of the Reagan foreign policy revolved around the conflict in Central America, which represented a strategic choke point with the potential to create tremendous strains in the ability of the United States to project power beyond Latin America. In a reversal from the Carter foreign policy, the Reagan administration actively worked to undermine the Sandinista regime and contributed millions of dollars in aid and military assistance to the governments of El Salvador and Honduras. Simultaneously, despite pressure from the Central American governments and the democratically controlled Congress to come to an accommodationist settlement and cut off the anti-Sandinista insurgency, the Reagan administration continued to attempt to foster conflict within the Marxist-Leninist alliance system in order to generate a Vietnam syndrome of attrition for the Soviet geopolitical system.

At the same time that the Reagan administration was pursuing a "negative" foreign policy in Central America, it was pursuing a "positive" foreign policy in South America, establishing AID programs to help build democratic infrastructures in the Andean region and working closely with the democratically elected governments in fighting against narcotics trafficking and guerrilla insurgency.

Cuba also began to come under direct pressure as well, as programs such as Radio Martí and a tightening of the trade embargo were implemented. Castro's freedom of manoeuvre was curtailed, and he was forced to spend valuable resources in combatting these new attacks at the same time that his troops were becoming increasingly bogged down in the struggles in Ethiopia and Angola where the Reagan administration was supporting the UNITA rebels.

The Reagan doctrine came under criticism at the time of its inception by those who were concerned that it raised tensions with the Soviet Union, would bog the United States down in protracted conflicts, and from those who felt that statist solutions were appropriate for Third World countries. It exacerbated internal divisions within the United States, especially among those who were sympathetic to the reform agendas of left wing regimes along with their allies in the U.S. Congress. Undoubtedly, the hostility that this conflict generated between the Administration and its critics in the Congress contributed to the budget deficit which continued to mount through the Reagan administration and on into the Bush administration. In order to garner support for its strategy of combatting Soviet surrogates and to build up its strategic defenses the Administration was unwilling to combat the large social spending agenda of the Democrats in Congress. The unfortunate consequence of this compromise was to push the U.S. budget deficit to ever-increasing levels and to confront American society in the 1990s with a tremendous deficit overhang.

Other, perhaps less long-term consequences, such as the deficit, was the Administration's willingness to interfere in the domestic electoral processes of fledgling democracies in order to obtain outcomes that would permit U.S. funding for the counter-insurgency programs. El Salvador is perhaps the most significant example of where the U.S. provided funds for one side of the domestic election in order to have a government that would be acceptable to the Democrat-controlled Congress. In the long run however, this sort of realpolitik has proved beneficial and El Salvador is on the path toward reconciliation since the January 1992 accords between the government and the FMLN.

One of the chief obstacles that the Reagan administration had to overcome was the domestic perception that it was allying itself with the reactionary military and oligarchic economic forces in the region. The fact of the matter was however, that the reforms initiated prior to Reagan's coming to office in El Salvador for example, had substituted statism for oligarchy and both had to be replaced.

However, as part of its pro-democracy agenda for the region, the Reagan administration equated the holding of elections with the establishment of real democracy. In a sense, this led to the disguising of very real social, economic and political problems which still persisted, and meant that in some cases, the basis for democracy was very fragile.

Under the Bush Administration, the United States continued its active pro-democracy policies by supporting the peaceful transition in Chile and the ouster of the criminal government of Manuel Noriega in Panama. Through an electoral strategy to resolve the problem, a successor non-communist regime replaced the Sandinistas in Managua.

In this series of setbacks, Castro watched his influence in the region and throughout the world decline. At the end of the 1970s, he seemed poised to make a bid for leadership in the Third World, but many of the developing nations decided to adopt different economic and political strategies from his own during the 1980s. The regimes backed by his forces in Angola and Ethiopia either accepted elections or fell to other military insurgencies. In Latin America, he continued to find support and friendship from Mexico, Ecuador, and Venezuela. Increasingly however, the Latin governments have turned a deaf ear to his pleas for political support and have opposed his calls for hostile cartels against the U.S.

Democratic movements also swept through the Eastern Bloc, undermining Castro's power position vis-a-vis the Warsaw Pact. Castro witnessed a growing reluctance of the Soviet Union under Gorbachev to provide him the economic and military backing to which he was accustomed. This development was perhaps the most troubling of all for Castro, but it may prove only a harbinger of the difficulties ahead, especially if Boris Yeltsin consolidates his power and the new Russia he heads, is transformed into a state with an anti-communist foreign policy.

The implications for Castro were immense. All of the evidence accumulated seems to indicate that Castro's effort to link Cuba to the Soviet Union had created a situation in which the Cuban political and economic support structures were almost inextricably entwined with Soviet interests. However, some sources have argued that this dependency is not as great as is popularly imagined and is being systematically reduced. By all accounts however, the developments in Russia will have enormous consequences for the Cuban regime as it can be assumed that the Boris Yeltsin-led Russian government will offer no support.

The inefficiencies of the central planning system were always corrected in part, by infusions of foreign aid from the Soviets. In addition, the Comecon structure of the Warsaw Pact countries gave the Cubans a guaranteed market for their sugar and any other goods they were able to muster for international consumption. Not only has Cuba suddenly lost its main source of aid to buttress the economy, but it has also witnessed a decline in the reliability of its major markets, as the old Soviet-dominated Marxist-Leninist regimes switch to hard currency and market trading.

For Cuba, the fall of the Soviet Empire may be as crucial an event in terms of the evolution of her political system as the Bay of Pigs. Once again, Cuba is caught in the coils of the revolution in the relations between the East and West. The Soviet experience is crucial, not only because it illustrates how Cuba's geopolitical situation has shifted over the course of the past decade, but also because it provides different models which Castro and the Cuban communist party might try to implement as they attempt to adapt to the times. At the same time, the emergence of alternative economic rivals to the U.S., like the European Community and Japan, and the nuanced foreign policy positions of the socialist/leftist regimes in Spain, Venezuela, and Mexico means that Cuba is not presented with a strictly either/or choice in how to come to terms with the United States.

What Reagan did in 1981, was change the terms of debate. By attacking the Soviet centers of weakness, the Soviet economy and promoting anti-communist resistance in the Soviet imperial periphery, the United States pushed the Soviet Union to reconsider its geopolitical strategy and implement a series of moves designed to counter these initiatives. Rather than remaining on the defensive, the United States developed a forward strategy, and in so doing, fundamentally altered the geopolitical position, not only of the Soviets, but of Castro as well.

ENDNOTES

1. This account does not enter into the discussion of the personal contribution of Reagan to the foreign policy agenda. Rather this is a characterization of the substantive implications of the prevailing foreign policy views of the intellectual movement in which Reagan took part. The debate about Reagan's contributions can be found in, among other books, David Stockman's *Triumph of Politics*, Gary Wills *Reagan's America*, Lou Cannon's *Reagan*, Martin Anderson's *Revolution*, William Ken Muir's *The Bully Pulpit*, and Edwin Meese's *With Reagan: The Inside Story*.

2. Principal officials with these views were Jeanne Kirkpatrick, the U.S. Ambassador to the United Nations, Constantine Menges, who worked with the Director of the CIA, William

Casey and then later served on the staff of the National Security Council.

3. Cf. Holly Sklar, *Washington's War on Nicaragua* (Boston, 1988), depicted the Committee as exaggerating the Soviet threat, and claimed that the high point of Soviet power had come in the 1950s. p. 59. Roy Gutman, in *Banana Diplomacy* (New York, 1988), attacked the approach towards resisting communism in Nicaragua, as "one of the most obscure events in Reagan's presidency."

4. Jeane Kirkpatrick, "Dictatorships and Double Standards," *Commentary*, November, 1979, vol. 68, p. 34.

CHAPTER XIV

The Soviet Need for Reform

The Soviet leadership seemed to be on the threshold of its greatest victories by the end of the 1970s, but even then it was beginning to feel the effects of the cost of empire. When the Reagan administration forced it to commit even more resources to its military-industrial complex to match the U.S. arms build-up, the lack of a domestic economic infrastructure to sustain that growth was keenly felt.

The challenge of the Reagan administration forced the Soviets into a position where they had to take risks with their political power in order to compete. They had to change the system enough to make it economically viable, but their political system could only sustain itself as it was through repression. Once the Soviets relaxed their security apparatus, they entered into a pre-revolutionary situation. The classic statement of this dynamic comes from Alexis de Tocqueville:

It is not always when things are going from bad to worse that revolutions break out. On the contrary, it more often happens that when a people which has put up with an oppressive rule over a long period without protest suddenly finds the government relaxing its pressure, it takes up arms against it. Thus the social order overthrown by a revolution is almost always better than the one immediately preceding it, and experience teaches us that, generally speaking, the most perilous moment for a bad government is one when it seeks to mend its ways.[1]

This was the situation which Mikhail Sergeyevich Gorbachev presided over when he came to power in March 1985.

The Roots of Reform in the Communist Party

Considerable material has come to light that suggests that there was an incipient reform movement developing within the Communist Party nearly three decades before Gorbachev came to power. The argument for this development is linked to the claim that Yuri Andropov was a reformer, Gorbachev was his protege, and Andropov in turn, was the protege of the real first revisionist of the Soviet system, Otto Wille Kuusinen.

The principal sources for this interpretation come from Fyodor Burlatsky, an editor of *Literaturnaya Gazeta*, Ivan Frolov, the editor-in-chief of *Pravda*, and Georgi Arbatov, head of the Institute of the United States and Canada. According to these writers' interpretation of the reform movement within the CPSU, Kuusinen undertook an official revision of a textbook on the foundations of Marxism-Leninism in 1958 with the intention to incorporate within it, the destalinization principles announced by the Twentieth Party Congress in 1956. Although the reforms were vague and did not lead to any specific recommendations for an alternative system, they nonetheless reflected an attitude about the need to develop democracy and a suggestion that the dictatorship of the proletariat had performed its historic role.

According to these sources, Khrushchev was not a member of this intra-party reform movement, and so his renewal program is in a sense, seen as having a different motivation and thrust than this group. Nonetheless, the historians of this reform group admit that Andropov upon becoming the head of the KGB in 1967, showed little signs of a reformist policy. They argue however, that he was placed in the KGB by the most ideologically orthodox elements of the Party, precisely to destroy his future in the Party. However that may be, they admit that Andropov became a hard-liner, but was able nonetheless to return to power in the Party, and ultimately achieved his goal of gaining its leadership.[2]

Gorbachev, in this light, is depicted as carrying out Andropov's intentions to reform the CPSU, not in terms of giving into the West, but in taking advantage of the development of favorable trends toward the Soviet Union. Like Andropov, Gorbachev's programs were fluid, even though his policy was clear. He did not know precisely what needed to be done with the Party, the Soviet government, and with Soviet society, but he knew that the international climate was well-disposed toward detente policies, and he knew that his domestic situation needed to be revitalized.[3]

In the wake of Mikhail Gorbachev's enunciation of the new Soviet policies of *glasnost* and *perestroika*, there was substantial uncertainty as to whether or not the Soviet Union could be maintained under a revitalized and renewed communist party or whether democratic changes and nationalism would lead to the breakup of the Soviet Union into a number of independent states. If the former were to occur as was clearly Gorbachev's intention, then a more progressive Soviet state could expect substantial assistance from the West. If the latter were to occur then the prospects for democracy would be contingent on developments in a host of new nationalistic states, and the entire Soviet Union would be an arena of complex inter-state relations.

Hard-line or orthodox communists who dominated the Party's Central Committee over the course of the Gorbachev era, became increasingly critical of and resistant to Gorbachev's reforms however. They accommodated Gorbachev at the outset because they did not foresee some of the costs to the Party's internal position in the Soviet Union and to the USSR's strategic international position. Nevertheless, they were clearly disturbed by both developments, and at every step along the way they attempted to impede any gains that anti-communist and pro-democratic forces made.

The reform communist group on the other hand, increasingly moved toward a position of justifying a multi-party system in the Soviet Union. A new democratic reform group within the Party, led by the former foreign minister, Eduard Shevardnadze and Gorbachev's former advisor, Alexander Yakovlev, was set up originally to provide an alternative to the orthodox CPSU. Two different policy agendas were set in motion by this action. One was to set up an internal dialectic within a Marxist-Leninist framework which would appear to be democratic enough for western governments to approve. The other was to provide a respectable party parachute for Gorbachev in case the CPSU were destroyed by the forces which he set in motion.

After Gorbachev's visit with the leading industrialized states in London in July 1991, he clearly indicated in an interview for Britain's independent television news, that he was moving more towards a market economy and toward a multi-party system, even though he felt that the communist party would retain influence throughout the Soviet Union. Gorbachev was caught between internal party politics and the economic imperatives of modernization.

At the same time, his course of action was also altered due to external events and pluralistic forces which his policies awakened. Gorbachev was seen to oscillate back and forth over the years, depending on where the center of power was within the Soviet Union at the time, in order to maintain his grip on the government apparatus. Yet despite all of the concessionary reforms which occurred, Gorbachev's position could not be seen for anything more than it was. He was not committed to democracy per se, but to the maintenance of power by his supporters, within a Soviet Union still committed to its historic political agenda of maintaining itself as a great power.

The key assumption of the Gorbachev-era Soviet strategy shift was the need to generate Western support for the renewal of the Soviet system. The economic failure of the regime began to have political consequences which the Soviets could not repair within their own system without some kind of restructuring. This realization began to spread to the various power centers within the Soviet government, and it received its key impetus from the military.

Reform in the Military

Just as the movement within the Communist structure led by Kuusinen and Andropov had developed, so an analogous movement developed within the Soviet military. Prior to Gorbachev's access to power, we find that the armed forces anticipated the need for a fundamental renovation of Soviet society and the Soviet military.

Several years before Gorbachev popularized the word *perestroika* in the West, Nikolai V. Ogarkov, Marshal of the Soviet Union, wrote *Always in Readiness to Defend the Motherland* in 1982.[4] In this work, Ogarkov called for perestroika as critically essential to the modernization of the Soviet military and for the USSR's capacity to stay competitive with the West. Ogarkov pointed to three conditions in the Soviet military and society that inhibited the military's competitiveness with the West.

The first obstacle was the engrained stagnant, parasitic nature of the Soviet bureaucracy. Both the military and State bureaucracies were fundamentally inhibiting the Soviet economy and society from international competitiveness. The second obstacle was the slow reaction time in the Soviet military to doctrinal changes in its opponents strategies and to bringing new weapons systems on line in an affordable and prompt manner in accordance with doctrine. The scientific technological innovative base upon which the military was dependent was inadequate.

Ogarkov argued that the Soviet military was deeply dependent on Soviet society to sustain it, and that the bureaucracies of both the military and state institutions were ossified. Without qualitative reform of both the society and the military the Soviet Union could not compete with the more technologically adaptive and economically innovative societies of the West. Ogarkov was removed from the Soviet ministry in 1984, but his ideas were continued by his successors, and he was identified as one of Gorbachev's military advisors.[5]

Ogarkov's successor, Marshal Akhromoyev and the Deputy Chief of the General Staff, General M. A Gareyev adopted and developed Ogarkov's views. Even before Gorbachev came to power the need to modernize Soviet society had become a matter of common sense for the reformers in the Soviet high command. When Gorbachev did assume leadership of the CPSU in early 1985, he brought with him a reform group which soon formed an alliance with the Ogarkov modernizers within the armed forces.

Rather than continue to see military superiority in strictly quantitative terms, i.e. who had the most guns, tanks, and soldiers, Soviet strategic thinking began to look at the quality of those guns, tanks, and soldiers. The Soviet military's view of perestroika was to bring about the long-range qualitative transformation of the Soviet military so that they would become more capable in both relative and absolute terms vis-a-vis the US. In this sense, some of the forces that were identified as the hard line resisters to Gorbachev's reforms appear—at the highest level of strategic thinking—to be its original godfathers.

Glasnost should not be confused with perestroika. Where it is certainly true that the Soviet military was thinking very seriously about the structural modernization of itself and Soviet society, it was not in favor of a policy that would remove secrecy from the development of Soviet military capabilities.[6] Glasnost, instead of being a move toward a pluralistic precondition for a democratic regime, was seen as a tool for strengthening the renewal of the Soviet system by shaking up the ossified bureaucracy and by providing the populace with the illusion of shared power.

Perestroika, instead of meaning restructuring the Soviet system in the sense of transformation, means remodelling, refurbishing, or renewing the existing system.[7] Such a restructuring would not only have the advantage of making the Soviet system more economically competitive, but also of making it more attractive to the West, while allowing the nomenklatura to maintain control over the government and economic apparatus of the country.

On the basis of this analysis, the military was not monolithically opposed to Gorbachev's reforms, but was in fact, identified in some of its top echelons as most sympathetic to the refurbishing of the Soviet system. Rather than being completely antagonistic to Gorbachev's reforms significant sectors within the military collaborated with him. To acquire aid from the West was an objective that all factions wanted. For this reason, Soviet domestic power politics took on the character of a "good cop-bad cop" scenario in the international arena.[8]

In this situation, one can see that for the military it was essential for Soviet foreign policy to stabilize the international environment. This process was needed so that the reform agenda could have the time necessary to bring the Soviet society and military into a competitive parity with the technological and innovative capabilities of the West.

This is not to say that genuine hard-liners did not exist before the August 19, 1991 coup. Just as genuine democratic reformers were engaged in an almost subterranean tug of war with the reform communists, so the hard line was also split into real and artificial divisions. Weeks before the August coup attempt, the *Washington Post* published accounts of hard-line Communists, including top figures in the army and the Interior Ministry police accusing "reformers in the Soviet government of leading the country to ruin and calling on the military and other 'healthy forces' to save the country from 'humiliation' and 'fratricidal war.'"[9] The existence of true hard line groups made the threat to Gorbachev all the more credible and his own political position that much more difficult.

In this light, pleasing the military was of paramount importance. Thus, in June 1989, a new Supreme Soviet Committee for Security and State Defense was created. Its mission was to evaluate how well the quality improvements of the military were being implemented. Gorbachev himself, repeatedly asserted the need to have the most modern of armed forces to guarantee the nation's security.[10]

ENDNOTES

1. Alexis de Tocqueville, *The Old Regime and the French Revolution*, translated by Stuart Gilbert (Garden City: Doubleday & Co., 1955) pp. 176-177.

2. Because Yuri Andropov is considered one of the predecessors for reform in the Soviet Union and Gorbachev's patron, it is particularly interesting to note his interpretation of the Carter Administration. On August 5, 1978, Andropov, then a Soviet Politburo member and KGB chief, gave his view of detente and the Carter Administration's response to it. He is quoted as saying:

The seventies, particularly the first half of the seventies, were marked by major steps forward in world policy and the growth of the positive processes that came to be called *razriadka* [in Western terms detente]. The principles of peaceful coexistence . . . have started to take their place more and more lastingly in relations between states with different social systems . . . The path ahead seemed clear . . . To make detente irreversible is the task history has set mankind . . . Even among conservative Western politicians the realization has appeared that there is and can be no reasonable alternative to *detente*.

The same source also noted that, "According to Andropov, three basic elements comprise these new realities: (1) 'our [Soviet] forces have grown immeasurably'; (2) 'the scale of the anti-imperialist struggle is growing in Asian, African and Latin American countries'; (3) 'the forces of fighters for democracy and social progress in capitalist countries are growing.' Accordingly, he went on, the entire international system has changed: 'An increasingly large place is beginning to be played in these relations by the principles of peaceful coexistence, equality and justice [i.e. Soviet causes], and an increasingly small place is being left for the policy of imperialist diktat [i.e. U.S. causes].' Furthermore, he claimed, these foreign policy changes are having a revolutionary impact domestically in the West: 'The lessening of international tension is stimulating the process of positive social changes and intensifying the influence of the working class and working people on the policy of bourgeois governments.'

3. Frederick Kagan "The Secret History of Perestroika" *The National Interest* Spring 1991, pp. 33-42. Kagan's discussion of this party reform group is a very interesting one, and draws together most of the information on it in the public record.

4. A memorandum prepared by the minority staff of the Senate Foreign Relations Committee on January 25, 1988 notes that Nikolay V. Ogarkov received from Andrei Gromyko the Order

of the October Revolution for "his service in the Soviet Army" on the occasion of his 70th birthday, October 30, 1987. Ogarkov created a doctrine that formed the basis for the massive reorganization of the Soviet military in 1981. The doctrine called for the Soviet Union to go on a war footing, with massive mobilization of all military, economic, industrial, and civil defense resources to defeat the imperialist enemy. Ogarkov argued that Europe could be dominated without triggering a nuclear exchange between the Soviet Union and the United States. He created three theater commands above the theaters of military operations. The most important of these theaters was the Western Theater where NATO could be confronted directly by the Soviet Union independently of the Warsaw Pact.

Thus, even before Ogarkov became chief of the general staff, the Soviet doctrine for fighting theater war was in place. This doctrine held that the Soviet armed forces could fight and achieve victory at the conventional level, while maintaining a posture to preempt enemy use of nuclear weapons. Finally, in his 1985 book, *History Teaches Vigilance*, Ogarkov stressed the importance of increasing the economic capability of the Soviet Union in order to provide the defense capability to counter and defeat the West. Cf. pp. 13-17.

5. Ilana Kass, and Fred Clark Boli, "The Soviet Military's Transcentury Agenda" *Comparative Strategy* vol. 9 no. 4. Oct.-Dec. 1990, ftnt. 27, p. 331.

6. Mikhail Tsypkin "The Soviet Military: *Glasnost'* Against Secrecy" *Problems of Communism* May-June 1991., pp. 51-66.

7. Ilana Kass "Gorbachev's Strategy: Is Our Perspective in Need of Restructuring." *Comparative Strategy* vol. 8, no. 2. Spring 1989, p. 183.

8. One student of Gorbachev's strategy notes that " . . . by fostering the perception that perestroika, indeed, Gorbachev himself, are vulnerable to a neo-Stalinist backlash, the Soviets

strive to persuade the West that unrequited concessions—as well as generous credits and technological transfers—are necessary to both the reform and the reformer." Kass, Ibid, p. 186.

9. David Remnick "Hard-Liners Appeal to Military to Prevent Soviet 'Humiliation'" *Washington Post* July 24, 1991, p. A23.

10. Kass and Boli op. cit. pp. 326-327.

CHAPTER XV

New Soviet Policies
for a New World Order

These developments occurred before the swift and decisive U.S. victory in the Persian Gulf in early 1991, and suggest that even if an important element of the military had backed the crackdowns of late 1990 and early 1991, the remarkable success of U.S. technological capability and new AirLand strategy must have convinced the top elements of the Soviet military again, that perestroika was essential for the long term competitiveness and modernization of the USSR. The pattern therefore, of seeking accommodation with the leading powers and exploiting their state interests as a basis for enhancing Soviet modernization was returned to as the only long-term viable option for Moscow.

Courtship of the West. This new pattern appeared to follow three tracks. The first was a change in Soviet perceptions of the West. Instead of seeing it as an enemy, the Soviets moved toward a perception of the West as an associate. Just as Margaret Thatcher proclaimed that "we can do business with [Gorbachev]," so Gorbachev's rise to power engendered a similar attitude in the Kremlin vis-a-vis the West. Rather than continuing to confront the industrialized capitalist countries solely on the basis of fundamental regime hostility and fear, the USSR decided to temper its overt military and covert subversive tactics in an attempt to create new patterns of expectations and develop a more fluid international environment within which to operate.

It now seems certain that the period between Gorbachev's rise to power and the outbreak of the revolutions in Eastern Europe was clearly an effort to renew the Soviet system internally and to buy time in the international environment to achieve this purpose. Gorbachev and his backers clearly and frankly recognized the weaknesses in the Soviet economy. Consequently, a drive developed within the Soviet party apparatus whose roots, as we have seen, extend back to the 1950s, to renew the country economically, while maintaining political control in the hands of the party.

The Gorbachev-led reform group embarked on a renewed peace offensive to give the Soviet economy a chance at renewal. They hoped to accomplish their objectives of opening up economic ties to the West and Japan, gaining a respite from the arms race and appealing to western elites who might be favorably disposed toward creating a new world economic order in which the Soviets could become participating members.

Gorbachev proclaimed his continued commitment to Marxist-Leninist orthodoxy while making clear that that orthodoxy did not require a confrontational position vis-a-vis the West. He anticipated that the concessions he was prepared to make to the West would produce a backlash against him within the traditional party apparatus. In order not to be a victim of such a backlash within the CPSU, as some of his predecessors had been—most notably Khrushchev in 1964—Gorbachev moved to consolidate a political base outside of the traditional Party apparatus. Rather than maintaining the formula of final power within the CPSU, Gorbachev strengthened the parallel powers of the Soviet government.

Subsequently he gave himself additional powers in these revitalized structures and moved to create a new commission, the Ideological Commission, which would supervise the work of the Communist Party's international department, the key agency for directing Soviet foreign policy in all of its facets. With these measures Gorbachev hoped to provide himself with a base which would allow him to resist anti-reformers within the party structure, and these changes had far-reaching consequences.

The International Department's leader, Valentin Falin succeeded Dobrynin, Gorbachev's first choice to direct the overall implementation of the new foreign policy, and became a key figure in implementing Soviet strategy of incorporating itself into the European Community. A former ambassador to Bonn, and a recent head of the KGB-controlled Novosti News Agency, Falin in an interview published in the spring of 1990 showed how far the Soviets were prepared to go to keep Western support—and to curry West German favor especially—during the renewal of the communist system in the Soviet Union.[1]

Certainly, the Soviets did not wish to lose Eastern Europe without moving toward the "Common European House". The policy of a "Common European House" goes back to ideas held by Stalin and Molotov in the 1950s, and to Brezhnev in the early 1980s. Gorbachev used the term first in his speech to the British House of Commons in December 1984, only a few months before he became Secretary General of the CPSU. For the Soviets, the Common European House meant a Europe that included the Soviet Union, but not the United States.

These initiatives recognized the growth in economic power of the European Community, and the nascent political power that it could hold as a bloc independent of the United States, but Soviet strategy was not only targeted at geopolitical blocs like the European Community, but at the leading actors within the geopolitical spheres like Japan and Germany. These two countries in particular, witnessed an extensive and intensive lobbying effort by the Soviet Union.

Japan

When Gorbachev first came to power, the pattern of attempting to intimidate Japan was openly stated. A *Pravda* article published June 22, 1985 stated that "if Japan did not seriously consider Soviet peace proposals, that Japan's sea lanes were vulnerable." It went on:

Japan depends greatly upon imported resources. Accordingly, Japan must be well aware that escalation of the arms race in sea lanes communication only increases Japan's vulnerability. The Soviet Union is ready to apply a proposed confidence-building measures as the Indian Ocean and the Pacific Ocean. Japan's acceptance of the

Soviet proposal will coincide well with Japan's vital interests.[2]

The tone could not be more different from that of the Gorbachev visit to Japan of April 17-19 1991, where the exchanges were warm and cordial. This visit included a Gorbachev speech to the Japanese Diet and a call for increased Japanese-Soviet cooperation. It is true that the outstanding issue between the two countries—the return of the Kuril islands was not resolved, but the change in tone and substance was one hundred and eighty degrees from when Gorbachev first came to power.

There are considerable indications that the Soviets grasped the changing nature of the Japanese view of international relations and sought to take advantage of a rising Japanese nationalism. After another long interval of Japanese timidity, signs of a new change in Japanese self-consciousness appeared. The Soviets, like the Americans, became well aware of this phenomena. But lest there be any doubt, a pirated and unauthorized translation of a book written by Sony Chairman Akio Morita and Liberal Democratic Party Diet member, Shintaro Ishihara has circulated widely among the U.S. government, trumpeting this change in attitude. (There is now an official version which includes only the parts, and not all of them, written by Ishihara.)

The Japan that Can Say No, sets forth a particularly sharp critique of the U.S. and a plea for a new Japanese self-assertiveness on the basis of its now large technological lead over the United States. In fact, Ishihara is particularly explicit in his demand for a change in Japanese self-consciousness. He points out that both the United States and the Soviet Union are far behind Japan in the semi-conductor technology essential for advanced military weaponry. He argues that if Japanese semi-conductors are not used in either country's technology, they would not be capable of implementing their strategic doctrines. He writes "the U.S. defense department's science commission recently prepared a huge confidential report on electronic engineering. Looking at this, one can well understand the sense of crisis the U.S. has [with respect to Japan]."[3]

The report states that if Japan is left to go as it is, it will be impossible to get the lead back. This report is very accurate in assessing the areas of weakness in the U.S. and the strengths of Japan, but only the president and a few select people have seen the report." He goes on to state "their sense of crisis stems from the fact that semi-conductor technology is absolutely vital in maintaining military superiority, and that this might flow from Japan to the Soviet Union."[4] Obviously the Soviets are as aware as the United States that Japan has complete dominance in the mega-byte semi-conductor industry.

It is in this context of Japan's high technology leadership, that Ishihara calls for a change in Japanese national consciousness. He writes "we Japanese now face choices on whether we can boldly proceed or stand back quietly. It may be possible that Japan can secure a new culture for itself based upon the skeleton of the development of new high-level technology."[5] Undoubtedly the Soviets recognized the enormous opportunities that would arise from working with Japan rather than continuing to present a threatening image to her.

Germany

The same sort of change occurred with respect to West Germany. West Germany, after Japan, is the leading regional economy, and it is clear that the Gorbachev regime agreed to come to terms with it over the reunification of East and West Germany. As a result of permitting reunification, there was an agreement to reduce the German armed forces to 370,000 men, to have a phased Soviet withdrawal from East Germany over a four year period, to provide the Soviets $7 billion to pay for ending the Soviet occupation, and to keep German and NATO forces from reoccupying East German territory. In fact, by July 1991, Germany committed itself to $31 billion in loans, grants and credits to the Soviet Union since Mr. Gorbachev agreed to the reunification of the two Germanys.

At a meeting in Kiev, USSR on July 5, 1991, Gorbachev asked for even more money from Chancellor Helmut Kohl. In pressing for additional aid from Kohl, President Gorbachev pointed to the rising internal strife in Yugoslavia as a "lesson and a warning." Gorbachev argued that he needed support in order to avoid the possibilities of such difficulties.[6] Apparently, President Gorbachev was quite convincing to Chancellor Kohl, and he responded "I would like to make clear to all citizens of the Soviet Union, without interfering in the internal affairs of your country, that the success of reforms in your country is not only in the interests of the Soviet population, but in the interests of all Europeans, and especially my compatriots."[7]

At the same meeting it was noted that "Mr. Kohl took pains to express his support for the beleaguered Soviet President declaring that the Germans—and he personally—were conscious of their debt to Mr. Gorbachev for enabling the two Germanys to unify. 'I simply do not intend to forget this,' the Chancellor said."[8]

In short, the Soviets returned to a policy of seeking relationships with the most developed Asian and European states, rather than relying on relationships with more revolutionary, but less developed countries. In addition, clear signs emerged that the Soviets hoped to gain economic cooperation from the entire North Atlantic community as a result of its initiatives toward the regional superpowers. However, the results of the London conference in July 1991 indicate that the agreed position of the seven industrial democratic powers was not to provide large infusions of funds without additional structural changes in the Soviet Union making it possible to assist both the market mechanisms to be implanted and the democratic structures to be installed.

From Clients to Powers

The second track was a shift in the USSR's approach toward regional politics. Instead of backing clients, the Soviets sought to work with regionally influential states. This shift in policy relieved some of the aid burden and cost of empire which the Soviets assumed. This policy also attempted to take advantage of the resolution of instability, and move away from the Soviet view of solely seeing the advantages of perpetuating conflict.

Signs of change were present with respect to the Middle East, Asia, and Africa. In the Middle East, the Soviets went along with the United Nations in condemning Iraq's invasion of Kuwait, and opened a dialogue with Israel. In Asia, they cut back their support for Vietnam. Now that nation is seeking to improve ties with the United States and other western powers. With Gorbachev's official visit to South Korea following his trip to Japan in early 1991, the USSR also signalled the end of its seeming blank check support for North Korea.

There are some signs that Castro and Gorbachev were at odds on the degree of cooperation necessary and desirable with the United States. Castro suppressed several Soviet journals from being sold in Cuba, including *Moscow News* and *Sputnik*, charging that these Soviet publications were hostile to socialism and the USSR, and pro-U.S. With respect to foreign policy, Castro described the United States as seeking and nearly achieving Hitler's dream of world domination, while the Soviets appeared to be mesmerized by good relations with the U.S.

To indicate at least the possibility that the Soviets reacted negatively to this prickly ally, there were foreign minister visits to Brazil and Argentina, and increased Soviet gestures to Mexico. Signs existed in the Latin American region as well, that the Soviets thought that it would be better to have relations with the leading states of the region, rather than to maintain an alliance predominantly with a heavily dependent, radically revolutionary client like Cuba.

If the August coup had not occurred this policy might have emerged in fuller focus. As such, it is very difficult to say how concrete these policy shifts were, and what Cuba's relationship to the USSR would have been. On the other hand, it is possible that just as Cuba was a potential ally to the hard line dialectic, it was also potentially an ally to the soft-line reform option. Within this option, it would have moved to open talks with the United States, and would seek at the appropriate moment, some joint economic cooperation. Probably the most attractive venture for Castro in this area would be the tourist industry. In this sector, he could rapidly expand Cuba's capacity to gain foreign exchange, while insulating the Cubans from any viruses of freedom that the tourists might bring with them by making the tourist areas off-limits to all Cubans except those employed in the resort areas.

Revitalizing the Military

The third track was to achieve military supremacy through asymmetrical military reductions in the new international environment while modernizing the military-industrial plant. At the same time that diplomatic glasnost was being pursued, Soviet military spending continued unabated. A spring 1991 report of the Committee on the Present Danger concluded that the Soviet Union continued to devote at least one-fifth to one-quarter of its GNP to the military prior to the August coup. The military-industrial complex of the Soviet Union was the only part of the economy which functioned normally, and it was the only sector of the economy that grew in 1990. The only cuts in Soviet defense spending that the Committee could detect were in some planned increases. Hence, there was in effect, no reduction in Soviet military procurement. The Soviets did not cut production of tanks, artillery, or aircraft, and the manufacture and deployment of strategic offensive and defensive weapons continued at standard rates.[9]

In addition, it is clear that the ongoing CFE talks with the United States showed that the Soviet Union saw arms control as a means of disarming the West without disarming themselves. Since 1989, the Soviets moved massive amounts of armaments east of the Ural mountains where the CFE treaty's terms did not apply. Before May 1990, the Soviets had in the treaty area more than 11,000 tanks than they previously had, nearly 20,000 more armored combat vehicles than they previously had, nearly 37,000 more artillery pieces than they previously had, some 45 more combat aircraft, and some 1,600 more attack helicopters. They still would have had to scrap large numbers of their military hardware to get them to levels that NATO had, but the Soviets had in fact, protected thousands of pieces of military equipment by their arms movements. The new strategy was clearly driven by the needs to economically refurbish Soviet society. The Soviets sought to do this without sacrificing their military power.

The independent observer may remark that the Soviet Union made too many concessions, or that Gorbachev's behavior was too contradictory to be planned, and that he was truly caught between different, antagonistic centers of power. The first interpretation argues that Gorbachev was sincerely trying to implement democracy within the Soviet Union, but that he was hampered by the powerful party apparatus and hard line elements in the military. In this interpretation it was in the U.S. interest to help Gorbachev as the most peaceful and smoothest way to effect a democratic transition in the Soviet Union. According to this view, a U.S. policy favorable to Boris Yeltsin before the August coup might have destabilized and polarized the country into intransigent factions, yielding to a scenario of instability and potential violence.

To say that Gorbachev tried to save his regime and personal power, especially in light of the fact that he always shunned democratic tests in his own right and his frequent avowals of Leninism, seems more credible, than to say that he was or is truly democratic. Events forced Gorbachev however, to embrace the democratic option after the coup. Therefore, it was more in the interests of the United States to adopt a wait-and-see attitude and to play the field, rather than to rush in and choose sides in an affair whose outcome was not determined. By adopting the Gorbachev-as-democrat outlook too soon, U.S. policy makers risked alienating the truly committed forces to democracy within the country, and perhaps risked making a historic mistake in allowing the reform communist forces to consolidate and perpetuate their hold on the country.

A second interpretation was that Gorbachev represented only one center of power within the Soviet Union, and that he was powerless in some sectors. His apparent authority was merely superficial and only maintained due to the consensus that he was a figurehead toward whom the West was well-disposed.

These scenarios do need to be taken into account, and not just for the sake of determining the future of Cuba. However, they do not have the same kind of grounding in the realities of power politics and the dialectical mode of thinking inherent in the country which began with the concessions of Brest-Litovsk.

For these reasons, despite the apparent hostility, it may well be that the Gorbachev-era Soviet strategy was supported at the highest levels by the so-called hard line elements or "reactionary

Leninists" of the Soviet system. The validity of this hypothesis would mean that the Soviet military was firmly behind perestroika, and that the so-called hard line-reform antithesis worked as a Marxist "good cop-bad cop" dialectic to extract the appropriate responses from the West.

The problem with such a scenario is that by definition, any opening of the system decreased the ability of the Soviet leadership to exercise total control over it. This factor complicates the situation in that there were both genuine as well as bogus reformers or hard-liners. As can be seen, in the process of implementing this dialectic, some of the reformers and reform movements, such as the Yeltsin-led Russian democratic movement, clearly spun out of control, and needed to be replaced. Gorbachev succeeded in creating a series of rival factions within the government, which he was able to play off of each other in order to accomplish his domestic agenda and maintain his international bargaining stature. In this context, Gorbachev most stood to lose if the democratic reform movement won on the one hand, or if there was a hard line reaction or coup d'etat on the other. If the democratic reform movement won then Gorbachev at least stood a chance of salvaging his position and declaring himself the father of Russian democracy. This is in fact what has occurred and what he claimed in his December 25 resignation speech. His place in history was seemingly assured by this outcome, and he personally benefitted, even if his original agenda failed.

Faced with losing power on the one hand, and a staying action (and perhaps an even greater crisis down the road) on the other, reform communism had to have been the most attractive option for the communist party apparatus and the Soviet military, as well as for Gorbachev. These players had everything to gain from Gorbachev's success: the renovation of the Soviet military, the refurbishing of the Soviet economy, the acquisition of foreign aid, and the maintenance of the CCCPs' political power.

In short, the argument here is that under Gorbachev there was a move to associate with Western powers and regionally influential states. He sought to gain economic benefits and technological transfers from the former, and regional influence and trade from the latter, while exploiting this original and creative detente policy to gain strategic leverage as the West disarmed asymmetrically. The success of this option would have meant the legitimation of the Soviet communist party at the same time that it would have thwarted true democratic reform. With the August coup, both the Soviet domestic political situation and the international arena became more complicated and finally led to the demise of the Soviet Union itself.

ENDNOTES

1. Falin said that "from the very beginning of 'new thinking,' we swore to ourselves that the right of national self-determination was not a declaration of words but a principle of practical policy. We were convinced that it could be no other way. Despite Panama, we were determined not to step into Eastern Europe to prop up falling regimes. We are determined not to be pushed off this track, this principle. We never made it a secret to anybody in the East German leadership that, whatever the developments, our forces were not stationed in the GDR to be a judge in domestic developments. They were there to fulfill a security mission for the Warsaw Pact." Valentin Falin, "The New World Disorder? the Collapse of Eastern Europe: Moscow's View" *New Perspectives Quarterly* vol. 7, no. 2 1990. p. 22.

2. Hiroshi Kimura "Soviet Focus on the Pacific" *Problems of Communism* May-June 1987, p. 14.

3. Shintaro Ishihara *The Japan That Can Say No* (New York: Simon & Schuster, 1991) p. 21.

4. Ibid., pp. 21-22.

5. Ibid., p. 25. I am using here the words of the unauthorized version. In the authorized version, Ishihara writes: "Our preeminence in technology must help us achieve a new consciousness without traumatic convulsions."

6. Serge Shmemann "Gorbachev Is Told by Kohl to Offer Proof of Reforms" *New York Times* July 6, 1991, p. 1.

7. Ibid.

8. Ibid., p. 6.

9. *Russian Military Expenditures* (Washington D.C.: Committee on the Present Danger, 1991).

CHAPTER XVI

1989-1991

The principal Soviet objective during the 1989 revolutions in Eastern Europe was to keep the option open of a Europe that would incorporate Eastern Europe and eventually welcome a reformed Soviet Union. At the beginning, the apparent loss of Eastern Europe held open for the hard-line Soviets the prospect to rejoin Europe later and to dominate it. This policy of apparent losses did not mean that the Soviets had either lost their interest in dividing Western Europe from the United States, or in enhancing their position in the Third World, but it did mean that they sought these objectives by other means.

In other words, the hard-line Soviets borrowed a page from Lenin, who gave away parts of the Tsarist Empire in order to consolidate his power on the greater whole. While this policy was daring, it was also a policy which fitted into the Marxist-Leninist dictum that the ends justified the means, and that long-term gains were worth short-term losses.

Events determined however, that these means were not to accomplish what the Old Guard communists hoped. Even before the events of the Fall of 1989, then Foreign Minister Eduard Shevardnadze outlined that these changes aimed to attract support from the Third World as well. In an important speech on October 23, 1989 in Latin America, he was "gladdened by the considerable positive changes in relations with Mexico, Argentina, and Brazil," with the "positive trends in political relations with Japan," and with "the further development of the project for an all-European home."[1]

With every estimate indicating that the Sandinistas would win the elections, both the Soviets and the Americans agreed to pull back.

A U.S. election monitoring team, headed by former president Jimmy Carter was on hand to sanction the election, and it seemed that the United States had agreed to go along with a process which would lead to the legitimization of Nicaragua as a Soviet client. Through July 4, 1989 U.S. intelligence reports claimed that the Soviet Bloc and Cuba had delivered about $300 million or about 500,000 metric tons of military associated cargo to Nicaragua from the beginning of 1989. According to a State Department source "if deliveries continue at this pace, 1989 will prove to be another record year. The military aid from the Soviet Union, Cuba, and the Eastern Bloc allows Nicaragua to maintain . . . about 80,000 active duty troops, militia, and reserves . . ."[2]

This interpretation of the situation between Cuba, Nicaragua, the Soviet Union, and the United States suggests a somewhat different analysis than was commonly expressed about the deterioration in Castro and Gorbachev's relations after the Gorbachev visit to Havana on April 3, 1989.

It is true that Castro did not give Gorbachev as much of a forum as Gorbachev had become accustomed to in Western capitals. Castro was not interested in implementing a Soviet-type perestroika reform for his own state, and Gorbachev's open call for "an end to military supplies to Central America from any quarter" was part of a Soviet effort to deal with the United States. Gorbachev's stance was in part determined by the hope of nursing a resolution of the Nicaraguan problem which most observers in both the Soviet Union and the United States felt would lead to the legitimization of the Sandinista regime. The full risks of the policy of relaxation in Eastern Europe were yet to be felt, and the surprising outcome of the February 1990 elections in Nicaragua were still in the future.[3]

With the extraordinary changes of 1989 in Eastern Europe, and the defeat of the Sandinistas in 1990, it was the unexpected external events which defeated the foreign policy intention of removing the Central American and Cuban sore point from the Soviet-US relationship. In these circumstances, Cuba was increasingly isolated and the Soviet Union was absolved from responsibility for continued aggressive action in the Americas. Should Castro now open a soft line towards the US, it would be interpreted as a sign of weakness.

Soviet-Cuban tensions were bound to come into the open because a soft line from the Soviets was still critical to its policy of gaining economic support from the West, while limiting its exposure in the various conflict regions around the world.

In fact, the Soviets were still seeking access to the World Bank, the International Monetary Fund, GATT, and other financial and economic institutions in order to assist its economic renovation. In this situation, domestic events began to impact even further on the Soviet position. Internal questions arose concerning its decision to continue reforms with their stimulation of internal dissent, opposition, and disintegration, or to move back toward a more repressive system.

In the years between 1985 and 1989, Gorbachev's effort to reform communism within the Soviet Union was the most extensive that had ever been attempted. He had provided more cultural freedom under *glasnost* than had ever been offered before, and he had begun a system of quasi-open elections which were providing him the possibility for all alternative sources of strength to deal with his old guard opponents.

But the restructuring of *perestroika* was really cosmetic as far as changing the Soviet Union to a market economy was concerned. Thus, by the end of 1989, the entire system of economic reform was a failure. The command system was paralyzed rather than reformed, and the prerequisites for a market system had not even been initiated. The paradox was that Gorbachev's policies of glasnost now made it possible for increasing numbers of people to point out and complain about the inadequacies of his economic reform policies.

In addition, the new basis of support that Gorbachev had created through his incipient election system, became a base of opposition, rather than of support for his policies. Vocal groups of critics developed in the new electoral bodies, and these groups began to distance themselves from Gorbachev's policies of renovating communism to policies of replacing it.

As the processes of reform escaped the control of the East European power groups in the fall of 1989, the pattern of this occurring within the Soviet Union was picking up speed through the winter, spring, and summer of 1990. The leadership of a genuinely democratic reform group gathered strength in the Soviet Union's major cities, and soon the sectors which Gorbachev thought would be his supporters were ahead of him on the reform agenda. Mayors in Moscow and Leningrad, and a former ally, Boris Yeltsin, moved to lead the Russian democratic reform movement, which threatened in effect, to break up the union of the Soviet Union, and to end the monopoly of power of the Communist Party.

Increasingly, Gorbachev was finding himself poised with one foot in the old Soviet Communist Party power base and with the other reaching to maintain a toe hold with the political and economic reformers who had moved well beyond any thought of renewing communism in the Soviet Union.

The Persian Gulf War. In this situation, the outbreak of potential hostilities in the Persian Gulf with the Saddam Hussein-led Iraqi invasion of Kuwait, provided the opportunity for a return of the hard line forces in the Soviet Union, and a retreat from the reforms which appeared to be harming the interests of the USSR and provoking a strategic weakening of its international position.

There were reports in the western press that Soviet military advisors were present in Iraq before and during the Kuwaiti invasion. In addition to providing advice on how to mount such an operation, Soviet military personnel were also present in Kuwait throughout the crisis, up to and including the outbreak of hostilities between the UN and Iraqi forces. This presence occurred while the Soviet Union itself, through its diplomatic representatives were supporting the UN action against Hussein.

In this same period, that is from the autumn of 1990 to March 1991, Gorbachev seemed to be aligning himself clearly with the hard-line forces seeking to reverse glasnost and perestroika as well as the more advanced agenda of the democratic reformers. The earlier economic reform plan, the so-called 500 day plan, was abandoned in October 1990, and by November, the rapprochement of the hard-liners with the Army and the KGB was in full swing. Reports out of Moscow in November 1990 clearly showed that the Soviet Union had entered into a post-perestroika era. Gorbachev accrued additional political powers, and the Supreme Soviet's legislative functions were virtually annulled. Foreign Minister Eduard Shevardnadze resigned, along with one of Gorbachev's key economic advisors who was considered the principal proponent of continuing economic market-oriented reforms. The new Ministers of Internal Affairs were hard-line KGB and army officers, and the new prime minister, Valentin Pavlov, was associated with the most reactionary Leninist elements in the CPSU. Soviet troops were sent in to repress the independence movements in Lithuania and Latvia, and Gorbachev moved against Soviet television which had showed some signs of independence.

Nonetheless, this process came to an end, and the Soviet Union entered into a third phase, in which the possibilities of a deeper reform including the transformation of the Soviet regime itself, could not be ruled out. But just as there was resistance in the previous stages, so there remained in place, elements which sought Soviet predominance by other means, and the maintenance of the Soviet internal regime by renewal rather than by change. The events of April and May of 1991 suggested the possibility of a return to the processes underway in the October-November counter-reforms, and these suspicions were vindicated in the August 1991 coup attempt.

On March 17, 1991 Gorbachev held a referendum on the need for preserving the Soviet Union, clearly designed in his mind to increase his authority in dealing with the breakaway Baltic republics, Yeltsin however, attached an additional proposition to the referendum which proved to be a stroke of genius. That amendment called for the direct election of the Russian president. When Gorbachev's referendum passed, so did Yeltsin's protocol. It was this which led to the attempt by the communist members of the Russian Parliament to seek to impeach him, but this impeachment effort failed, and Yeltsin was subsequently overwhelmingly elected President of Russia. In retrospect, this move formed the basis for a growth of alternative governmental structures to the communist-dominated central apparatus, and Yeltsin was able to use his position as President of the Russian Republic as an effective legitimate counterweight to the putschists.

In addition to gaining this extraordinary legitimacy through his election by the largest republic of the Soviet Union, Yeltsin worked out an agreement between presidents of nine of the other constituent republics and with Gorbachev, which transferred substantial economic and administrative powers from the Soviet center to the administrations of the republics. Yeltsin also obtained an independent television station for his republic, and partial control over the Russian KGB. The two concessions that Gorbachev received in return, were a ban on strikes, and work discipline in the context of Yeltsin's successful effort to end a two month long miner's strike in Siberia.

In an extraordinary situation, popular-based power in the Soviet Union was moving increasingly toward the republics and the reform democratic movements. Gorbachev sought a measure of support with these forces, but reactionary Leninist forces, which he had appointed, continued to occupy the internal security ministries, the prime minister's office, and other key posts inside the central government.

The August Coup

The prospect of the total collapse of Soviet power, did not seem nearly so close at hand in the first weeks of August, as it has become in the aftermath of the events of August 19-25. Prompted perhaps, by the fear that the All Union Treaty would decentralize their authority beyond all recognition, eight of Gorbachev's most senior cabinet members organized the putsch. Gennady Yanayev, the vice president of the USSR claimed that Gorbachev was seriously ill, and announced the creation of the State Emergency Committee to govern the country during the crisis. Calling for a return to law and order, but noticeably short on Marxist-Leninist rhetoric, the Gang of Eight, as the coup leaders were called, wanted to retrench from Gorbachev's internal glasnost policies, even as they sent out signals that they wanted to continue their good relations with the West, and continue their policies of perestroika. In this light, the example of the Tiananmen crackdown may have been a pattern which the coup leaders tried to imitate: bring in the army, quell domestic dissent, maintain economic restructuring, and continue detente policies with the West.

Seen as a union between the military-industrial complex and the KGB, the coup leaders strategy was complicated and risky, but it was doomed to fail because they misunderstood where the center of their opposition lay.

Gorbachev was much easier to neutralize than Yeltsin, for by the time of the coup, Gorbachev's constituency had diminished dramatically as increasingly popular sentiment and political support moved away from a reform communist option to genuine democratic renovation. Yeltsin however, became the symbol of both USSR democracy and Russian nationalism, and he mounted the opposition campaign to the Gang of Eight.

By the time that Gorbachev was able to fly back to Moscow, Yeltsin had gained enormous political clout and the momentum for radical change in the Soviet Union had increased dramatically. Gorbachev, in confirmation of his reform communist tendencies, either did not recognize the full magnitude of the changes which had taken place, or tried to coopt the situation into continuing his crypto-communist agenda by appointing General Moiseyev to take the place of Dmitri Yazov as Defense Minister, and Anatoli Kryuchkov's Deputy for External Security to take his place as head of the KGB. Yeltsin displayed his hard-won political authority by replacing these appointees only a day later, with his own reform-minded people. The CPSU was discredited and many of its top leaders were linked to the coup, and Gorbachev was forced to take the extraordinary step of resigning from the party, even as it was being banned in most of the republics.

At the same time that the top ranks of the armed forces, KGB, and communist party were being purged, the disintegration of the Soviet Union continued apace. Eight of the fifteen republics declared independence, including Byelorussia and the Ukraine.

Thus, what was already a very difficult situation for Castro became even more complicated. His isolation has become so desperate that he has been forced to put his economy on an emergency footing. Yeltsin is on record as saying that charity begins at home, and that he would cut the Cuban subsidy immediately. It looked like the Soviet Union would follow the example of both the Austro-Hungarian and Ottoman Empires and break into more representative ethnic states. In addition, Yeltsin repudiated Marxism-Leninism and the commitments of the Soviet regime abroad.

Future Scenarios

Studies on countries while they are still engaged in their revolutions very quickly run the risk of becoming dated. Nevertheless, it is interesting to explore them with the idea of demonstrating the contingent possibilities which they are seen to hold rather than simply viewing them as historical chains of inevitable causes and effects.

The Soviet Union is now dead, and in its place are numerous new states, essentially defined by ethnic nationalities, with practically non-existent traditions of democratic self-rule. Boris Yeltsin is the head of a new Russian republic, and has gathered most of the strategic resources into his hands which were formerly controlled by the Soviet Union. His primary political agenda is domestic reform, and he has clearly dropped the international expansionist policies of the former Soviet Union.

The major immediate variable which the democratic republic and republican revolution in Russia faces is the continuing economic crisis likely to last for several years. Undoubtedly, extreme hardships in this period could have a decisive impact on the attitudes of the Russian peoples in terms of their evaluation of the emerging Russian republic and its alliance with the other republics of the former Soviet Union. Several potentially severe winters loom with prospects of extreme scarcity and accompanying social disturbances. Government dilatoriness in extricating Russia from its economic hardship could provoke a return of hard line forces. These forces would probably assume some sort of authoritarian nationalist agenda for the resolution of Russia's problems. In the six years of Gorbachev rule, no alternative economic structures to the inefficient and demoralized bureaucratic regime had been implemented. Consequently, the new republican experiment enters into government with a collapsing statist economy and no alternative free market, private property, and national capital financial system in place.

Given these difficulties, the country will undergo severe hardships in the near term. If those hardships are not seen as necessary, and are not also to some degree mitigated by foreign assistance, *then disorder is likely and the involvement of security* forces in the maintenance of peace may be inevitable. One could then expect the possibility of a creeping coup or an outright return to power of the reactionary statists under the guise of nationalism or national socialism.

It must be understood that there is no protracted experience with democratic procedures in Russia, and no consensus that those procedures take precedence over the economic well-being of the population as a whole. The growth in the belief that the primary responsibility of government is economic well-being, and not mechanisms for limiting its power, may occur in circumstances of serious economic deprivation.

However, should the fledgling experiment with republicanism survive the next few years, and should the mechanisms for operating a market economy be put in place, then the chances for a consolidation of Russia's move towards republicanism would seem to have a very substantial chance. In effect, we would argue that the most crucial period for the consolidation of the transformation rather than its reversal will be determined before the end of Yeltsin's term in office.

Russian nationalism has the potential for moving in several directions, and in conflicting directions. That is, it can move and be channeled by the authoritarian interpreters of Russian history and experience, and it can be led and shaped by those who are now committed to checking arbitrary power as the preeminent lesson of the Soviet experience. There are substantial examples from history that prolonged experience under repressive regimes have had the effect of creating a consensus among a nation's leaders, even when they disagree on a host of economic, social, and political matters. This consensus would focus on controls over arbitrary political power. These agreements reflect an understanding of the nation's history as being remiss in not addressing as its primary concern, the dangers to the entire people from arbitrary political power. If Britain came to this conclusion in 1688, and France at the end of the Napoleonic era, and Spain after the demise of Franco, there is every reason to believe that Russia could reach a similar conclusion at the end of the communist era.

The Russian revolution movement in this analysis depends on its authoritarian or democratic bent on the basis of whether immediate economic pressures or historic political lessons prevail. One suspects, having now watched the extraordinary events of the failed coup of 1991, that the political lessons are the most important ones for most of the leading elements of the nation. So that the economic deprivation will have to be severe and deep in order to provide the more authoritarian leaders the mass base for an alternative regime.

This argument suggests that communism in its old transnational or international form is nearly finished. On the other hand, statist structures bottomed on a nationalist justification may still be revived. Due to the community particularisms that so undergird modern national identities, it is extremely difficult for elites to impose their statist solutions on multi-ethnic populations. On the other hand, to the degree that the deprivation is seen to be particular to a national community, the possibility of a statist elite justifying its authoritarianism for the benefit exclusively of that ethnic group is still not out of the question.

The most likely scenario for a return of a statist nationalist solution under a Russian rubric, would be for the old disgruntled communist hard line elements in the party, police and armed services to form coalitions with the managers of the state industries and their workers as a socio-economic coalition to sustain a Russian statist solution to its economic problems. They would restore government planning, they would restore rationing, they would restore communications censorship, but they would do it under the restored symbols of Russian nationalism: the tricolor, Mother Russia, the state-controlled church, and the duty to protect the greater Slavic nation in the old Soviet Union and Eastern Europe. They would probably be able to justify such a coup with a nation-wide referendum as an emergency measure to restore the economic well-being of the Russian peoples. In this regard, they would be taking a leaf out of Castro's policies, where he wedded communist methods of political control to a powerful strand of anti-American Cuban nationalism. If Castro's Cuba survives until that occurred in Russia, then Moscow will reforge its alliances with Cuba and the other radical statist regimes of the world in a refurbishment of the anti-American alliance, but this time under the far more powerful sentiment of nationalism rather than communism.

These scenarios suggest that the most critical decisions with respect to Moscow and the constituent republics of the former USSR will have to be taken during the early years of the Yeltsin administration. The model here must be that of assisting Russia and the other republics through the economic crisis, and assisting them in forming a cooperative confederation which will maximize their interests in developing a system of checked power. The dilemma for the United States, in assisting the former states of the Soviet Union is very similar to the dilemma that faced the Founding Fathers in Philadelphia when they were attempting to overcome the defects of the Confederation. On the one hand, there was the need to avoid tyranny with excessive power in the central government, and on the other hand, there was the need to avoid anarchy from too little authority and decision-making at the center. The degree the United States can politically assist the republics in coming up with mechanisms which will avoid either extreme will be decisive in assisting the evolution of the democratic regime forces in all the republics. It may be remembered that among the most critical elements for the founders of the United States in Philadelphia were to resolve the representation in the central government, the commercial relationships between the state governments, and the sphere of autonomy that was to be relegated to the central and state authorities. The compromises that will be made in the former Soviet arena will be undoubtedly different from those that were made in the United States but will be no less decisive as to whether or not the new states of the former Soviet Union conflict and disintegrate and the forces of authoritarianism rise, or that the new states manage to cooperate and the forces of democracy are reinforced.

ENDNOTES

1. Eduard A. Shevardnadze "Foreign Policy and Perestroika" FBIS-Sov. 24 Oct. 1989 pp. 47, 51. In this speech on page 42, Shevardnadze also indicated how the Soviets were moving towards accommodating Washington in the Central American and Caribbean region: "The situation around Nicaragua is different now. The Sandinist leadership's flexible line and the activity carried out by the institution of the presidents of five countries of the region are bearing fruit. Washington is also displaying realism and giving precedence to a political settlement. We attach great significance to the Secretary of State's statement that the United States will accept any results of elections in Nicaragua provided those elections are 'clean.' As is well known, Managua agreed to ensure that the February general elections take place under international supervision.

    The joint decision we have taken with our friends to suspend our arms shipments to Nicaragua also contributes to stabilization."

2. *Human Events* July 28, 1989, p. 3. In this same speech, Shevardnadze made it clear that Castro was at this point, sympathetic to what the Soviets were trying to do: "We had a thorough exchange of opinions on a broad range of questions in Havana with Comrade Fidel Castro and the members of the Cuban leadership. We informed our friends about our talks in the United States and in Nicaragua and also about the progress of perestroyka. Comrade Fidel showed tremendous interest in the processes taking place in our country and stressed the importance of the successful implementation of the aims of perestroyka for Cuba and the entire world. The priority task in Soviet-Cuban relations is to improve the mechanism for economic cooperation and sharply boost its effectiveness and mutual advantageousness. Substantial work lies ahead in this direction.

    In connection with Cuba I would like to single out something that we said to the Americans: U.S. policy toward

Cuba does not fit in with the current situation. It presents a very stark contrast against the general background of the warming of the international climate. The very terms 'blockade' and 'embargo' grate on one's ears. Washington should give some thought to the signal given by the world community when it elected Cuba a member of the UN Security Council. If there are problems, they must be resolved through dialogue. As far as we know, the Cuban leadership is ready for this." Shevardnadze, op. cit., p. 43.

3.   To understand that the new Soviet foreign policy establishment put in place by Gorbachev continued to desire a pro-Castro alignment one need only hear Valentin Falin in his spring 1990 interview: "With perestroika, many people wonder about our Party's relations with Cuba. Let's [sic] look at the map. For 30 years, Fidel Castro has lived under the conditions of economic blockade and of persistent animosity on the part of his northern neighbor. When we understand this, we can understand Fidel much better. His emotions and his attitudes may be difficult to grasp from the luxury of an armchair in Moscow or Washington. It is not with our own scales that we should judge the things that bother our Cuban comrades. As a matter of fact, the most unproductive part of our conversation at Malta with the US was on the Cuban trade embargo and Nicaragua. I can attest that this was not through fault of the Soviet side, but resulted from the dogmatic, fixed positions of the US Administration." op. cit. p. 26.

PART IV

THE REVOLUTION
IN CRISIS

If we use the definitions of Crane Brinton, Castro, like Mao, has presided over every stage of his personal revolution. He started out a member of the Ortodoxo party, the principal moderate, democratic counter-weight to the tyranny of Batista's ancien regime. He moved to the radical opposition and the resort to arms. Then he seemed about to establish a constitutional democratic system during 1959, only to proceed to a radical Jacobin period, characterized by a reign of terror and demagogic, populist measures, succeeded by his personal tyranny, and attempted Napoleonic posture vis-a-vis the Third World.

As happened with Napoleon, Castro has outpaced the strength of the ideology which supported him. His external support base evaporated, Castro can no longer maintain the outward-looking regime orientation that he had before. Just as with every dictatorship in the throws of old age, there comes an increasing need to concentrate on internal repression, a more desperate search for sources of foreign aid, and an increasingly defensive posture vis-a-vis an ever-more strident and comprehensive critique of his regime from both internal and external sources.

CHAPTER XVII

The Continuing Crisis: The Status Quo

Castro's Attitude Toward the USSR

A survey of Castro's relationship with Gorbachev's new thinking in 1990 indicated that Castro was both understanding of the political agenda and fearful of some of the risks that it might entail. The possibility of maintaining political control and simultaneously gaining greater access to foreign products and improving the regime's economic competitiveness was surely a tantalizing goal. The decoupling of the external empire and the events transpiring in Eastern Europe indicated however, that the Soviets were losing their ability to maintain their foreign commitments at the same time that the satellite countries underwent change that was more revolution than it was reform. As the months rolled by, it became increasingly apparent that the reforms which Gorbachev had set in motion were very difficult to contain and soon developed an impetus of their own. The divergence in the paths between the Soviet Union and Cuba crystallized even before the August coup. Its failure confirmed that the Gorbachev experiment had led to a logic of dissolution of both the country, the communist experiment, and its overseas commitments.

What the Soviet experience did then was show Castro the limits and the dangers of attempting to revitalize his own Marxist-Leninist regime. This is not to say that Castro abandoned all attempts at revitalizing his own regime. He practiced his own form of disguised rapprochement with the United States while attempting to pursue his revolutionary international agenda. In this context, while the events in the Soviet Union were of greater significance in terms of Castro's international posture and his economic survival, the events in China, may have proved just as important in showing him possible ways to perpetuate his own regime.

Castro was sympathetic to the hard-line elements in the Soviet Union and shared their concern at Soviet strategic losses in Eastern Europe. He welcomed the support of those in the Soviet Union who fought any suggestions that the Soviet Union should disengage itself from its Cuban alliance. In this respect, his most visible allies in the Politburo were Alexander Dzasokhov and Gorbachev's advisor Yevgeny Primakov, and elements in the Foreign Ministry and the Armed Forces.[1] Castro attempted to keep his relations open to the reform groups even though he did not refrain from criticizing them.

His strategy prior to the collapse in the Soviet Union, had been to gain support from either a hard-line or reform communist regime in that country. Castro was, nonetheless, more sympathetic to the hard-liners than he was to Gorbachev. He had argued that the pro-perestroika movement did not accomplish what it set out to do with respect to the consolidation of Soviet-Cuban positions in Central America and with respect to the revitalization of the socialist economy, and instead had led to the overthrow of Marxism-Leninism in the Soviet Union.

On the economic front, Castro pointed out that perestroika reduced the Soviet capacity to assist the Cuban economy, and therefore placed an even greater load on it. In fact in a June 6, 1991 speech, Castro said there was no reason for Cuba to copy Soviet-style perestroika. He went on to add

> We are two different countries, we respect the Soviets very much and I am fond of them, but the USSR is a multi-ethnic state and we are not. There is no reason for us in Cuba to rectify mistakes that were made in other places ... There was no forced land collectivism; Stalinism, a phenomena of abuse of power, of authority,

of personality cult, and of statues, did not take place here, was not seen in our country.[2]

There is some evidence that Castro began his own Rectification Campaign in Cuba before Gorbachev started his perestroika. In 1984, Castro was concerned about the need to increase the productivity of his hard-pressed economy, but unlike Gorbachev's perestroika, Castro sought to strengthen state control and centralized planning. In order to do this, Castro, like Gorbachev, encouraged criticism within the party organization, but did this on his own, without encouraging autonomous centers of self-criticism. Later, as Gorbachev's perestroika and glasnost became increasingly prominent, Castro claimed in an interview with NBC in 1988, that glasnost had always existed in Cuba. He said, "we have glasnost, we have always had it. No party in the world has been more self-critical than the communist party in Cuba. None. Examine our history and you will see glasnost on a large scale."[3]

In a statement calling for a meeting of the Central Committee of Cuba's communist party to meet in October 1991 to "perfect and revitalize" its organization, the Central Committee reaffirmed its commitment to a one party Marxist-Leninist system. The statement also made clear that the Castro-led party intended to continue its rejection of pluralist democracy despite recent events in Eastern Europe and tendencies in the Soviet Union. The fact that these statements came out in February 1990 show that Castro was feeling the pressures for reform prior to Gorbachev's return to the reform movement in the spring of 1991.[4]

When Castro began his program of rectification in April 1986, he indicated that he was attempting to remain in sync with what he thought were the initial intentions of Gorbachev's reforms. Nonetheless, this new perfecting of the Cuban system was more Chinese than Soviet in terms of its reform model, in that the Cubans sought to improve the economy rather than open up participation in the political system.

The economic pressure on Cuba was only beginning to grow at that time. William Safire reported in the *New York Times* that "an academicians' article in *Muskavskie Novosti* revealed that Moscow was spending proportionately six times as much as the U.S. on foreign aid, the largest portion of this unsustainable cost of empire going to Cuba. That sort of Soviet article is now banned in Cuba. The Cuban dictator has said he banned such publications of perestroika as Moscow News 'without vacillation' because they cast aspersions on Lenin and socialism itself."[5]

Castro began to align himself at least de facto, with those forces in the central government which were hostile to not only the Yeltsin-led Russian democratic reform movement, but also Gorbachev's perestroika. Certainly Castro would have remained sympathetic to the Gorbachev efforts if they had been successful. He would have welcomed the prospect of a revitalized Soviet regime and economy providing the opportunity for Cuba to open negotiations with the United States and the West for assistance as well.

But in the context of the debilitation of the Soviet-Cuban position in the Third World and the collapse of a central government holding the Soviet Union together, Castro was forced into a serious policy readjustment. He could set Cuba's development up as an alternative route and offer himself as an alternative model of communist evolution and adaptation. As in the case of China, this alternative route embraces an effort to gain investment from the West without abandoning the predominantly socialist system or an ideologically revolutionary agenda. The problem is that this model increasingly appears to be economically unsustainable.

Cuba Without Moscow

Cuba remains a dependent country, yet despite its hardship it is more ideologically orthodox than its former patron. However, with the collapse of its former patron, Cuba is faced with the prospect of either finding alternative financial patrons or changing its regime. This current period presents the spectacle of a country which is not accustomed to sustaining itself on its own. As a result, Castro has been forced to make two decisions: reach out diplomatically to other potential patrons, and place the economy in a state of siege in anticipation that foreign aid will not suffice to meet the needs of his people.

Given the uncertain and increasingly hostile international climate, Castro has to consider what options are available to him for continuing to dominate the Cuban scene. We would suggest that he has four main options. These options are all based on the premise that he would want to continue in power, or that he would want to perpetuate the Revolution as a force even greater than himself. In this light, he can adopt a China solution, a Gorbachev solution, a Sandinista solution, or finally, make a Martí type of gesture. We do not expect him to go gently into the good night.

The first option is the China solution, or the hard-line option. In this solution he cracks down relentlessly on all dissent, and in effect places the country on a nearly continuous war footing. In this scenario, nothing much changes. Cuba remains committed to statism, but needs alternative sources of financing to sustain her economy, and attempts to get by using fear and altruism as the only incentives to get workers to function.

Castro has been trying to renew the Leninist system in Cuba without fundamentally abandoning the socialist system. To the degree one downplays the extent of the Soviet subsidy, the more attractive a potential reform communist option is to Castro. If that subsidy was only about 2 to 2.5 billion annually for the 1989-1991 period versus the CIA estimated 4.2 billion then it may be possible for Castro to diversify his economic support base without abandoning an essentially statist regime.[6]

The political indications of this reform communist line are also reasonably apparent. The spring 1990 speech of Raul Castro calling for "democratic discussions before the proposed Fourth Party Congress to be held in the fall of 1991" proposed a reform "within the revolution."

Castro has sought joint ventures and investments from abroad. For example during 1989, the country's tourist industry earned about $149 million. This industry is being set up with Spanish, German, French, and Italian investors, and the tourist operations they run have been given complete control over management and work rules.

Another area where modern investment and technology has been applied has been at the center of Biotechnology and Genetic Engineering. The scientists working at this complex have developed medicines and vaccines which have been commercially marketed. This evidence indicates that Castro has, at least to some extent, begun his own restructuring while firmly claiming that he has not.

On a political level, if he is choosing a reform or the Gorbachev option, Castro still needs additional support bases now that the Soviet Union has collapsed. Castro has been interested in gaining this support from Latin America, but in the present circumstances, it seems that he will not receive support from the three largest Latin American states. Mexico, which has long had a pattern of sympathetic cooperation with Cuba is now moving sharply to open its economy and develop free trade arrangements with the United States. It is unlikely that Mexico would jeopardize this policy by being excessively supportive of *Castro* in Cuba. Brazil is also unlikely to provide substantial assistance, not only because of its historic ties to the United States, but also because its present government is particularly pro-U.S. An Alfonsin-led Argentina might have been the best candidate for support, but President Carlos Menem has been particularly critical of Castro, and has called for both political pluralism and the market economy in order for Cuba to integrate itself into the new political realities of Latin America.

Probably Castro is attempting to combine political and economic support from Latin America, China, and Europe. Between 1985 and 1988, trade with Latin America tripled. Brazil has exchanged petroleum products for Cuban pharmaceuticals, particularly meningitis B vaccine. China has been receiving large increases in Cuban sugar exports, and Castro has hosted visits of potential Japanese investors. There is a chance Castro will get political support from China, but that may be a risk given China's bad odor in the U.S.

Apparently, the principal external support base in Europe for a reform communism in Cuba may be provided by Spain. Spain because of its position in Europe and because of its historical links to Latin America is looking to restore its ties in the region. Furthermore, the socialist government of Felipe Gonzalez has less of an ideological distance to travel in terms of its ability to reach a structural accommodation with Cuba. The promotion of relations with Cuba should not be seen as an isolated event, but placed in the context of the European state's over-all Latin American strategy designed to give it maximum influence and economic ties to the region. It is only natural that Spain would want to reach outside of the European continent for some kind of buttressing support against the obvious strength of Germany on the continent.

Given the vast numbers of first and second generation Galicians and Asturians in Cuba, relations with Cuba are a matter of political concern to one of the chiefs of the conservative Popular Party, the governor of Galicia, Manuel Fraga. As a result, Spain enjoys bi-partisan support for what might be called a Spanish Gaullist strategy in Latin America.

Adolfo Suarez, who was the King's principal agent for bringing about the regime transition in Spain has brought to Castro an offer from his international political group to help bring about a seeming opening of the political process in Cuba. According to Armando Valladares, as reported in *Diario Las Americas*, this effort would guarantee the continuation of Castro in power while, at the same time, providing an apparent opening of the political process. There is as a result of the private meetings that Castro had with both King Juan Carlos and Felipe Gonzales, at the Ibero-American summit in Guadalajara in July 1991, a sense that Castro and the Spaniards may be exploring a reform process which will have Spanish backing. It is already clear that diasporan Cubans will oppose this arrangement bitterly, and fear that it is already taking place.[7]

The former Spanish Foreign Minister, Francisco Fernández Ordoñez, has supported the internal dialogue option with Castro. This gesture has been seen by diasporan Cubans as part of the continuation of Castro's regime by means of a reform communist movement. The diasporan Cubans seem to think that if Castro will just give the appearance of opening up his regime, that countries like Spain will support him as though his regime were a true democracy.

The third option would be the Sandinista solution. In this situation, Castro would permit a substantial opening up of the political process. He might allow elections in which he would try to stack the odds in his favor, and thus renew his legitimacy. If he were to lose, there would be a nominal transition to others holding the reins of government, but he and his core group would continue to control the reins of power by dominating the military.

All three of these options represent a form of *continuismo*, with the first being the most openly communist, and the third, the least. All of them presuppose the continued strength of the communist party in Cuba, whether overt or disguised. While Cuba may have been dependent on the Soviet Union to the extent that Soviet actions generated Cuban reactions, the Castro regime has still had the capacity to carry on in one form or another, and the democratic forces have not initially had sufficient strength to dislodge it.

The fourth option would be the Martí solution. This option would represent a recognition that the regime would not have the resources to perpetuate itself by normal means, and might instead seek a mythic or historical solution. Here Castro would seek a dramatic act probably leading to his own heroic death, with the expectant effect of solidifying the Cuban nationalist consciousness in terms of the Castro myth. One cannot rule out that chaos abroad and severe unrest at home would lead Castro to conclude that the communist experiment has failed, and that only an extraordinarily dramatic act could resuscitate the spiritual enthusiasm of Cuban and other anti-American forces.

Castro's options have radically changed now that the Soviet Union no longer exists. Previously, he could keep his options open to either of the two possible outcomes in the Soviet Union which would assist his continuation in power. If the hardliners had won in Moscow, it would have been easy for Castro to maintain a hard line regime with their backing. If the communist reformers had won in Moscow, then Castro could have embarked on his own Marxist reform program.

Now however, with the Russian republic showing clear signs of hostility to him and the entire communist enterprise, he must work out his options without expecting any support from the remnants of the former Soviet Union. In this regard, if he decides to maintain a hard line communist regime in Cuba, he must find a major alternative source of economic support. If he were to find additional sources of support from various democratic regimes, he would at least have to call for some reformation of his regime.

Castro, unlike Gorbachev, has a hard line option as well as a soft line reform communist or "perestroika" solution for Cuba. Castro has not ruled out a repressive or China-like response to dissidents and democratic reformers as Gorbachev seemed to have done after the failure of the coup attempt. In addition to these two options, Castro has retained the possibility of initiating a Managua-type solution without any risks. Of course, at the time that the Ortega brothers embarked on opening up their leadership to a democratic test, it was inconceivable to them that they would lose the elections. Castro has the benefit of their experience, and he too could now move towards a Managua-type solution without risking a loss at the polls. What this solution would entail would be that he would remain as president and head of the armed forces on the basis of revolutionary legitimacy, and open up the election of his prime minister to electoral competition. He would undoubtedly expect the Cuban people to elect in this scenario a left-leaning, or socialist candidate. This option would be geared not so much to regaining support from a Yeltsin-led Russia, but to making Cuba acceptable to U.S. economic support and the lifting of U.S. economic sanctions.

For Castro, the status quo is untenable and yet the future may be worse. The Cuban economy, as he has managed it, is incapable of sustaining itself in isolation. By 1989, the Soviets were subsidizing it to a tune of well over $5 billion per annum. At the same time, Castro is faced with the prospect that any real reaching out to Cuba's natural trading partner, the United States, would force unwelcome political changes upon him. Castro, has to be worried about the forces which may trigger domestic unrest such as the human rights movement, and the close links between the Cubans and their diasporan brethren, and about the forces which may trigger international pressure for change such as the international human rights movement, U.S. concerns about narcotics, and U.S. concerns about the future of the Cuban nuclear program.

ENDNOTES

1. Jiri Valenta, "Cuba in a Changing World: The U.S.-Soviet-Cuba Triangle" *Testimony for the House Foreign Affairs Sub-Committee* April 30, 1991 (Washington, D.C.: Cuban-American National Foundation, 1991).

2. FBIS-LAT, 7 June 1991, p. 4.

3. Quoted in Sebastian Balfour *Castro* (London and New York, 1990) p. 153.

4. Julia Preston, "Cuba Vows to 'Perfect' Its Communist Party" *Washington Post* Feb. 18, 1990., p. A1.

5. William Safire, "Castro's Last Stand" *New York Times* Feb. 19, 1990. p. 17.

6. Gillian Gunn, "Cuba in Crisis" *Current History* March 1991, pp. 101-104, 113.

7. Ariel Remos, "Adolfo Suarez Llevo a Castro un Mensaje Para el Dialogo" *Diario Las Americas* July 16, 1991, pp. 1A, 11A.

CHAPTER XVIII

Emigration and Human Rights

Totalitarian regimes are very rarely completely closed. Opposition is never completely suppressed. For Castro, his main political problem is how to prevent an alternative power structure from emerging which could destroy his power. For these reasons, over the course of the past thirty years, Castro has transformed Cuba into a security state, and he has employed other mechanisms to ensure that opposition to his regime does not become too extensive.

In the new situation, where the Soviet Union no longer exists and a Boris Yeltsin-led Russia can no longer be expected to support either a hard line or a reform communist regime in Cuba, most of the disturbances arising in Cuba and impacting on the United States can not be expected to provoke a major crisis between the two countries.

If Castro continues a reformist line in Cuba, there would not be a major crisis situation with the United States. Some minor crises might arise from substantial increases in Cubans fleeing their island for economic reasons, and the possibility that Castro might once again unload his jails and insane asylums into the United States. But one suspects that the type of crises that might arise under a reform option within Cuba would be perceived as essentially economic or internal ones, and not produce in the short run, any flashpoint in U.S.-Cuban relations.

Mariel. The least aggravating crisis would be a Mariel type problem. In 1981, Castro opened the borders of Cuba and allowed many people to emigrate to the United States. There was a long-standing concern among the exile community of rescuing their

183

family members who were imprisoned for political reasons. Castro, nominally accommodating these wishes opened up the port of Mariel, but in the process also unloaded hardened criminals and insane asylum inmates. Over 125,000 Cubans left the island.

The United States has traditionally pursued an open door policy with regards to Cuban exiles because they were seen to be victims of political persecution. But the United States has never accepted refugees who have fled their countries for economic or criminal motives.

Castro used the ambiguity of the situation to at once "purify" Cuba, and place further stress on American social service institutions. For Castro, migration has always been one of the safety valves of the regime. By allowing periodic migrations, Castro has been able to limit dissent within the country.

Nonetheless, the United States is becoming increasingly sensitive and hostile toward government-induced migrations which have strained particularly such regions as Florida and Southwestern United States.

These government-induced migrations include not only the economic catastrophe communist-statist regimes impose on their own people such as in Cuba, but also their support for insurgencies in Central America and the Andean region which have produced mass migrations to the United States and a host population to provide distribution networks for their drug war assault on the United States. The growing awareness of the American people that large criminal mafia organizations have infiltrated the migrations has further antagonized the United States to Castro's intimate support of these insurgencies.

Although one cannot perceive this provoking a collective or direct unilateral action against Castro, it will certainly fuel the growing impatience felt throughout the United States with the continuation of his regime.

Human Rights. The Castro regime, like every other closed, totalitarian regime which does not believe in the basic worth of the individual, has committed many crimes against its own people. Yet for some reason, the Cuban human rights record has not been subjected to the kind of scrutiny one would think it would deserve. Because of the lack of information, the victims of the Castro regime are truly "desaparecidos," disowned by their own government, unknown to the world outside. Perhaps, as more information does become available, international pressure could be brought to bear on the Cuban government, and the result could be disturbing to the security of the regime.

The continuing difficulty of getting human rights reports out on the Castro regime have bedeviled the UN, where there has been long resistance to publishing the Cuban government's rights abuse record, and where other human rights agencies have directed more of their attention toward governments that would receive them, than those that would not. Castro's own response to human rights charges is to deny them absolutely. He claimed in an interview for the "MacNeil-Lehrer News Hour" in response to a question on his human rights record, that he had "no political prisoners in any unjustified sense."[1]

Armando Valladares' firsthand account leads to an understanding of how many of the people in Castro's prisons were there because of their political beliefs. Valladares explains the attempts to indoctrination and horrors that prisoners of conscience face, "Marxist theory was explained there. There were talks about defending communism, and the students had to participate in activities in support of the revolution. Meanwhile, every night patriots were falling before the firing squads."[2]

Another example of the difficulty intellectuals have had with coming to grips with the human rights abuses in Cuba is chronicled by Herberto Padilla in his *Self-Portrait of the Other: A Memoir*. This famous Cuban poet recounts how the state security official assigned to his case told him, "we have to put an end to the problem of intellectuals in Cuba." The official went on to say, "we can destroy you even though you know that we have no legal justification for doing so" and "the moment will come when every citizen will be a member of the Interior Ministry, just as Fidel wants."[3] What is fascinating about this account is that pro-Castro intellectuals continue to defend him. Padilla reports that the Colombian writer, Gabriel Garcia Marquez refused to intervene with Castro on his behalf because if Padilla left Cuba, it would "harm the revolution."[4]

The reason both of these scenarios have to be classified as minor, is that similar behavior on the part of the Castro regime has been tolerated and condoned by the international community in the past. Foreign policy priorities would have to be reshuffled to make these problems more pressing and generate more international censure. Immigration is widely seen as a problem of individual conscience, and most countries are more willing to treat the symptom by accommodating immigrants, rather than confronting Cuba as a cause of it. Furthermore, extensive education would be needed to make people acquainted with Cuba's human rights record, and the Castro regime has successfully stonewalled most attempts to get this kind of information.

The problem is that human rights, and human rights organizations may play the same role in Cuba that Solidarity played in Poland, and the intellectual movement played in the Velvet Revolution in Czechoslovakia. Human rights has always been a double-edged sword in Latin American internal politics, and in relations between the United States and Latin America. On the one hand, it has been used to destabilize authoritarian regimes, and unify U.S. public opinion against a regime. On the other hand, it has often been a cloak for communist or socialist movements to pursue their own anti-democratic agendas. As a result, foreign powers are often placed in an invidious position of having to discern between authentic democratic human rights organizations and false front human rights organizations.

The problem in Cuba is that because of Castro's ruthlessness in suppressing alternative intellectual currents and political parties to his own, other vehicles for dissent have been very limited. However, the Castro regime has needed to have nominally independent human rights groups for its own political purposes, and independent-minded thinkers have seized on this avenue to voice their criticisms of the country.

Already within Cuba, the first organized demonstration against Castro took place under the direction of an umbrella human rights coalition led by the Aspillaga brothers. This group, called the Concertación por la Democracia en Cuba (CDC), have taken it upon themselves to call for resistance to the regime, and are opposed to its very foundations.

However, another coalition human rights group has also developed. It is composed of dissenters who disagree with parts of the Castroite regime, but are not opposed to a dialogue with it. They are led by Elizardo Sanchez, a former teacher of Marxism at the University of Havana, and Gustavo Arcos Bergnes, a Sierra Maestra veteran and former ambassador to Belgium. Both of these men have credentials as dissidents; Bergnes was a political prisoner for ten years, yet their authenticity is uncertain, and has the earmarks of an intelligence operation.

Like the Concertación Democrática, this group also has the initials CDC (Convergencia Democrática Cubana). As such, enormous confusion has been generated in the international community as to the exact nature of the human rights opposition in Cuba. While Castro has imprisoned the Aspillaga brothers and tried to cripple the Plantado movement of political prisoners of conscience, he has indicated a willingness to deal with the various human rights organizations subscribed in Convergencia.

The leaders of Convergencia have had their authenticity questioned in the exile community. Valladares and other exile leaders believe Castro may exploit the group for the reform Communist option. As a loyal opposition, they could lend added legitimacy to a neo-communist regime still in keeping with the general tenor of the Castroite revolution. Should the situation in Cuba worsen, the Castroites, if not Castro himself, may find themselves a ready-made legitimating institution, and foreign powers may use the affirmations of these "human rights" groups to legitimate an opening of relations with a new superficially reconstituted regime.

A Democratic Upheaval

On the other hand, unrest could become articulated in some form of a mass movement. This scenario would form a different set of challenges for the Castro regime and the world community. If the Ministry of Interior were unable to contain the seeds of a democratic movement, and the army were still to remain loyal to Castro, a conflict between the state and society could force the United States to consider various forms of reaction to the continuation of the Cuban regime.

The crushing of a democratic movement, whether that movement took the form of a protest or an effort to bring about a democratic regime would have serious ramifications. Probably the first example of this sort of crisis occurred in China, with the tragedy of the student pro-democracy movement in Tiananmen Square. The crushing of that movement, widely publicized as it was because of the presence of American television, was indelibly etched in the American mind.

To some degree the publicity of that movement and its opportunity to arise occurred because of events external to the domestic politics of China. The Chinese leadership was awaiting a friendly visit from Gorbachev and was seeking to project the most favorable image possible throughout the world, it permitted the students to gather before and during the visit. The American media was there in force. Undoubtedly this had a synergistic effect on the growth of the protest movement.

Such triggering events could occur in Cuba as well. When Cuba prepared to host the Pan American games in Havana in August 1991, Castro wanted to put on a big show for the world, and he was afraid precisely such a movement might develop during the Games. He stockpiled food and other commodities to have as little unrest and dissension as possible during the games. Furthermore, he formed Rapid Reaction Brigades which were designed to respond to unrest and eliminate it before it came to the attention of reporters attending the Pan Am games.

Given the amount of world attention focussed on the Pan Am games, a spontaneous movement would have proved immensely destabilizing to the regime, but it was willing to take that risk in pursuance of its "bread and circuses" strategy of appeasing the Cuban people. The lack of resources in Cuba made the gesture of hosting the games politically and economically irresponsible, but Castro used the events to reaffirm his populist ties to the people. Paradoxically, it was precisely through such events as the Pan Am games that Castro has historically sought to arrest the developments of any democratic movements and deepen his own cult of personality.

The ruthless use of the security apparatus combined with control of the press have meant that the Castro regime has been able to nip these forces before they could begin. The difficulty of such policies is that as the regime becomes more isolated and resources become increasingly scarce, it will no longer be able to sustain its repression at such a high level. The corruption of the regime may then lead to a very dangerous and violent situation indeed. Democratic forces will begin to coalesce, and the regime will be forced to act with even greater force to counteract this opposition and do so in a more public, less clandestine manner.

The most dangerous situation for U.S.-Cuban relations might occur in a hard line scenario, if Castro, following the Chinese example, crushes such a democratic reform movement. A repression of a democratic movement would entail substantial media criticism, rhetoric, punitive legislative initiatives in Congress, and warnings from the Administration. There is moreover, some reason to believe that in the present international climate, the U.S. could be pressured to take more vigorous action against an open, bloody, and widespread repression of a democratic and anti-Castro movement. Should this repression emerge into an insurgency situation, it would undoubtedly involve the expatriate Cuban community sooner or later, and the pressure for U.S. involvement would surely be enhanced.

Should that be the case, the United States, for the first time in over a decade, could turn possibly to the OAS to provide a collective justification for a regional intervention. At the spring 1991 OAS meeting in Santiago, Chile, the foreign ministers did indeed agree to consult within ten days when a democratic regime was overthrown. An existing authoritarian regime repressing a democratic movement might prove to be an analogous situation, and the action at Santiago suggests that the OAS may be more available for such a contingency than it has been in the past.

Should the OAS prove unavailable for such an extreme situation, then it is possible that the U.S. could turn to the UN for the legitimation of some sort of collective response to either a widespread, bloody repression or a protracted civil conflict.

Since the Congress very nearly blocked the U.S. intervention against Iraq after such action had been authorized by the UN Security Council, the prospects for the U.S. use of force as a response even to a bloody repression and/or civil war just ninety miles off the U.S. coast would be unlikely.   On balance therefore, one would expect, despite enormously critical rhetoric, that Castro and/or his successor regime can get away with a Tiananmen Square-like repression, and at least enter into a civil war situation without outside intervention. The longer however, such a civil war went on, the less certain the repressive forces in Cuba could be that the U.S. would not become involved, even if that involvement were to be unilateral.

Opposition to Castro is still seen as more likely emerging from the human rights organizations.   They represent perhaps, the greatest opportunity as well as the greatest danger to his regime. While they have formed the core mobilizing institutions against his government, they may also form the core legitimating institutions for a successor government, and they may prove a significant vehicle for the renovation of the regime before a drastic crisis involving a widespread mass movement does occur. Emigration in conjunction with repression and censorship are the two vehicles of choice from preventing such a scenario from occurring, but the Cuban government is finding it increasingly economically and politically difficult to maintain its traditional policies. For these reasons, some kind of orchestrated transition which superficially produces change, but institutionalizes a successor regime may be the most strategic way that the Castro regime will handle its domestic discontent. If this were to be the case, international response might be hesitant and unclear, where it would be more concerted if an obvious crisis were to emerge.

ENDNOTES

1.   Here is an excerpt from the interview:
    Castro: What are the violations of human rights in Cuba? Tell me. Which ones? Invent one. Do we have disappeared people here? Look, if the United States--
    MacNeil: Well, let me give you an example of what he [White House spokesman Larry Speakes] said. For

instance, human rights organizations, like Amnesty International, estimate that you have up to 1,000 political prisoners still in your jails here. Do you have political prisoners still in jail in Cuba?

Castro: Yes, we have them. We have a few hundred political prisoners. Is that a violation of human rights?

MacNeil: In democracies it is considered a violation of human rights to imprison somebody for his political beliefs.

Castro: I will give you an example. In Spain there are many Basque nationalists in prison. They're not political prisoners? What are they? Because you also have to analyze what is a political prisoner and what is not a political prisoner. Now then, those who committed crimes during Batista's time, did we have the right to put them on trial or not? Okay. Those who invaded Cuba through Playa Giron. Did we have the right to try them or not? Those who became CIA agents, those who placed bombs, those who brought about the deaths of peasants, workers, teachers, do we have the right to bring them to trial or nor? Those who, in agreement with a foreign power like the United States and inspired by the United States, conspired in our country and who struggle and fight against our people in this revolution--because this revolution is not of a minority; this is a revolution of the overwhelming majority of people. What are these people? What are they? Political prisoners? Those who have infiltrated through our coasts, those who have been trained by the CIA to kill, to place bombs: Do we have the right to bring them to trial or not? Are they political prisoners? They're something more than political prisoners. They're traitors to the homeland.

2.   Armando Valladares, *Against All Hope* (New York: Alfred A. Knopf, 1987) pp. 92-93.

3. Herberto Padilla, *Self-Portrait of the Other* trans. by Alexander Coleman (New York: Farrar, Straus, Giroux, 1990) p. 144.

4. Ibid., p. 213.

CHAPTER XIX

Narcotics

With the Soviet Union no longer in existence or capable of backing Cuba, Castro's options for maintaining his regime have been drastically reduced to either a bunker or a hard line maintenance of his existing system or a Nicaraguan solution without the risk of democratization. The first option would preclude Castro from getting economic assistance that he needs from the United States while only the Nicaraguan option provides him the chance of convincing the United States to lift the economic embargo. Lifting the economic embargo is critical to Castro's survival and the Managua solution must be a great temptation. It can be assumed that Castro will be able to activate an extensive support mechanism in the United States to end the embargo if he embarks on a Managua-type solution. The great barrier to the success of this continued sustenance of a disguised communist regime will be his continuing involvement in narcotics trafficking.

If Castro does not choose the Managua solution, but a hard line response, then it is inevitable that Cuba will continue to further its links with narcotics trafficking in order to finance his regime. To some degree, Castro's support of M-19 in Colombia and its increasing influence in the Colombian government suggest that such an enterprise could find substantial support from the international narcotic mafia networks inside and outside of governments.

Castro's personal ties to drug trafficking extend back into the 1950s. A former Mexican Federal Police officer who was involved in the Santa Rosa raid, A. Gutierrez Barrios, has subsequently been identified by Castro as his personal friend.[1] He had become the head of the Mexican Federal police at the time of the brutal torture and slaying of US Drug Enforcement Agency (DEA) agent Enrique Camarena Salazar ("Kiki" Camarena). He was subsequently fired. This connection needs some elaboration because it shows the long association that Castro has had with elements in Mexico which are deeply involved in the drug trade.

DEA agent Enrique Camarena Salazar was tortured and killed in February 1985. The order to kill him came from Miguel Felix Gallardo, who led the Los Manosos gang of narcotics traffickers. The motive behind the elimination of Camarena was the discovery and destruction of 8,000 tons of marijuana in the province of Chihuahua. The two authors of the crime were Rafael Caro Quintero and Ernesto Fonseca Carrillo. Caro Quintero escaped from the chief of the DFS (Direccion Federal de Seguridad) by paying him some 60 million pesos at the Guadalajara airport. In his escape, Caro Quintero used credentials signed by the head of the DFS José Antonio Zorilla. (Zorilla later fled to Spain, which has no extradition treaty with Mexico.)[2]

Gutierrez Barrios rose in the DFS under the presidencies of Luis Echeverria and José Lopez Portillo. In fact Gutierrez Barrios has been accused in Mexico as being linked to the group which eliminated thirteen Colombians from a rival drug trafficking gang. This was the famous killing of the Rio Tula, by the Group Jaguar, allegedly directed by a high Mexican officer. Gutierrez Barrios is also part of the alleged narco-communist element inside the Mexican services who were involved in the purge of Miguel Nassar Haro, the top police officer who had cooperated with the DEA in Mexico. Clearly, Castro's friendship was not used to dissuade Barrios from joining the most corrupt elements inside the Mexican police system since the mid-1950s.

Drugs as Strategy. Moving from a personal to a political level, it should not be a surprise that the Soviet-Cuban connection to drug trafficking in this hemisphere has endured for several decades. Narcotics was developed as a sub-component of Soviet global strategy in the 1954-1956 period. This strategy began to be implemented with the development and training of leaders for the revolutionary movements throughout the world at key centers like the Patrice Lumumba University.[3]

The second element was the actual training of terrorists, and the third component was the incorporation of narcotics trafficking into the revolutionary strategy. The final two components of this revolutionary activity was to penetrate organized crime, and to actually initiate subversive operations.

According to Joseph S. Douglass, Khrushchev decided either in late 1955 or early 1956 to integrate narcotics into the Soviet revolutionary strategy. The Soviet Defense Council was the organ chosen to subvert such western targets as the United States, Canada, West Germany, and France. The key source for this intelligence on this Soviet strategy was the high level Soviet intelligence defector, Sejna, who tied Raúl Castro to this strategy and subsequently Fidel.

Cuba was brought into this operation during Raúl Castro's visit to Czechoslovakia in the summer of 1960. In the beginning, the principal target for initiating the drug trafficking operation was Mexico. While the Soviets studied the feasibility of the operation on a worldwide scale, Mexico was critical because of its long border and easy access to the United States. According to Joseph Douglass,

> Recognizing the strategic location of Mexico, the Soviets directed the establishment of a second Czechoslovak operation in Mexico that was designed to complement the Rhine operation. The code name of this second operation was "Full Moon." This operation had two purposes. The first was to develop an extensive network for smuggling drugs into the United States. The second was to train intelligence agents who would then be inserted into the United States and Canada. This was a "push-pull" drug operation. The name "Full Moon" referred to the time when the Soviet Bloc agents would be in control of most major groups in the United States and Canada.[4]

Indeed, El Paso DEA agent Jacques Kiere testified before the then 1975 House Armed Services Committee that five out of the known

Mexican Marxist groups were trading Mexican heroin and other drugs for US guns.[5]

The DEA dates Cuba's involvement in drug trafficking from 1961. A secret report was published in November 1983 by the *Miami Herald*, which indicates that the DEA failed to attach a strategic motive to the Castro regime's drug trafficking against the U.S. internally. The DEA believed that the drug trade was conducted for profit primarily, and to move arms and other illegal goods for insurgencies. The report concluded, "considering the increasing volume of drug-trafficking activity in the Caribbean, the proximity of Cuba to the United States, the benefits to be derived from minimal participation, and the motivating ideas of the government of Cuba, it is likely that Cuba's involvement with drug trafficking will continue and possibly increase."[6]

The Soviets have seen narcotics as a basis for their long-term strategy to defeat the West, and they found in Castro, a willing supporter of this strategy. Joseph Douglass writes that:

> Castro was particularly forceful in presenting his position to the Czechoslovak and Soviet officials. He argued that it was important to push this aspect of the drug trafficking [the crippling of bourgeois society] even harder, and to advance the onset of stagnation by targeting younger students, specifically, high school students and children. The Soviets were thinking in terms of forty or fifty years to bring about the desired results. Castro believed it could be accomplished in thirty-five years. The Soviets were more conservative because of the social changes they believed were necessary to achieve in parallel and because they had coordinated these changes with other events in their long-range plan to destroy the West. The Soviets were also concerned that pushing drugs on high school students and children might be too radical and cause an undesirable counter-reaction. In their plan, the Soviet-preferred bourgeois targets were the technical elite, intellectuals, soldiers, and college students.[7]

Castro is on the public record, as stating the natural marriage that existed between the insurgency and the drug trade.[8] Indeed, a DEA report cited in the 1989 testimony of Melvyn Levitsky, then the assistant secretary for international narcotics matters, stated that Castro's involvement in narcotics trafficking and gunrunning had begun at least by 1961, corroborating the *Miami Herald* report.[9]

This involvement of state-sponsored drug trafficking is very important for appreciating how supply created demand. While demand has been a part of the problem, it has not been the primary or most sinister element. The information we have now on state-support for the drug habit clearly indicates that suppliers were out to create demand, and suggests why price may remain low around targeted communities when over-all supplies may be scarce. Clearly targeted communities have been American bases, high-tech personnel, and particularly vulnerable minorities. Minorities too, have been particularly useful as couriers, and this is one of the reasons why Jamaicans, Haitians, and Dominicans have been effective in exploiting the black community in the United States. The result is that at the same time that significant sectors of the country become addicted, that addiction also becomes part of the U.S. cultural-ethnic problem. As Douglass wrote: it was hoped that "by the year 2000, people with a lack of morals created mainly through drugs, people who were willing to take whatever actions were necessary to support the revolution, would have expanded to encompass forty-two percent of the population."[10]

Castro has long attempted to aggravate racial conflict in the U.S. as part of his strategic attack on the U.S. internally. Hence his alliance with Nelson Mandela must not be seen as only an altruistic opposition to Apartheid in South Africa. This alliance has permitted penetration of the U.S. black community under allegedly human rights motivations, and to divide the diasporan Cuban community from U.S. and Cuban blacks. Castro's narcotics politics reveals his true motives and suggest another reason for his extreme measures for disguising his participation.[11]

Narco-terrorism. Needless to say, there was a close connection between drug trafficking and terrorist revolutionary activities.[12] Castro's revolutionary war strategy vis-a-vis Latin America was to "ignite the continent with the total revolutionary war" and eventually move his field of operations from Cuba to a liberated territory in Latin America. One of the preferred areas was the Andean region, with its supportive population base and cocaine basin in the Alto Huallaga valley. It had been singled out ever since "Che" Guevara's efforts in Bolivia in the late 1960s. Castro's strategy derived from Mao's revolutionary strategy and has subsequently been picked up by the Abimael Guzmán-led Sendero Luminoso in Peru.

Mao drew heavily on Sun Tzu for his tactics and strategy. It was Mao who originated the idea of using drug trafficking to destroy the West. As early as 1928, Mao employed the narcotics weapon against his enemies among the Nationalists, and later, after the Long March, used it against the Japanese. Mao flooded a targeted area with drugs to destroy its military and civilian populations while he prohibited its use among his troops and civilian supporters. Later after completely controlling all of China, he established control over the export of narcotics through his narcotics export trade center located near Macao. Through this organization he targeted the French in Vietnam, and later, the Americans in Korea, and after that, the Americans again in Vietnam.

Castro has forged an alliance already with the narcotics trafficking groups in Colombia, Panama, and Nicaragua. In Colombia Marxist narco-guerrillas were tied directly to the Cuban ambassador, himself indicted by the U.S., Fernando Rovello Renedo. There have been of course, mafia groups not controlled by the communist insurgents but there is no doubt about their involvement in pushing narcotics into the United States. The possibilities of Castro's becoming more firmly identified with these narco-guerrilla insurgencies cannot but exacerbate the US concern about him and his successor government.

Another related possibility, is that elements tied to the ideological and/or-narco-guerrilla insurgencies may commit serious terrorist acts within the United States. Depending again on the scale and significance of these attacks, which (conceiving the worst) could include nuclear, political and economic targets, a US response cannot be ruled out. Nonetheless, drawing on the experience of the Kennedy assassination in 1963, there is considerable reason to believe that the provocation would have to be extraordinary and the connection to Castro unambiguous to fire a direct US retaliation. Both these conditions are unlikely to be met.

The response to the growing region-wide narco-fueled guerrilla insurgencies has been to react to their local manifestations rather than their ideological and organizational core. Again one expects from past performance, that the United States would continue to respond in this manner, rather than at the center of its operation and core capabilities. Signs of a change in US policy in this regard would be the use of massive and effective eradication agents and direct strikes at the center of operations. Such a change would involve strong cooperation among the Andean states. While Cuban assets might be involved in such a strategy, direct conflict might still be minimized or downplayed diplomatically.

Cuban Regime Involvement. Indictments against four high ranking Cuban officials for drug trafficking were certified by grand juries in Miami and Tampa, Florida in 1990. The growing charges and evidence against the Castro regime led to the preemptive move in June 1989 against General Arnaldo Ochoa Sanchez who was a hero of Castro's Angolan adventure, and other top members of the Castroite armed forces and the Ministry of Interior. In a highly publicized trial, Fidel Castro and his brother tried to give the appearance of uninvolvement, surprise, and a sense of betrayal on the part of the government by rogue elements inside the military and security bureaucracy. Castro and his brother made highly public denunciations of General Ochoa.

Raúl Castro was particularly strenuous in his efforts to distance himself from the military officers directly under his command. Raúl called Ochoa's activities "a stab in the back and a slap in the face of the fatherland."[13] The American press thought that this was a kangaroo court and that the defendant had been drugged. According to the *New York Times* "the defendant's behavior and his long, downcast gaze which he appeared to hold his eyes fully closed, led diplomats here to speculate that he had been given a drug to prepare him for the appearance. But no foreign reporters or spectators were permitted to attend the tribunal's proceedings, and it was impossible to verify such allegations."[14]

Besides Ochoa, Castro ordered the arrest and trial of six other officers. Among them was Brigadier General Patricio de la Guardia, who was the commander of the special forces charged with Castro's personal security. It was truly astounding that de la

Guardia could have been involved with drug trafficking without Castro's approval. In addition, Castro fired his Interior Minister, General José Abrahantes Fernandez who had been associated with Castro since his takeover of power and had been trained in Eastern Europe.

Two of the defendants who were sentenced to death, General Antonio de la Guardia Font and Major Armando Patrón worked for Abrahantes. La Guardia testified that he had turned monies earned from the drug operations over to the Ministry of Interior. It was necessary for Abrahantes to be arrested to protect the Castro brothers from having knowledge about drug trafficking. It is interesting to note that Abrahantes has reportedly died of a heart attack while serving a twenty year prison term in the Guanajay prison.[15]

In addition, the former Air Force Chief of Staff who was the Minister of Transportation and Vice President of Cuba's Council of Ministers was also dismissed. This official, Diocles Torralba Gonzalez, was close to Ochoa, having studied with him in Moscow during the 1960s. The best interpretation of this purge was that it accomplished two main objectives for Castro. On the one hand, he received unmerited credit in the U.S. for opposing narcotics and purging corrupt government officials. On the other hand, Castro eliminated possible centers of resistance to him within his own military and security establishments.

Undoubtedly Castro was also attempting to keep his reputation as honest and forthcoming and as unbesmirched as possible.[16] In Ochoa's alleged defense at his trial, which reminded most observers of Stalin's show trials so brilliantly described by Arthur Koestler, he denounced himself and said that if he died before a firing squad, that his last thoughts would be of Fidel. What might have obviously induced this brave general to submit to this obviously set-up procedure was that immediately after his sentence, his three young daughters went into exile to Eastern Europe.

It has been in fact, a tactic of Castro's to use narcotics since the very beginning of his revolutionary era in the Sierra mountains. Castro used drugs not only in his insurgency stage, but from the very beginning to help his new regime's economic activities.[17]

The Noriega trial has revealed additional evidence of Fidel Castro's direct involvement in international narcotics trafficking. Carlos Lehder, the convicted Colombian drug trafficker testified that Raúl Castro directly aided the Colombian drug cartel's efforts to smuggle cocaine into the United States throughout the 1980s. In addition, Lehder identified the former president of Colombia and the current president of the ruling Liberal Party Alfonso Lopez Michelson as the cartel's chief government contact in Colombia. Lehder said that during the 1982 presidential campaign the cartel funded more than $900,000 to Lopez Michelson, and ordered the assassination of the Justice Minister Rodrigo Lara Bonilla two years later in part, because he was about to reveal cartel connections with Lopez Michelson.[18]

The importance of Lehder's testimony, is the fact that the M-19 which has long had links with Castro, had its leader Jaime Bateman chair the Constituent Assembly which reformed the Colombian constitution and excised the extradition treaty with the United States.

The brief period (1977-1979) of Cuban cooperation with the U.S. Coast Guard for interdicting narcotics traffic in Cuban and U.S. waters ended in a 1979 meeting in Spain. The contact for the Medellin cartel with Cuba was made by Mr. Guillot-Lara and the Cuban ambassador to Colombia Fernando Ravelo Renedo. Ravelo Renedo had fought with Castro in the Sierra Maestra and was apparently a member of the Americas Department. At the meeting between Guillot-Lara and Ravelo Renedo an agreement was concluded whereby Cuba would assist drug boats flying the Panamanian flag and bearing the name "Viviana."[19]

Guillot-Lara had long been associated with the M-19 leader, Jaime Bateman. Guillot-Lara has admitted to shipping arms to M-19 terrorists in 1980 on behalf of Cuba. The Cuban embassies in Mexico and Colombia provided funds for these shipments which included Uzi submachine guns, pistols, and AR-15 rifles.[20]

It should be kept in mind that since the M-19 has moved into the Colombian political system, its leaders have presided over the demise of the extradition treaty with the United States, and thereby provided a safe haven within Colombia for those indicted for narcotics trafficking and a substantially lessened threat to the communist narcotics traffickers who remain in opposition to the government. Indeed, a book by the recently retired army colonel, Agusto Bahamon, charges that Colombia lost its war against the narco-trafficking mafias when Pablo Escobar surrendered to the Colombian penal system in June 1991, without fear of extradition. Bahamon's book, *Mi Guerra en Medellin*, argued that it was not Escobar who surrendered to the justice system, but the constituent national assembly which surrendered to the narcotics mafias.

The penetration of the Colombian government from above and within by the Marxist narcotics trafficking interests suggests both a highly sophisticated Gramscian strategy for subverting a democratic regime and a possible alternative alliance structure for Castro without having to transform even cosmetically, his regime in order to seek external financing from the United States despite the wishes of the U.S. government.

In conclusion, it seems apparent that Cuban involvement in narcotics has evolved over the course of time. At first, narcotics trafficking was seen as part of an overall Soviet strategy attacking the United States through a weakening of U.S. morale and infrastructure. Increasingly however, Cuban emphasis has shifted from what cocaine does to consumers to what it can do for producers. In this sense, narcotics have helped terrorist movements sustain their operations, or in an even more advanced stage, penetrate established governments. In Cuba's own case, a government with increasingly limited resources, scarcity may lead to a further criminalization and perversion of the Marxist-nationalist idea, as clandestine activity in cocaine may become one of the regime's chief financial supports as a substitute for lost Soviet subsidies.

ENDNOTES

1. Regino Diaz Redondo *Endeudamiento y Subversion: America Latina Entrevista a Fidel Castro* (Mexico: Collecion Enlace-Girjalbo, 1985) p. 122.

2. For an extensive discussion of this case in English see Elaine Shannon, *Desperados* (New York: Viking, 1988)

3. Robert B. Workman in his June 1984 study *International Drug Trafficking: A Threat to National Security* wrote that "Defecting Soviet Ambassador, Raya Kiselnikova, tells us that in 1971 *Movimiento de Acción Revolucionaria* (MAR) was founded under the auspices of the KGB with ten Mexicans who were attending the Patrice Lumumba University in Moscow. They returned to Mexico City and recruited fifty people for intensive guerrilla training in North Korea. By 1975, the *Marxista Revolucionaria*, now a part of the 23 September League was attracting the attention of US law enforcement officials by trading significant amounts of brown heroin for military weapons across the Mexican-US border." p. 2.

4. Joseph S. Douglass. *Red Cocaine: The Drugging of America* (Atlanta: Clarion House, 1990) p. 30.

5. Workman, op. cit. p. 2.

6. Rachel Ehrenfeld, *Narco-terrorism and the Cuban Connection* (Washington D.C.: Cuban-American National Foundation, 1988), p. 4.

7. Douglass, op. cit. p. 83.

8. *Drugs, Law Enforcement, and Foreign Policy* Douglass, p. 65.

9. House Foreign Relations Committee, "Cuban Involvement in International Narcotics Trafficking" Washington D.C. 1989, p. 74.

10. Ibid., p. 90.

11. Most recently, Castro used Mandela again to support his revolution at its July 26, 1991 celebration. Mandela helps Castro with Castro's poor black population as well. Mandela said: "Cuba is my friend, and if by visiting this country I am going to cause tension in Miami, I am very sorry because I have come here in a spirit of peace." New York Times News Service and Lee Hocksteder "Castro Heaps Praise on Visiting Mandela" *Washington Post*, July 28, 1991 pp. A29, A32.

12. One of the most interesting testimonies to this connection is provided by Jose Blandon Castillo, a former intelligence aide to General Manuel Noriega. He testified before a Miami Grand Jury and the Senate Foreign Relations Committee in January 1988. This testimony speaks for itself. "Fernando Ravelo-Renedo, the Cuban Ambassador to Colombia was the contact person between the guerrilla movement, the M-19, and the drug movement . . . In the case of Colombia, there is a link between drug trafficking and the guerrilla movement, and part of their coordination is done by the Latin American Department [sic] of the Communist Party of Cuba, led by Manuel Pinero [sic], who is also the head of all subversive movements in Latin America. . . . Ravel traveled to Panama and dealt with Noriega as an officer in charge of those operations . . . The Republic of Panama was converted into a huge empire in order to commit certain crimes, and it was part of a general project in the hands of Colombia's drug traffickers. This project aimed to penetrate other countries like Nicaragua and other armed forces, such as in Honduras . . . Only two or three months ago, there was a large shipment which was hidden in lumber exported from Honduras to the United States [and seized in Miami]. This international network has been able to penetrate the Central American armed forces and, because of this, security problems . . . affecting the democracies in Latin America, especially in Central America, are jeopardized [sic]. Quoted

in Rachel Ehrenfeld. op. cit, p. 3. And *Narco Terrorism* (New York, 1990), pp. 44-45.

13. *New York Times*, June 27, 1989, p. A3.

14. Ibid.

15. *Miami Herald* 23 January 1991, cited in *Update on Cuba* (Washington: Cuban American National Foundation) 23 March 1991, p. 12.

16. In an interview that he gave in 1985, when questioned about whether Cuba was actively involved in drug trafficking, he responded, "One of the Ten Commandments says: 'Thou shalt not bear false witness against thy neighbor.' The Reagan administration should constantly be reminded of this commandment. Besides, I believe that the people of the U.S. and the U.S. Congress deserve more respect. It's absolutely impossible for the U.S. government to have a single shred of evidence of this kind. These are, in my view, dirty, infamous methods, a totally dishonest way of conducting foreign policy. If we stick to facts, during the last twenty-six years, Cuba's record in this regard has been spotless. In our country, prior to the revolution, drugs were used, sold, and produced. The very first thing the revolution did was to eradicate that problem. Strict measures were taken to destroy marijuana fields and to strongly punish all forms of drug production and trafficking. Since the victory of the revolution, no drugs have been brought into Cuba, nor has any money been made from drugs coming from anywhere else.

Moreover, during the twenty-six years since the revolution, I haven't heard of a single case of any official who was ever involved in drug trafficking—not one. I ask if the same could be said in the United States, or if it could be said in any other Latin American or Caribbean country or in the rest of the Western world." Quoted from *Nothing Can Stop the Course of History* op. cit. p. 61.

17. Workman, op. cit. p. 21.

18. *Washington Post.* Michael Isikoff "Noriega Trial Told of Cuban Drug Link" November 21, 1991, p. A40.

19. Workman, op. cit. pp. 23-24.

20. Ibid.

CHAPTER XX

The Cuban Martyr Complex and Apocalypse

If Castro's alternative programs of economic development fail, and Cuba is unable to find other sources of financing, given the intransigence of Castro and the mixed legacy of Martí, apocalyptic scenarios could unfold. Castro has taken Cuba to the brink of destruction before; a combination of nuclear complications whether through some kind of missile development or reactor breakdown and the prospect of standing up to the United States one more time, is a particularly dangerous prospect. Given the record of self-emolation of Cuban leaders in the past, the pattern of symbolic transcendence through self-destruction is a particularly powerful motif in Cuban politics. Castro may not be susceptible to that temptation, but nevertheless, Cuba's access to nuclear products must be viewed with grave concern by the international community.

Castro has been fascinated with nuclear programs almost from the beginning of his regime. The fact that his son, popularly known as "Fidelito" has been in charge of Cuba's nuclear program, attests to his close personal interest. The oil crunch resulting from the cut of the Russian oil subsidy has left his government scrambling for answers, and placed an added premium in bringing the Cienfuegos nuclear reactors on line very rapidly.

Cuban Nuclear Capability. The completion of Castro's nuclear facilities and the evidence that substantial nuclear weapons grade material are being accumulated for Cuban-made atomic weapons has to be a cause for global alarm. Reports from defectors who have worked on the Cienfuegos nuclear power plants indicate that the Cuban government is placing a premium on completing the projects at the expense of international safety codes. With the disengagement of Russia from Cuba, the Cubans are contemplating continuing the project alone, despite their lack of expertise and the lack of hard currency which they will need in order to import vital equipment which they cannot produce on the island.

Lessons of the Cuban Missile Crisis

Castro's behavior during the Cuban Missile Crisis indicates that the United States could be threatened by a regime which has expressed willingness to use nuclear weapons in the past.

Interesting recent information on the attitude of Castro toward the Cuban Missile Crisis comes from the reunion of many of the still living participants in that crisis at a Tripartite Conference in Moscow in January 1989. This conference built on the earlier U.S.-Soviet conference held in Cambridge, Massachusetts in October 1987. For our purposes the most important information concerns the attitudes of the Cubans and the Soviets. According to the conference reports, Khrushchev made the decision to send missiles to Cuba at the end of April 1962. According to Khrushchev's son, Anastas Mikoyan had serious reservations about this step. The only other member to express doubts to Khrushchev in the Presidium meetings was Otto Kuusinen.

The Soviets chose at this time as their new ambassador to Cuba, Aleksandr Alekseev. He was sent to replace Sergei M. Kudryavetsev who was persona non grata for Castro. Alekseev was informed by Khrushchev of the plan to deploy missiles to Cuba, and apparently from this moment on was among the inner circle. Khrushchev asked Alekseev, who had been in Cuba as a Soviet press representative for some time and was friendly with Castro, how Castro would react to the missile installation. Alekseev reported that he thought that Castro might be reluctant, so he was sent on a ten day agricultural mission with several other high ranking Soviets to find out if Castro would agree and to determine whether or not the missiles could be installed secretly.

One of the members of the mission was the actual commander of the Soviet strategic rocket forces, S.S. Biryuzov. He, along with

Alekseev, met with Fidel Castro, Raúl Castro, "Che" Guevara, President Osvaldo Dorticós, and Blas Roca. The other member of the group from the Cuban side who is a source for this information, was Emilio Argones. Alekseev reports that Fidel Castro and the other members of the Cuban group were keenly interested in the proposal, and the Soviet group returned to Moscow with Castro's agreement to the proposal, and with an optimistic evaluation of their chances to secretly deploy the missiles. The actual agreement for the deployment was subsequently signed between Raúl Castro and Soviet Marshal Malinovsky. This agreement was signed in Moscow, and as a part of the operation, some 40,000 Soviet troops were sent to Cuba with the utmost secrecy. The first intermediate range ballistic missiles arrived in Cuba on September 15, 1963. Apparently President Kennedy did not learn of the deployment until October 16, and did not inform the American people until October 22.

After the Crisis was resolved, the deterioration in the Castro-Soviet relationship became quite marked. According to the Conference Report, Castro urged Khrushchev to fire the nuclear missiles in Cuba against the United States.[1]

Castro's reaction to the deal between Moscow and Washington was one of fury. The Soviet Ambassador Alekseev reports "I felt myself the most unhappy man on earth, as I imagined what Fidel's reaction to this would be."[2] Apparently, Castro would not see the Soviet Ambassador for several days, and apparently Cuban troops surrounded the missile sites on October 28, and could be only persuaded to stand down from an imminent confrontation after the arrival of Mikoyan, who convinced Castro to go along with the Washington-Moscow accord. There is some confusion however, as to whether or not there was a possible clash between Soviet and Cuban forces. The Soviet Ambassador says that there was no such danger, because the troops surrounding the Soviet missile sites were Soviet soldiers in Cuban uniforms, but the Cuban conferees insist that the troops were Cuban, but that they were there to protect the missile sites from low level attack. An additional aggravation to the Soviet-Cuban relationship was the withdrawal of the Soviet bombers.[3]

It is well worth noting that at a time of an acute Soviet-U.S. crisis, that from all accounts, Castro was urging a nuclear strike on the United States. With the recent but unconfirmed reports that prohibited SS-20 rockets had been seen again in Cuba, the possibility of demented action on a far wider scope has to be considered. Such a situation would truly force the United States to evaluate its options.

The Martí Solution. The most dangerous scenario is if Castro adopts a Martí solution. This scenario would probably be dependent on a very serious implosion of the situation in Cuba and would clearly involve vital U.S. interests. An aging or desperate Castro might contemplate provoking an apocalyptic resolution of his relationship with the United States.

Castro has had a visceral anti-Americanism that antedates even his coming to power. An example of this is a letter he wrote to Cecilia Sanchez dated July 6, 1958 while he was still in the Sierra Maestra. This letter was published twenty years later by Carlos Franqui. In it Castro wrote that his principal aim was to fight relentlessly against the United States, and that he would do so after the revolution had succeeded: "once this war is over, I will start what for me is a much longer and bigger war, the war I am going to wage against them [the Americans]. I realize that this will be my true destiny."[4]

This situation may also be linked to Castro's narcotics weapon as it is directed against the United States. John Barron, in a March 1990 article in *Reader's Digest* relying on the testimony of former Cuban intelligence officer Juan Antonio Rodriguez, speculates that Castro's drug dealing is linked to an effort to build a Cuban atomic bomb. Rodriguez recalls a conversation he had with Castro's interior minister in the 1970s, Rolando Castaneda, in which he quotes Castaneda as saying "as long as we produce dollars we are safe. Fidel craves them for the bomb."[5]

According to Barron's article, Cuba's atomic bomb program goes back to the 1970s, when Cuba began training atomic scientists in the Eastern Bloc. Again according to Rodriguez, Castro's son, José Raúl Castro Diaz-Belart, told him that Cuba was very close to acquiring the knowledge necessary for the manufacture of a nuclear device.

When this information is added to Cuba's civilian nuclear program with its capacity to make weapons' grade nuclear material, and the reports that prohibited SS-20 rockets have been seen in Cuba, the possibility of Cuba taking a spectacular action vis-a-vis the United States cannot be ruled out. One fear that has been raised would be a possible Cuban attack on an American nuclear facility such as that of Turkey Point in Florida.

It is well known that Castro considered such an attack in 1983 after the U.S. invasion of Grenada. The intention was to lead the United States not merely into conflict with Cuba, but into a struggle with the Soviet Union. There was in this respect, considerable fear that the hard line elements in the Soviet Union, opposed to Gorbachev, would not have been adverse to such a provocative action if it would have caused a reversal of course in Moscow.

Obviously, if more and more evidence accumulates as to a connection between narcotics trafficking and an aging and increasingly irrational Castro dictatorship, with the approaching capacity to deliver a final historic blow at the United States, the possibilities of a preemptive U.S. response cannot be ruled out. In this situation, it would not be expected that moves by the OAS and the UN would proceed a US action. Moreover, it cannot be ruled out that the U.S. might still have difficulty attacking Castro, despite such a capability, because of the lack of information on both Castro's capabilities and intentions.

If the US experience with Saddam Hussein tells us anything, it tells how woeful the understanding of his motives were, and how inadequate the intelligence was about his nuclear capability, even after the war was over. In the summer of 1992, a year and a half after the war was concluded, the United States was still seeking Iraqi weapons grade nuclear materials and secret production sites for its atomic bomb, which was being developed with the type of technology the US had long declassified around the Manhattan Project.

Although this possibility cannot be ruled out because of the demise of the Soviet Union and the unlikelihood of Russian support for Castro, the chances of Castro utilizing this option is low. He has a much greater possibility of maintaining himself in a hard line position through a pro-narcotics strategy or through an apparent regime transformation and, consequently, should not be tempted by such an apocalyptic resolution.

ENDNOTES

1.   This is the way Khrushchev is reported to have received the Castro communication in an unpublished passage of his memoirs: "Suddenly, we received through our Ambassador a cable from Castro. The Ambassador reported that Castro had given him the report face-to-face. Castro informed him that he had reliable information that an American invasion would take place within a few hours. Therefore, he was proposing to preempt the invasion and inflict a nuclear strike on the U.S." Taken from Bruce J. Allyn et. al. "Essence of Revision: Moscow, Havana, and the Cuban Missile Crisis" *International Security* winter 1989-90, vol. 14, no. 3. p. 167 [pp. 136-172].

2.   Ibid., p. 168.

3.   Further light has been shed on the Castro-Khrushchev relationship at the fifth conference between the surviving participants of the Cuban Missile Crisis held in Havana in January 1992. General Anatoly Gribkov provided the participants with the information that there were some 43,000 Soviet troops in Cuba at the time, and that the Soviet forces had nuclear warheads that were both strategic and tactical. According to Gribkov, the Soviets had six tactical missile launchers with nine nuclear warheads, and were permitted to use the tactical weapons against an invading American force without prior clearance from Moscow.

    This report provided by Arthur Schlesinger Jr.("Four Days with Fidel: A Havana Diary" *The New York Review of Books* March 26, 1992 pp. 22-29), has been challenged by critics as inaccurate and unbelievable. According to Mark Kramer, "in short, *there is no basis for concluding that Soviet forces in Cuba in October 1962 were ready to use tactical nuclear weapons against incoming US troops.* Khrushchev was not so foolhardy." (Letter to the editor, *The New York Review of Books* May 28, 1992, p. 54. italics in the original.) Schlesinger has responded by noting a Soviet General Staff retrospective assessment of the operation unearthed by Bruce Allyn which notes that, in the event of an invasion, and "if there is no possibility to retrieve directives from the Ministry of Defense of the USSR," the Soviet commander in Cuba was allowed "as an exception, personally to take the decision to apply tactical nuclear weapons as a means of local war for the destruction of the opponent . . . on the territory of Cuba."(Ibid., pp. 55-56).

4.   Carlos Alberto Montaner, *Fidel Castro and the Cuban Revolution* (New Brunswick: Transaction Publishers, 1989). p. 10.

5.   John Barron, "Castro, Cocaine, and the A-Bomb Connection" *Reader's Digest* March 1990, p. 65.

PART V

THE FUTURE OF THE REVOLUTION

Castro's regime has acted as an artificial break on the dynamism of the Cuban political spirit and the development of a Cuban modern economic model. Yet Castro's revolutionary posture also forms a part of a powerful tendency in Western thought. It is impossible to expect Cuba to enter docilely the fold of Western nations upon Castro's removal. There are serious, elemental questions concerning the direction of Cuban society which still need to be decided; a dialogue which Castro suspended, but did not terminate upon his accession to power in 1959.

Will Cuba revert to a form of government and society in which the forms of democracy and free market economics are subscribed to, but which in substance, are subverted and controlled? How will Cuba reconcile the differences between diasporans and those who have stayed on the island? What will happen to the Communist party apparatus and the military machine which are the chief legacies of Castro's institution-building, and how will the Cubans succeed in converting the out-moded and disastrously inefficient command economy, education and health systems which are institutionally destroying Cuba's viability in the world arena?

The world is only just beginning to discover the truth behind the propaganda machines of the Soviets, the Eastern Europeans, and the Sandinistas. What horrors await the lifting of the veil from Castro's government? What environmental disasters caused by negligence and lack of accountability wait to be discovered? How many murders and tortures has Castro presided over which remain yet to be revealed?

Castro's end will not mark the end of the problems for Cuban society, and at the end of his long revolutionary struggle, still greater revolutionary struggles remain for the Cuban people. At the present, we have witnessed the destruction of the Marxist-Leninist model as a viable vehicle for economic and social development, and free market practices have swept the hemisphere, taking root in such havens of statism as Venezuela, Mexico, and Argentina. But as the Latins are discovering, the rejection of statism has been fraught with difficulty, and even beyond that lurk fundamental problems over the nature of Latin society.

CHAPTER XXI

Potential Transition Scenarios

With the extraordinary events in Eastern Europe in 1989 and the demise of the Soviet Union in 1991, increasing discussion has been focussed on the possible scenarios for the Castro's regime's last years. Because of the international climate, the perilous Cuban economic situation, and Castro's advancing age, hardly any international observer believes that Cuba will be able to maintain its current status quo. As a result, a variety of commentators have speculated on the variables which may lead to change, and the Cuban response to such changes.

The three independent variables that are most discussed with respect to the possible scenarios for the Castro regimes' last years are what Castro does, what the Cubans do in Cuba and in the diaspora, and what the United States does.

While these factors certainly must be taken into account, the fact of the matter is that the Cuban population has been passive and acquiescent in Cuba for the past thirty years despite Castro's oppression and various opportunities for rebellion. The diasporan population, though vocal and politically active, has been largely ineffective as far as direct action is concerned. The United States itself, has apparently become accustomed to living with Castro.

In light of these considerations, the principal decision-maker and arbiter of events over the years has proved to be Castro himself. Hence, if these three possibilities are the independent variables, then it seems far more likely that Castro will decide what the possible scenarios for the future are, rather than any of the other players involved.

If this is the case, we would argue that there are only two highly likely scenarios. The first would be that Castro stays in power without any substantial change until his death. The second would be that if there is to be a change, it would be very much like Paul's on the road to Damascus. There would be a sudden "conversion." Castro would preside over a transition to democracy which would be greeted by everyone with amazement, wonder, and joy.

Nonetheless, just as the possibility of an internal movement bringing Castro down against his will seems unlikely, neither does this last scenario. The reason for this point of view is that the changes in Eastern Europe did not come about because of the native strength of the indigenous forces, but as ramifications of the changes in the Soviet Union and their foreign policy imperatives. In fact, the nudges on the Eastern European governments to reform came from the Soviet Union. Many, if not all of the actual leaders in those countries resisted reform. Because many of the Eastern European leaders did not get out ahead of the reforming impulse as the Soviets wished, they lost control of the reforming process.

The Soviets did not want to see these countries move away from communism. Rather they sought to install reform communist regimes which could be assisted by the West. This conversion would thereby reduce the drain on Soviet resources that their unreconstructed economies represented. Because of the twin forces of Soviet persuasion and the Soviets' simultaneous inability to continue to support these economically bankrupt regimes, the old East European governments were forced to open the political process to new political actors with different political agendas.

This argument would seem to be true for Cuba as well. The objective from the Soviet point of view, was not to bring a change in regime, but to renew communism. The most recent evidence on the economic relationships between the Soviet Union and Cuba suggest that the Soviets continued to assist the island dictatorship despite their own crumbling resources.

It was Soviet assistance to reform forces in its erstwhile allies that inadvertently began the process of disintegration, not the inherent strength of those movements. Earlier movements which had been crushed by the Soviets, such as Hungary in 1956 or

Czechoslovakia in 1968, showed that there existed considerable antipathy to communist rule, but also that the communists could effectively stifle it when they chose to. Gorbachev indicated not only that the Soviet Union would no longer interfere in its satellite's domestic affairs, but suggested that they follow the USSR's example, something which the Soviet satellites attempted to do with greater or lesser skill. During 1989, Gorbachev seemed to be the chief catalyst for pro-democratic movements. Two of his direct actions sparked events like the intensification of the Tiananmen Movement (and the subsequent crackdown by the Chinese), and his visit to East Germany resulted in the deposition of Honecker.

The post-Castro era will undoubtedly bring increasing pressures for a transition to a more open political and economic system. Even if Castro is able to stay in power and pass on leadership to Raul Castro or Carlos Aldana, or whoever else finds favor after his death, the pressures to transform the Cuban system will not be contained.

Nevertheless, it seems very likely that we are witnessing the initial steps of Castro's previously made decision to bring about a reform communism that will last after his demise. In this regard, the new Havana-based Cuban Committee for Human Rights led by Gustavo Arcos Bergnes,[1] and the new Union Liberal Cubana, the soft-line political party in the Cuban exile community, are part of the effort to initiate reform communism within Cuba. It should be noted that even though Castro's regime has denounced Arcos and his followers, it has said it will talk with these "dissidents and discontents" but not with its diasporan opponents. The function of these groups would be to preempt the Cuban forces which would seek democratic and market solutions for the Cuban transition. As a result, "dissidents" has become a term within the exile Cuban community for defining the reform communist option in Cuba, and "opposition" for the supporters of a democratic transition.

Nonetheless, it should not be interpreted that Castro likes these "acceptable" reformers or that they are insincere in their reform agendas. Gustavo Arcos Bergnes was jailed again in the spring of 1992; Maria Elena Cruz Varela was severely harassed and "repudiated" by an organized "spontaneous" gathering at her house, and Elizardo Sanchez, often cited as a spokesman for these groups, has been harassed by Castroite forces. Their position of condoning parts of Castro's agenda at the same time that they repudiate him, places these dissidents in an enormously difficult role. They are not welcomed by the Castro regime, and yet they are greeted with suspicion by more outright opponents of the Castro regime.

Castro, given the evidence, may already be embarked upon a reform solution, managed by himself, which the Soviets had desired the Eastern European hard-liners to do. If this is the case, then we can expect in due time, that there will be increased calls for economic assistance for him, and for substantial easing of the trade restrictions against Cuba. It is for these reasons that exile Cuban leaders will be fearful of assisting reform communism in Cuba, initiated from the top.

The U.S. Position

Just as changing circumstances have forced the Soviets, and by extension Cuba, to qualitatively reevaluate their traditional attitudes toward foreign policy and their regime security, so the United States must realize that its policy attitudes should adapt to these changing visions. The basic guidelines of the Reagan foreign policy: aid to pro-democratic and anti-communist movements, a commitment to economic growth based on free trade principles, and a military build-up to forestall military superiority have turned out to be the crux of the political, economic, and ideological combination which caused the Soviet to rethink their geopolitical position. George Bush, in continuing these basic guidelines has had the good fortune to preside over the tangible outcomes of these policy directives.

But this was a foreign policy which was designed to cope with Marxist-Leninist ideological momentum, expanding Soviet power and influence, and a strong network of allies and client states working in the USSR's behalf. In light of the changing nature of the international problems, the U.S. foreign policy vision needs to be expanded. While its basic tenets still maintain their validity, it is necessary for the Bush administration to move into a second phase.

In the case of Cuba, the U.S. should have a long-term commitment to see that democracy and social market practices are established. U.S. policy makers must understand that while most Marxist-Leninist regimes now recognize the need to import market principles into their economic systems, they wish to do so with as little transfer of political power as possible. These regimes need economic aid and reform, they do not necessarily want political reform. China is an exaggerated form of this phenomena, Cuba is a disguised form of it.

In its eagerness to implant market economies in these countries, the United States needs to insure that it does not end up abetting the relegitimization and/or reconsolidation of Marxist-Leninist one party authority. The political process should be opened.

However in calling for political pluralism, the United States must not be content with half-way measures. As we have seen, part of the Marxist-Leninist strategy has been to adopt a dialectical approach to internal reform. With reformers on one side and hard-liners on the other, Marxist leaders can appear to be pursuing moderate policies, when in fact all three wings may share the same goals and may be operating in tandem. Furthermore, reform parties can nominally coopt the agendas of genuine democratic movements and thereby channel democratic support for what is in reality, a subterfuge for *continuismo*. Obviously, the United States is therefore placed in the difficult and invidious position of having to decide if a reform movement is genuine or artificial.

The United States is faced with four alternatives, and degrees of response within each of these viewpoints. It can seek change from above and advocate internal reform. It can seek change from below, either through support of revolution or mass movement, or it can sit on the sidelines abetting both reform and revolution, or it can remain strictly neutral and let the regime crisis play itself out. To complicate matters still further, the U.S. may want to adopt one strategy for China and another for Cuba, as indeed it seems to be doing currently.

The U.S. has been pursuing a reform strategy with China. This analysis has already investigated some of the perils in such a policy, but it also has the effect of encouraging other Marxist-Leninist regimes to embark on similar courses of action. Where there was no political opening before, this is a benefit, as would be any move by Castro to open up the system politically, but if the U.S. were to consistently follow this process it would be inadvertently conforming to Gorbachev's agenda by propping up Marxist-Leninist pseudo-democratic groups, rather than moving toward a democratic regime.

Given the Marxist-Leninist regime control over the military and security apparatus, support for revolution from below could potentially entail a long and drawn out affair. Such a process occurred in Nicaragua. It might have the benefit of crystallizing the political spectrum, and of ultimately exhausting the regime, but it could also be costly and dangerous to long-term U.S. interests, not only in terms of the regime involved, but also in terms of hostile Marxist-Leninist propaganda value, and in the effect on internal politics within the U.S.

One of the historical lessons that an outside regime should learn when attempting to take advantage of a regime crisis, is that direct intervention almost never works and almost always backfires. The allied invasion of France in 1792 and their defeat at Valmy helped consolidate the republican regime as the French rallied around the flag. Saddam Hussein sought to take advantage of Iranian disarray and was badly mauled. The United States should proceed gingerly and cautiously with respect to Cuba.

ENDNOTES

1. This dialogue dissident group is led by the Arcos Bergnes brothers, Gustavo and Sebastían. It includes Jesus Llanes Pelletier, Julio Ruiz Pittaluga, and Aida Valdés Santana. Gustavo Arcos fought with Castro against Batista and was his ambassador to Belgium. He has apparently been at odds with Castro for nearly a decade to the extent of having been imprisoned by him. Sebastian Arcos has also been jailed as recently as January 1992.

CHAPTER XXII

The Legal Foundation
of a Transition

Castro cannot be seen as falling in a simple comparative category with either the leaders of Eastern Europe or with Gorbachev himself. The communist leaders of Eastern Europe were all products of a system that was imposed upon their peoples, with the weight of the Soviet army behind them. Gorbachev himself, represents a second generation of bureaucratic leaders from the originators of the Bolshevik revolution.

Castro on the other hand, is an originator of a communist nationalist revolution himself, and thus must be compared to figures like Lenin, Stalin, Mao, Ho Chi Minh, to see the intensity with which he holds the revolutionary faith and the degree of sacrifices he is willing to make in order to secure his political destiny. In this context, Castro cannot be expected to have either the more dispassionate view of a revolution that has lost its progenitors that a Gorbachev has, or the fearful attitude of an imposed dictator that the European communists have had. Castro sees himself in the same pantheon as the great communist fathers and so his attitude must be seen as one of far greater determination, tenacity, and illusion, than that of those in Moscow and Eastern Europe. The somewhat cosmetic reforms which were initiated in Santiago de Cuba in October 1991 only further underline this difference.

There is a profound difference in a leadership which originates a revolution, and a leadership which comes from within a previously established order. Gorbachev is a different caliber of leader than Castro.

One of the more interesting questions arising over the Castro experience is whether or not some governments operate so beyond the pale of legality and the norms of political accountability that the leaders exercising power should be tried as criminals. The typical grounds for this kind of judgment have been since the Nuremberg and Tokyo War Trials, crimes of embarking on aggressive war and crimes against humanity or human rights.

What are the present charges and evidence for Castro's violation of the prohibition against aggressive war? If insurgency, terrorism, and conventional attacks against people without the normal justifications for the use of force are absent, then there is a prima facie case for saying that a state has embarked on aggressive war. Was Castro's support of insurgency in Venezuela, the Dominican Republic, Central America, the Andean region, and the Southern Cone authorized by any invitation on the part of the governments of the countries? The evidence for his support of these insurgencies is overwhelming, so that one might assume that he could be held to be a practitioner of aggressive war.

He certainly was excluded from the OAS in 1961 on the grounds of his support of the insurgency that was mounted against the elected Venezuelan government. He also has a record of involving his armed forces in the wars of Angola, Ethiopia, Syria, and Israel, which might also be added to the charges which could be filed against him.

Regarding the crimes against humanity and human rights, there is very substantial evidence of Castro's torture, imprisonment, and liquidation of those who opposed him on political grounds in which was no hint of the use of force in their opposition to his regime. In addition, there are innumerable incidents of assassination and acts against the lives and property of individuals associated with his insurgency conflicts.

Finally, there seems to be considerable testimony about the Castro regime's involvement in international drug trafficking, implicating Castro himself, in a worldwide criminal conspiracy against the lives, health, and well-being of literally millions of people.

The jurisdiction for such charges could certainly be held in Cuban courts after his government collapses. It is also possible under the present practices of the U.S. government that should Castro be brought to the United States a la Noriega, he could find himself subject to the criminal laws of the United States.

This vast criminal record suggests that he would face many of the charges that have been leveled against Stalin and other communist mass murderers. He might therefore, be extremely reluctant to relinquish power during his lifetime.

The over-riding interest of the Cuban people and the United States is to bring about a transition to a democratic government so that the Cuban people can live in a normal society, and we can all share a more peaceful international environment. With those objectives, it is not too much to assume that the United States would probably seek to grant Castro immunity from prosecutions if he would be willing to permit his regime to be transformed into a democracy. This choice was certainly offered to Noriega, and he obviously did not think that he needed to accept it. It is hard to believe therefore, that Castro would accept a similar offer.

Consequently, should Castro survive the demise of his regime, which given his psychology seems highly unlikely, he may very well find himself in the dock either in Cuba or in the United States. The greater likelihood will be that proceedings against Castro will go forward in Cuba.

The Problem with Vindictive Policies Against Past Regimes

The best policy of overcoming the past is reconstruction. Reconstruction must be understood as something that goes beyond economic concerns, to moral, spiritual and communal concerns. The spiritual is the root of the moral and the communal life. So the capacity of the people to form around their sense of the ultimate essence of their beings must be allowed to flourish again. In the Cuban case, that means that the first step of the spiritual rejuvenation of their moral and communal life must come with the rejuvenation of the Catholic church.

The moral life is rooted in the spiritual life. It is the source of the way of dealing with people and the social environment. A restored moral sensibility infuses the language, which ultimately provides the basis of the inter-subjective communication with others, and that ultimately provides the basis for a sense of community and trust. So by the reconstruction of the spiritual, the communal bases are constructed, which in turn set the civil society's standards of what is and is not permitted in a free market economy and the arena of political discourse.

Indeed, it was the breakdown of communal standards which points to both the failure of statism and capitalism. Statism fails because it denies that community, and large scale capitalism fails because it ignores it. The presupposition of a statist mentality is that economic creation and distribution are decided by elites unaccountable to the community, whereas large-scale capitalism with its extreme rationalization of the factors of production ignores community.

So one of the primary elements of the restoration of Cuba after Castro's demise will be to foster the spiritual links common to all of the Cuban people, and to promote economic activity appropriate to the existing habits of the population. The Cuban community will have to encourage local economic activity and not introduce large-scale private economies in areas where the people have no experience with them. Privatization and the conditions for the free market encouragement of small and medium-sized businesses are not the same thing. Privatization should not lead merely to the transfer of a state monopoly into a private monopoly.

This discussion provides the key to how the U.S. should approach the continuation of the embargo in the post-Gorbachev era. Economic coercion is a very imprecise, and usually, a very ineffective tool. Nonetheless, it is justified in circumstances where it has a chance of bringing about more good than harm. The rule for bringing about more good than harm lies in whether pain is, in fact, inflicted on the appropriate political target, and benefits are conferred on the most deserving. Whenever the pattern is reversed, the economic pressure of an embargo is inappropriate.

For example, in the recent case of Haiti, the economic pain fell on the least culpable elements of society. In the case of Cuba, the embargo was designed to punish the Soviet Union and the Cuban regime. Now it must be designed to address the people. The difference between the two embargos is that when the state controls the economic resources, it does not matter to the people how much or how little foreign exchange there is, because they do not receive the benefits. But it does matter to the extent that the more resources the state has, the greater its ability to coerce them. In a case like Haiti, the embargo impacts on the independent economic sectors, and abets centralization of state power, so that it has precisely the opposite effect that would be desirable, in terms of promoting greater state power at the expense of the private citizen. Instead, the objective of an embargo vis-a-vis Castro must be to harm state power while increasing societal independence.

The primary justification for the embargo during the hegemonic drives of the Soviet regime was to increase the cost of empire to the Soviet Union. With the demise of the Soviet regime, the embargo must be approached with a different perspective.

It can be continued merely as a means for expressing U.S. displeasure with the Castro government. However, the post-Soviet Cuban policy of the U.S. must go beyond a simple punitive attitude towards Cuba. The new question is whether or not the continuation of the embargo or its lifting would be most helpful to a democratic transition under Castro or in a post-Castro environment. Looking at the transition to democratic regimes in other contexts, there does not appear to be any clear answer as to whether economic prosperity or economic distress furthers a transition except as it impacts in leaders' perceptions of their relative power. Thus, one must focus on what will influence the will of Castro and his successors.

There are probably two targets for impacting on Castro's and his political successors' will. The first is the elite, and the second is the people. The question for the elite is whether or not the policy makes them more able and willing to keep control or to give up control. For the people the question is what will contribute toward more dependency or more self-control. Self-control comes from the ability to have an independent economic life from the state.

If these considerations are appropriate, then there should be a nuanced embargo policy for the post-Castro transition. The embargo should continue to exist for those economic activities which accrue directly to the benefit of the ruling elite. On this basis, the U.S. should continue to discourage investment in Cuba's tourist and extractive industries. That is, U.S. policy should be aimed to prevent economic investments which are primarily beneficial to continuing state control of the economy.

On the other hand, the U.S. could ease the embargo with respect to investment which enhanced the societal strength of the Cuban people. Investments which provide private Cuban citizens with franchises, and other economic activities which primarily strengthen the society at the expense of the state should be the ones the United States should support. This strategy would make it clear to Castro that he could not have development without private sector capitalism, and that if the country were not to develop, the primary and exclusive responsibility lies with the Castro regime.

The U.S. embargo had been aimed at raising the costs for the Soviet Union, now it should be retargeted toward promoting the creation of an independent economic middle class. Until now Castro has maintained such total control over the means of production of the Cuban economy, that any easing of the embargo would not necessarily contribute to the welfare of the people, but to his continued control over them. Opponents of the embargo argue that lifting the embargo is a humanitarian act, but in reality, it would allow Castro to sustain his repressive regime by giving him increased access to foreign exchange. The essential precondition for any lifting of the embargo would have to be change in the legal structure of the Cuban economy so that the people could participate directly as owners and consumers in a market economy.

What this leads to is that Cuba can no longer operate on the arbitrary will of the absolute dictator, and needs to make a transition to a political and economic state of law. In this analysis the political question of what to do with Castro and how to deal with the embargo needs to come down not to piecemeal concessions to Castro, but to a structured reordering of his political and economic system on a constitutional and legal basis.

CHAPTER XXIII

Future Regimes

It is a widespread practice within the comparative government field to classify regimes on the degree of political participation of the populace. Robert A. Dahl in his book *Polyarchy* provides one such model, Giovanni Sartori, through the medium of political parties, provides another. In a study of pure politics such as this, an informal typology is important, but this analysis has to, by definition, reject the implications of rigidity and theoretical coherence that such models provide. In this study, political systems are not seen to be permanent structures, but are rather transient articulations of the interaction between state and society.

Political systems can evolve within themselves while maintaining their formal characteristics. The United States is a case in point. It continues to formally embrace the 1788 Constitution, but its government has actually changed dramatically since that time. At the same time, discontinuities between governmental practice and social development can lead to crisis situations in which the governing regime is swept away. In these situations, regimes which come to power do not necessarily reflect greater alignment between state and society. Rather, they may simply have been formed by an able political elite within the society, able to capitalize on public dissatisfaction for the time necessary to consolidate its own rule.

The political actors within the regime establish their own codes for the mechanism of perpetuating the regime. In some cases, the principle of power sharing arises to ensure regime stability by providing a vehicle for the regime to reflect different concerns of the society, and to give it a means to adapt to changing social and political conditions in a way that static bureaucratic models cannot.

The means of choice in modern society is the electoral process. Not only are elections seen to be the most feasible way of reconciling the will of the people to the necessity of having a central government, but they are also seen to be legitimating acts which provide the government with authority and moral force.

Nevertheless, solely having an electoral system does not guarantee that the regime is truly committed to reflecting the will of the people. The Partido Revolucionario Institucional (PRI) of Mexico has ruled that country since 1917, using elections to continue to justify its government, even as it has subverted the electoral process to its own ends, and has prevented other political parties from effectively participating in the government.

As can be seen, formal political structures do not necessarily convey the true nature of the state, and for these reasons, attention needs to be focussed on the principles upon which the state is organized as well. Fidel Castro has long disparaged the U.S. form of political organization as not being genuinely democratic, while touting his own as a model of political participation. What Castro has done however, is create an effective grass roots system which responds to direction from central authority, not a grass roots system which directs the central authority.

As this model has increasingly proven to be politically unviable, there have been four modern attempts to reconcile the desire to maintain a leadership principle at the expense of genuine pluralistic competition. These four different regime types, are not all equally attractive to Castro, but they do represent possible models for an attempt to maintain rule from above with apparent liberalization. These could be titled the Chinese, Pinochet, Nicaraguan, and Mexican efforts.

The China Model

After the Mao era ended, the leaders of the PRC moved to revitalize the economy without changing their authoritarian political rule. According to their political calculations, any aperture in the political system would result in severe unrest, possibly leading to their overthrow. For these reasons, the Chinese leadership under the direction of Deng Xiao Ping, attempted to maintain as much political control as was feasible, while maximizing economic freedom. Nonetheless, in this process of economic revitalization, some movement toward political change was made, but this was effectively crushed in Tiananmen Square.

What Castro can do to solve his political problems is likewise move to revitalize the Cuban economy, without giving any hints that there will be any change in Cuban communist political authority. This economic revitalization will be spearheaded, as in the PRC model by offering attractive sectors of the Cuban markets to foreign investors, including from the United States.

Since it appears that China has had some success with this experiment, it cannot be ruled out that it will not work to some degree for Castro as well. In this light, lifting the U.S. embargo would constitute a political victory for Castro, which might further cement his determination to adopt such a politically authoritarian and economically liberal policy for his continuation in power. The political consequences of lifting the U.S. embargo therefore need to be emphasized in any debate on its merits.

What the Chinese model accomplishes, is that it allows Castro to maintain his political authority as much as possible, while it provides an escape valve, in terms of channeling Cuban incentives toward increasing their material well-being. The problem that this model faces, is that as long as there is no political liberalization, the regime runs the risk of remaining internationally isolated, and cannot gain access to the foreign investment the economic opening would naturally require. In addition, any time there is independent economic activity, some political leeway is introduced into the system, and Castro wants to make sure that the political order he has imposed on Cuba does not unravel because of the rise of independent economic actors whom he cannot control.

The Pinochet Model

When the coup first occurred against President Salvador Allende's government in September 1973, it was not immediately apparent how long the military regime would endure. The Pinochet government soon emerged however, as making an effort to preclude the return to the "politics as usual" that had preceded the coup. Pinochet formed a constitutional commission which rewrote the constitution, and among other things, outlawed the Communist Party. It provided a mechanism whereby the military could legitimately intervene in the political process to prevent the communization of the nation's polity. This constitution was submitted to a plebiscite, and was ratified in that plebiscite although it was criticized by its opponents as unfair to them because of their limited access to the means of communication in fighting its ratification.

Subsequently, Pinochet moved further to have his rule extended in another plebiscite which the traditional political parties of the country with the exception of the communist party, opposed. Pinochet had hoped to prevail in this contest, because he had substantially opened up the economy both internationally and domestically, and had presided over the most successful economic development the country had seen in this century. Nonetheless, even with his defeat and the return of the country to a competitive party system, Pinochet remained commander-in-chief of the army and in this position remains as a potential check on any constitutional changes.

To the degree this model would recommend itself to Castro, it would do so because his brother would remain in control of the armed forces, and it is undoubtedly clear that Castro could get plebiscites to ratify his permanence in office as the head of state. In this two step process, Castro would first run against an opening up of the system, and if this failed, would then still secure a preeminent position within the new system whatever it is, and perhaps expect to win.

The Nicaraguan Model

As already touched on, the United States government, was aware even before the Sandinistas came to power, that they were led by Marxist-Leninist revolutionaries. There was a direct effort on the part of the Carter administration to co-opt the Sandinista Revolution. What was particularly interesting about this was that the Sandinistas and Castro realized that they might gain assistance from the United States in the implementation of their revolution because of the U.S. desire to get along with them, and minimize the importance of the region as an area of conflict. When the Carter policy of co-option failed and Carter was forced to come to the aid of El Salvador, where the Salvadoran rebels were aided by the FSLN, the United States fell into a decade-long conflict in the region.

Nonetheless, when the Bush Administration came to office, it sought to terminate its conflict with Nicaragua by accepting an electoral solution which everybody expected at the time the policy was announced, would confirm the Sandinista leadership in power. Since this outcome was also expected by the Sandinistas, they agreed to an open election, closely monitored by international observers. When the vote turned out to grant a majority to an anti-Sandinista coalition, the UNO umbrella of parties, the Sandinistas had to go along with the election of the opposition. Nonetheless, the Sandinistas retained control of the armed forces, and were able, despite the election of Violeta Chamorro, to retain control of the permanent structures of the government.

Castro could expect, even if he put his own chances for direct election in jeopardy, that he could win this election, even if, as in the case of the Nicaraguan election, U.S. or other international interests funneled money to his opponents. What the Sandinistas succeeded in doing was interpreting very cannily two distinct U.S. foreign policy stances to their favor. Under Carter, the U.S. administration policy could be characterized as appeasement and attempted co-option of the Sandinista government. Under Bush, the motivation was not appeasement, rather it was an attempt to reduce conflict in the region in light of the changing nature of the U.S.-Soviet rivalry and the desire to cooperate with a Democratic-controlled Congress.

What the Sandinistas have accomplished is that they have managed to maintain control of the permanent government apparatus and funnel U.S. aid to their supporters and networks, while nominally being subordinate to the Chamorro government. Under the Chamorro government, they have escaped responsibility for the problems facing the government, yet they have retained a broad measure of power and the capacity to disrupt significant reforms such as the implementation of new property laws and security reforms. The Sandinistas have no hopes of finding a patron powerful enough to counter-act the United States, so what they have tried to do is work out a role for themselves where they are not seen as threatening the U.S. per se, but still maintain their left-wing posture, and institutional power. In this model, the big risk is a complete collapse of any ideological authority which still may exist, and the exposure of the hypocrisy of the ruling Cuban elites, such as what has happened to the Sandinista leadership, and their corrupt seizure of property prior to the inauguration of President Chamorro.

The PRI Model

One of the patterns that appears to be emerging since the Fourth Communist Party Congress of October 1991, is a growing sense that Castro is attempting to do what Plutarco Diaz Calles did with the Mexican Revolution in the late 1920s. Having watched the leaders of the Mexican Revolution assassinate each other in the succession struggles for power, Calles formed a party of the revolution which was designed to both maintain the revolutionary elite or family in power without any serious possibility of it being replaced, and prevent the internal struggles for political power leading to schisms or murders of elite candidates. The solution was the creation of what is known today as the Institutional Party of the Revolution (PRI), which gives various sectors of the revolutionary movement corporate representation within the party, while the inner circles decide who will rule for six year terms without the possibility of reelection. This model may prove attractive to Castro for the institutionalization of his following after his demise.

The Mexican system has proved remarkably adaptive to a wide variety of challenges and even now, under the enormous pressures of the world wide collapse of one party systems, it has found a method of revival on the basis of a renovating technological elite, that consolidated its influence within the key sectors of the political apparatus during the sexenio of Miguel de la Madrid, and is now seeking to revitalize the Mexican economy through a free trade agreement with the United States under the Carlos Salinas de Gortari government.

What this model offers Castro is the continuation of one party domination within Cuba, with the prospects of controlled liberalizations, followed by controlled limitations on the political process, while gaining United States economic support during the periods of liberalization. The Mexican Revolutionary family has found this to be a very effective mechanism for obtaining U.S. assistance and for undermining the capacities of internal opposition groups effectively challenging their power. It is also true that the Mexican system has been able to justify itself on the grounds that its legitimacy derives from a revolutionary process, rather than popular elections, and that this origin of power is superior to that of the electoral process.

Should Castro choose this option he could very well find substantial political support within the United States for lifting the trade embargo, providing him with economic assistance, because of the continuing attraction revolutionary statist nationalism has for intellectual and fashionable opinion in the United States, Latin America, and Europe.

In this regard, it should be recognized that in the United States and Latin America, there is a growing belief that the new world order is one to be based on technology and economic efficiency, rather than on a humanistic civilization represented through democratic institutions. To the degree both the Gorbachev and Salinas reform efforts were designed to reform rather than transform, they demonstrated a parallel understanding that liberalization of elitist regimes could obtain substantial international financial, technological, and political support. Castro might very well try to move in this direction foreseeing that the revolutionary authoritarian regime with commercial, rather than political reforms could obtain the international economic support Cuba needs to survive. Paradoxically, the economic salvation of Castro would not come from Spain and Europe or Japan and China or Mexico and Latin America, but from the United States.

All of these different models are predicated on the understanding that old-fashioned Marxist orthodoxy on the economic sphere is obsolete, and that Castro's power in Cuba cannot endure if he continues the status quo. Castro's calculations may depend on the amount of genuine popular support he thinks he has among the people. The less he has, the more appealing the China solution is; the more he has, the more appealing the Pinochet solution is. Another calculation must be the amount of weight the institutional apparatus around him has. If it is very strong, the Mexican PRI solution must be attractive; if it is weaker, the Nicaraguan model may develop. Popular strength, institutional support, and the dictates of circumstance combined with Castro's psychology will all determine whether a departure from the status quo is contemplated by the Cuban leadership, and what direction that departure might take. It is highly dubious however, that genuine democracy would emerge as a first option of this current leadership.

CHAPTER XXIV

The Continuing Revolution

It is becoming increasingly clear that W. W. Rostow's insight into communism as a source of political, rather than economic power, and the particular vulnerability of regimes during the period of transition from early or pre-capitalist economies to this phenomena, has a great deal of validity. The Cuban Revolution was fundamentally a takeover of the state on the presumption that controlling the levers of power would create the changes in the society above and beyond the personal power ambitions of Castro. As Mr. Rostow would allege, Castro's revolution was a revolution of transition—to the extent that Castro was able to generate popular support for his anti-capitalist agenda, it was due to the legitimate concerns about the dehumanizing tendencies of the trend toward a globally interdependent economy.

However in this regard, a distinction needs to be made because the Cuban revolution developed in two stages. There was much deeper, widespread support for the end of the Batista dictatorship, the desire for the end of autocratic rule, and a genuine longing of the people for self-government. The second stage was the takeover of that movement by a complex of forces—in part the furtherance of the elite ambitions of Castro, his core of supporters, and the communist/materialist leftist forces who sought to remake Cuba entirely within a secular, utopian framework.

In a sense, the Cuban revolution was one of the last waves of the first stage of the intellectual war against democratic self-government. The structure of the Castroist revolution was that of a declasse intellectual elite, spearheading a force of *guajiro* and peasant cadres against the middle class. The state takeover was not predicated on the development of economic shocks, but on the use of force by a dedicated minority. It was this implicit use of force, once the regime was established, that was seen as the predicate underlying a politics of persuasion designed to make the population accept the regime and legitimize its vision of the good person and good citizen.

The Continuing Appeal of Utopian Politics

As the failure of this experiment becomes more apparent, the second great gnostic challenge is underway; however, it has developed two distinct, though perhaps not mutually exclusive patterns. These two patterns are radically nationalistic historicist societies or permanently revolutionary ones until the extra-historical group can bring utopia. Both gnostic revolutionary ideologies have their supporters in the developed as well as the developing nations. As a result, a Castro continues to have his supporters in the developed West either among the revolutionary nationalist interpreters of revolution or among the Western Marxists or New Left (in contradistinction to the outmoded Marxist-Leninist or Old Left schools of thought.) Where these two new anti-democratic challenges, which, we would argue, find their clearest articulations in the Heideggerian and Frankfurt schools of thought, differ is in their concentration on nationalist or transnationalist cleavages.

Once the people accept the materialist, utopian mind-set, it does not matter what the organization of the state is. Rather than force, persuasion becomes the key tool in the remaking of the society-state dynamic. Control of the institutions of persuasion becomes the key battlefield, and the revolutionary endeavor shifts from a focus on government to a focus on the churches, schools, media, and arts of the society.

But just as the materialist ethic becomes more clearly engrained in these institutions, so new paradigms and mind-sets arise which are, if not diametrically (or dialectically) opposed to this mind-set, at least representative of the perceived reality of the self-governing group. The battle between autocrats and democrats takes on a new guise, but in such a way that the autocrats paradoxically dress as democrats and the democrats as elitists. These perceptions already represent a victory for the gnostic revolution, but are a blow to the cause of republican self-government.

In this regard, the revolution moves into a different phase, one in which countries on the periphery of the great powers are diminished in the influence that they wield, except in so far as they form one more battlefield among the rest. Paradoxically, the former Marxist-Leninist nations become the strongest opponents of the gnostic march through the institutions. Cuba, in this light, is still struggling to emerge from the first gnostic revolution, but it may well find that its international role is increasingly diminished.

Although it is true that the gnostic problem for western civilization starts at the beginning of the Christian era, and thus in the first centuries of the Roman Empire, and continues through the Middle Ages and the Renaissance, it is the Enlightenment which inaugurates on the political scene, movements expressing the autonomous reason of man as the characteristic feature of human nature. This autonomy first expresses itself in the French Revolution and produces the first mass movement in the Christian cultural milieu that places the secular cultural intelligentsia as the arbiters of the political world. The reaction to this phenomena in the European scene was the Romantic movement which in both its epistemology and philosophy of history denied both the exclusive autonomy of human reason and the rational teleology of the Enlightenment.

In this situation Hegel emerges as the father of modern gnosticism in an effort to bring back a metaphysical basis to the unity of European peoples which overcomes the radical autonomy of the Enlightenment and accommodates the expressive yearnings for community of Romanticism without succumbing to either radical freedom or communal irrationalism. Hegel's logic is therefore clearly an effort to respond to the loss of a common metaphysic for the European peoples. Hegel, in effect, attempts a new grounding or a new definition for what the people are in a theory of the absolute spirit, the *Geist*, actualizing itself in history.

Nietzsche represents the ending of this effort to provide a metaphysic behind the meaning of modern man with his announcement that God is dead. That statement in this context, means that Nietzsche has declared that the effort to explain man and the natural world with a transcendent metaphysic in any of its forms is now meaningless. This in effect, creates a fundamental nihilistic situation which Heidegger will attempt to resolve by making all transcendent positions finite.

Nietzsche's solution to the metaphysical tradition of Western civilization is not appreciated for its full implications until World War I and the defeat of the Prussian monarchy which had been the ultimate end of history in Hegel's thought. With this defeat, the effort to bring back some sort of a unity to the metaphysically bereft German and other European peoples was undertaken by Martin Heidegger. Heidegger attempts to reverse the reversal of Nietszche and he does this through the creation of a finite transcendental position, but this of course in turn, reintroduces a radical subjectivity into the philosophical political discourse and means that nationalisms based on it will not be subjected to a common standard that could be shared by different peoples.

This radical subjectivity of historical understanding is basic to Heidegger's gnosticism, even though he attempts to purge subjectivity from his philosophy, explicitly in his post-"turn." For our purposes, the stages of Heidegger's philosophy do not change the essentially gnostic element of his political thought—the self-salvation of man in history by the all knowing political leader or philosopher-king. Where dasein—the authentic human knower of Being has precedence in *Being and Time*, and Being takes precedence in the Turning essays of "What is Metaphysics," "The Essence of Truth," and "Plato's Doctrine of Truth," the alleged residues of metaphysics are expunged in the post-Turn thought as developed in the Nietszche volumes. Whatever the phase of his thought, Heidegger still remains the thinker who has exclusive access to understanding the significance of Being for modern man.

In effect, Heidegger throughout the course of his thought remains a gnostic, but clearly Heidegger thought that by moving from a posture of an authentic human thinker discovering being, to Being revealing itself to the human thinker that he had purged subjectivity and metaphysics from his philosophy. Metaphysics in Heidegger's sense was man projecting his categories of analysis onto the world rather than receiving authentic being. Heidegger tries to undermine Aristotle's rational man and Kant's metaphysical man and postulate that the key understanding should be that of ontological man, and his unfolding through time.

Castro, as a heterodox Marxist, has adapted, though probably unconsciously, many of these principles. Elements of this kind of thinking are apparent in his concepts of "the leadership principle" and of the "*hombre nuevo*." In this sense, he is closer to fascism, with anti-Americanism substituted for anti-semitism, than he is to Marxism. This philosophical orientation would in part explain the attraction of the existential Marxists such as Sartre, for Castro. This post-modernist analysis fuels an understanding of the Cuban ruling class as elitist and dirigiste for the sake of a pseudo-idealistic philosophy rather than the one-dimensional materialism that Marxism espouses.

Heidegger's essential argument was to attempt a radical critique of Western metaphysical thought which he grounded on an analysis of the pre-Socratics. The essential error of Western civilization he stated occurred later. Heidegger argued that authentic self-conscious understanding involved a partial unveiling of being. The great error occurred in his judgment, when Plato and Aristotle interpreted the original Greek efforts at unveiling as implying that the explanation of being must lie beyond the totality of materially existent things. This mistake began, in Heidegger's view, the historic Western search for an explanation beyond existent beings to explain the existence of existent beings. In the Heideggerian view, the last form of this search had been Hegel's affirmation of the *geist* and that search had been closed when Nietzsche declared that all further metaphysical possibilities were foreclosed because of the death of God.

This return to the pre-Socratic position placed Germany and other European and Western cultures in the common Greek position of recreating their own Holy of Holies on the basis of a radical new understanding of the nature of being. George Steiner has captured this insight when he writes that philosophy in the Heideggerian sense "is a thinking that breaks the paths for, that opens the perspective of, that kind of knowing which sets the norms and values of the knowledge in and through which a people fulfills itself historically and culturally. The knowledge that comes of such thinking kindles and necessitates all inquiries, and thereby threatens all values."[1]

Heidegger in this regard, makes his understanding of small being (dasein) and Being (Sein) as immanent, rather than transcendent. Where traditional metaphysics went beyond nature searching for a universal experience to explain reality, Heidegger's being (dasein) is explained by the finite beings of this world. In this regard, Heidegger is anti-Kantian because unlike Kant things can be known to being (dasein). What is unknown is Being (Sein) for Heidegger.

The starting point for Heidegger is being (dasein) and it searches for authenticity through its effort to come to grips with having been thrown into the world out of nothing and having to leave the world into nothing. The authentic being (dasein) experiences angst which is its awareness of nothingness. It is in effect, anxiety over its condition and responding from this condition with an act of freedom which leads to the self-creation of an authentic being.

The key decision for the modern gnostic movement which must undoubtedly come more to the fore as the materialistic form of the Hegelian solution collapses in the international arena at least in its Marxist-Leninist form, is the decision of beings choosing to belong to other beings in order to have a collective destiny. In the Heideggerian sense "destiny is fate made authentic on the national or ethnic level."[2]

What emerges then, is what may well become the new nationalist response to the crisis of capitalism and materialistic gnosticism in a naturalistic theology that finds authentic collective being arising from history and flowing into the future. The nationalist socialism of Germany was a primitive form of this philosophy, and this current is a determined effort to think against the theological solutions of revealed religion and may be one of the responses of the anti-traditionalist movements to the stresses placed on secularized segments of the population by the continuation of the capitalist revolution in the twenty first century.

This is not to say that the materialist position is dead. Unlike the Heideggerians, the neo-Kantians continue to believe in a phenomenology that provides certainty with respect to subjective understandings, but abandons an understanding of things as they are. They remain in the position of the Enlightenment. Whereas these later nationalisms are more expressions of the reality of where large portions of the population who have been both dechristianized and derationalized are. The neo-Kantians still believe that they can create ideas and structures which can do away with sovereignty, religion, and the state whereas the gnostic anti-metaphysical tradition maintains that individuals and peoples can not and will not live under and within structures created by metaphysically and culturally disembodied minds.

To the degree the international regional regimes and transnational regimes are products of these self-defining mental structures, they will be challenged as well by the anti-metaphysical gnostics who endow the nation with its own soul and the people with a self-defining transcendent idealism for identifying with such nations.

The Frankfurt school represents another alternative for the revival of a radical attack on modern society without falling into the positivistic nationalism of the Heideggerian response to modernity. Often understood as a "western marxism" responding to the failure of the proletarian revolution in the developed countries, this school draws heavily on the thought of not only Marx, but also Hegel, Heidegger, Spengler, Nietszche, Freud, and a secularized messianism. The leadership of Max Horkheimer in the school's second period—which occurred during the exile of many of the group to North America between 1933 and 1950—crystallized this thought. The leading proponents of the School were Walter Benjamin, Theodor W. Adorno, Herbert Marcuse, Frederick Pollack, and of course, Max Horkheimer. Enormously influenced by the Holocaust, the School attempted to reconcile their continued confidence in human reason while denying the certainty of modernity's progressiveness. Their hostility was not to the ever-increasing poverty of modern society as projected by Marx, but the philistinism of the ever-growing affluence of the modern state. They drew on Marx for their insights into the possibility for the end of scarcity, but they also drew on Freud for their understanding of the human psyche and for their understanding of the "New Man" whose psyche was liberated. They overcome Freud's death wish

243

with Marx's ending of scarcity and they overcome Marx's materialism with Freud's pleasure principle.

From Hegel, they remained concerned with the problems of history, but reject his view that the problems of society will be resolved within a historical dialectic. They argued for a permanent negative dialectic against a positive historical outcome as they no longer agreed with Hegel's view that the state can become both rational and real within the historical process. This conclusion was reached, in their thought, through their views about what had happened in Nazi Germany. They argued that Hegel's positive view of historical development had culminated in a disaster. Thus, for this school something had gone wrong with history, and they did not think that there could ever be a final synthesis within an historical dialectic which would create a perfect society.

On the other hand, they did not abandon the idea of a utopian solution for mankind. On this more positive side of their thought, they drew on Nietzsche's criticism of the Enlightenment, Heidegger's ontology, and Spengler's prognosis for a new caesarism in modern society. Nietzsche was important for them because his critique of the Enlightenment demonstrated that the excessive rationalism of the Enlightenment had itself become a myth, and it was a myth that reason itself could resolve the problems of modernity which the school felt was impossible. Thus Heidegger's destruction of the metaphysical tradition of the West with his concern for restoring Being as the central concern of man was an important contribution to the school's efforts to be critical of modernist beliefs. Finally, Oswald Spengler was significant for the school because he saw the rise of a new caesarism which was to have cataclysmic effect on the outcome of modernity. It is in this context that the cultural background of these writers was critical to the way they saw a new utopia occurring. Instead of the solution coming from within modernity and the historical process, there would have to be a messianic break with the past, an exogenous intervention into history from forces that had been marginalized by history. Thus this school was extraordinarily encouraged by the student revolts of the 1960s, the possibilities of a revolutionary black movement, and of revolutionary Third World states. These potentially revolutionary groups which included the woman's movement were the new substitutes for the failure of a revolutionary self-consciousness of the proletariat in the developed West.

These new groups—students, women, blacks, and Third World nations, according to the critical theorists—were particularly attracted to the pleasure principle as a new myth which could transform the consciousness of marginalized or unintegrated groups in the modernization process. If these groups could have their consciousness transformed, unlike what had happened with the proletariat, then they could become the exogenous revolutionary force which transforms the historical process from without. This is a new lease on the revolutionary tradition which is transnationalist since it seeks student groups anywhere or potentially schismatic groups as the exogenous catalysts for revolutionary change. Castro's Cuba was one such Third World revolutionary movement that some believed might have held such revolutionary potential.

To return to Cuba, Castro has served as a carrier of the radical Jacobin nationalism, and materialistic internationalism has deeply cleaved his society between the traditional transcendent metaphysic of Catholicism and the radical secular challenges to the historic metaphysic. In this context, the choices for Cuba seem to be very much like those of the other Latin American nations which have faced this crisis. Either it returns to a constitutional democratic regime based on a traditional metaphysic postulating the finitude of rulers and ruled, or they are likely to fall into the Heideggerian effort to formulate a new nationalism based on the finite transcendentalism of a dechristianized population.

Thus the Cuban Revolution is seen by Western Marxists as an authentic revolutionary response to underdevelopment and capitalist dependency. For them, it is not even appropriate to interpret Cuba as either pro-Soviet or as an example of a classical proletarian Marxist experiment. Accordingly for them, Castro brings a correct self-consciousness to the Cuban people. Castro explicitly noted in 1985, that "the people had to be led to the road of revolution by stages, step by step, until they achieved full political awareness and confidence in their future."[3] This statement is a classic formulation of the Western Marxist perspective, albeit wedded to Castro's brand of Marxist-Leninism.

It seems unlikely that the Cubans in a post-Castro order could join a regional arrangement that was based on a neo-Kantian or scientistic foundation. Such a solution would appear to be an imperial imposition on a people who have been both unified on a common anti-Enlightenment view of imperialism and have been divided in their metaphysical understandings. In other words, their natural evolution would not allow them to have a simple liberal constitution. To the degree the new regional order is seen as a rationalist order it will not come to grips with the crisis in the value system which currently exists in Cuba. It is impossible for the Cubans to come into a system of uniform law that will not take into account the peculiar complexities that have developed in the nation's psyche as a result of being both Catholic and Marxist.

To the degree the United States attempts to impose a political and cultural form on these societies that is alien to them, they will forego the economic cooperation that seems to be imperative in the expansion of the benefits of the modern international capitalist system. What must be done is to create cultural and political structures that can take advantage of those economic benefits without aggravating the cultural and political crises that have been plaguing Western civilization since the Enlightenment and producing gnostic movements which have been unable to cooperate with other societies.

The best form we have found for doing this has been the constitutionalist regime which permits the traditional cultural values to promote accountable governments over substantially self-governing peoples. This was due to the fact that the religious and customary norms of the people were sustained on the basis of the historic beliefs in a transcendent metaphysic.

ENDNOTES

1. George Steiner, *Martin Heidegger* (Chicago: University of Chicago Press, 1978) p. 36.

2. Ibid., p. 113.

3. Balfour, *op. cit.*, p. 163.

Conclusion

The Importance of Democracy

Cuba, as much as any country in the world, has incarnated the revolutionary struggles of the twentieth century. It may well represent the last gasp of the crisis of transition from the conflicts of the twentieth century to those of the twenty-first. Despite the collapse of communism in the Soviet Union and Eastern Europe, Castro continues to pledge allegiance to his brand of revolutionary statism. Yet there is a sense of profound crisis in Cuba; a sense that Cuba has entered into a time of transition. A change of government, if not of regime, is therefore anticipated at any moment. What remains to be seen is whether Cuba will flower into an autonomous, democratic state, or whether she will continue to be a bellwether of the continuing political conflicts of our time. In this struggle, Cuba has had to grapple not only with the revolutionary principles of her democracy and national identity, but with her involvement with external actors, in particular the United States.

Why the emphasis on democracy? For the United States, advocacy of democracy has been one of the key principles of her foreign policy under the Reagan and Bush administrations. For Cuba, democracy, along with national identity, has been one of the chief forces behind her continuing revolution.

One of the chief characteristics of U.S. foreign policy is the inadequacy of *raison d'etat* as a justification for action in the international arena. U.S. policy makers have a very difficult time justifying actions which are not seen as promoting liberal democratic values. The concept of democracy takes on special significance for the United States as a basis for legitimating its role in the international arena. Democracy therefore takes on a moral quality and a revolutionary tinge. In some cases this can result in insensitivity to indigenous political organizations, but in other cases, this emphasis on democracy can result in U.S. advocacy for revolutionary change. The problem is that not all movements which claim to be democratic are democratic.

The Sandinistas came to power in Nicaragua with U.S. approval by claiming to be a democratic alternative to the oligarchic *caudillismo* of Somoza. In turn, the Sandinistas established their own tyranny. The model they followed was that of Fidel Castro and his July 26 movement.

Nevertheless, despite the uncertainty generated by false democratic claims, "democracy" has achieved enormous prestige as the most legitimate and most appropriate regime for modern circumstances. Just as absolute monarchies dominated the world in the Age of Enlightenment, now democracy has established itself as the political organization most suitable to modern sensibilities.

Historically speaking, this is ironic. The term "democracy" as it was used in the time of the ancient Greeks was a term for a deformed system of government. In Aristotle's famous typology of regimes democracy ranked behind monarchy and aristocracy as the least best regime. Aristotle considered democracy to be inefficient and not conducive for producing virtuous leadership. In the Greek conception, the rule of the many had to be at the service of all sectors of society for it to be considered good. Democracy too often degenerated into the rule of the many for the many based on the lowest common denominator of appetite.

Aristotle contributed to an understanding of civic culture which conflated the private and public roles of the individual. The greatest fulfillment of the individual was as a citizen within the state. Hence, in ancient democratic theory there was no legitimate civic counterpoise to the state's power. In many ways, this historic understanding would form the basis for Rousseauvian and Marxian reinterpretations of democracy and would be especially significant for Cuba's own revolutionary development. In many ways, the endurance of concepts of ancient democracy and their reinterpretations have played an integral role in the history of twentieth century Cuba. These ideas are also in dialectical relation to the understanding of modern democracy as it has developed in the United States.

The roots of modern democracy are quite distinct. It developed in the Anglo-American context out of the protracted struggle in Great Britain generated by Henry VIII's break with the Catholic Church. This event, occurring in the context of the Protestant Reformation, ushered in a nearly century and a half struggle between the claims of absolute monarchy and Stuart crypto-catholicism on the one hand, and representative government and Calvinist protestantism on the other. Because neither side could effect a decisive, total victory, the system of checks and balances began to emerge. Parliament emerged as the dominant political institution of England, but the monarchy continued under a constitutionalist theory of limited sovereignty.

One of the overlooked aspects of this struggle is that it was predicated implicitly, if not explicitly, on three fundamental Christian doctrines. In opposition to the hierarchical, absolutist order the Stuarts represented, this developing political understanding was revolutionary.

The first part of this understanding saw citizenship as only one aspect of personhood. This idea mandated that government be limited and instrumental to allow each person to work out their individual destinies. The second doctrine was that each person was equal in the eyes of God. This did not mean that all people were blessed with the same skills and talents, but that they were all entitled to work out their individual destinies. The third doctrine was the doctrine of Original Sin, which held that people were fallen (if not depraved, as some of the more radical protestants argued). Governors could not be trusted absolutely. They needed to be checked in their capacity to do harm.

These principles were established in both secular and religious versions as natural law by the English political class. Through force of circumstance these principles were imperfectly applied in the practical context of the English political system, but they formed the core ideas of its political evolution. In retrospect, John Locke's *Two Treatises on Government* and the Glorious Revolution and the English Bill of Rights were only theoretical and practical capstones of a 150 year old conflict. This long struggle provided the particular historical background to the founding of the United States. The political wisdom of the founders of the American constitution was based on the belief that the most powerful institution that had emerged in the struggles between monarchy and Parliament was the legislature. What the American colonists came to realize was that even the legislature had to be checked. This development was based on the premise that no center of power could be trusted not to threaten the freedom of the people. Even though the legislature was the body which was supposed to represent the people most directly, the people did not feel that they could rely solely on its sense of accountability. Institutional mechanisms as well as elections had to be created.

Modern democratic theory therefore represents a dramatic reversal in the classical Greek approval of the homogeneity of society and the power of the government. In the Greek theory of good democracy, decisions were made collectively in the interest of the whole. The predicate of such a system was that the population was small and homogeneous in order for it to function. The modern idea of the democratic regime sees society as divided by competing value systems, and concentration of power anywhere in the ruling system is undesirable. The protection of the individual in the context of a pluralistic society and the maintenance of the freedom of civil society are the primary goals. Secular modern democratic theory requires that there be dissent, diversity, and parts represented by more than one party in the polity. Difference, not uniformity, is the essence of the good state, and a multi-party system is essential to the freedom of the individual and to the limitation of regime power.

This view was synthesized in the Federalist Papers, which were used to get the various new states in the American union to accept the Constitution. In the famous formulation of Federalist 51, it was held that since men were not angels they required governors, and since governors were not angels, they required checks and balances. Governors have a moral obligation to be accountable to the people, but there are political safeguards in case they are not.

For these reasons, process norms (such as elections, reliable and fair mechanisms for securing the vote, access to the population by competing political parties, and access to the media) are among the ends the democratic regime constantly seeks to protect or implement. These ideals are freedom of the individual, the right of association, security of the person, and the private and social pursuit of fulfillment or happiness as it was stated in the U.S. Declaration of Independence.

The democratic system is a mechanism designed to allow society to flourish because it is based on freedom. Freedom in turn is based on an acceptance of transience and an antipathy to the maintenance of vested interests. The democratic system ideally accommodates the ability of people to fail or succeed according to their own merits. Political and economic structures which create privileged classes instead of promoting natural aristocracies are seen as ultimately leading to economic and political inefficiency, corruption, ossification, and the breakdown of the economy of government.

This understanding argues that if the evil propensities of men in society can be checked that the creative and social capabilities of the society will flourish. The democratic regime presupposes that the individual's creative and spiritual fulfillment occurs more in society than it does in government. Government is a necessity for society, but should be at its service rather than dominate it.

Democracy is only possible when the political culture can sustain self-government. Rather than seeing this process as an overnight development, validated by an election or two, a much longer view of the historical struggle would probably be more accurate. The ability of the people to be self-aware needs to be emphasized. Often it does not happen, except through a process of breakdown of past structures of power in conjunction with the growth of independent political classes and democratic sensitivity to the corrupting nature of power. Democracy can often be derailed or side-tracked by other powerful ideas which grip the political imagination of a society such as communism and some forms of nationalism.

Democracy is not a panacea. The problem with other forms of modern government such as authoritarian and totalitarian regimes which Cuba has struggled with, is that these regimes essentially dominate the civil society. Authoritarian governments isolate themselves from accountability to the civil society. Totalitarian regimes seek to absorb civil society completely.

In this sense, totalitarian regimes are closer to ancient democracy than modern democracies are, but they are antithetical to the preconditions that we posit are natural and necessary in an open, democratic polity. The totalitarian regime of Castro shows just how far the quest for democracy in Cuba has been derailed.

Yet the Cuban people may have gained an understanding of what the democratic conscience might be, and the international situation is propitious for a new transition to take place. There have been a number of authoritarian and totalitarian regime transitions in recent years. In Spain, the transition was brokered by a monarch who acted, in a sense, above the political system. In a number of Latin American countries, the transitions were principally prepared by agreements between the major political parties. In the Warsaw Pact, there have been transitions through transaction, transitions through revolution, and transitions through plebiscite. The fact that the Soviet Union has collapsed is of extraordinary significance because it served as both patron and exemplar to Cuba. These processes, once set in motion, have led to more open political systems, even if it is still too early to say that they are definitively so.

For countries in transition to democracy, whose populations have suffered deeply from the exploitation of government, the principal problem is the establishment of democratic procedures. People anxious for civic responsibility need to have the chance to exercise it. These societies also face the problem of transferring economic activity substantially to the civic society. Society also has to have the economic capability of holding its political officials accountable. As long as an independent economic sector does not develop, the country has no alternative recourse from the state.

This economic dependence on the state is one of the chief adverse developments of the modern era. Instead of society preserving its autonomy through a multiplicity of intermediary associations and holding the regime accountable to the interests of the people, statism has imperilled democratic institutions in many regimes. Not only has statism fostered a climate propitious for the development of corruption, graft, and administrative inefficiency, but it also creates a bureaucratic mentality completely alien to the democratic principle of self-government.

The democratic regime is an historical development that worked itself out in the interaction of the norms of people and their experience with both the problems of anarchy and tyranny. With regard to civil society, diversity has come to be recognized as an asset. Individual and social rights need to be protected. Regimes have to be accountable to a healthy civic society. Claims of absolute sovereignty, whether by kings, peoples, or parties have been rejected and systems of checks and balances have been embraced. For these reasons, multi-party systems have emerged as the critical mediating process between diverse societies and accountable governments. We must understand therefore, that the word "democracy" is a highly simplified term for an extremely complex political understanding developed over centuries of political experience.

As we have argued, the continuing revolution in Cuba was not solely about democracy, but about developing an autonomous national identity.

The revolution in Cuba is illustrative of a part of the overall international regime crises of the twentieth century. If those crises can be seen as beginning with World War I, it may very well be that we are watching the ending of these characteristic crises of the twentieth century with the events in Eastern Europe of 1989. What was particularly characteristic of these tumultuous years between 1914 and 1989 was that the international conflict between the great powers became intimately connected to the nature of the regimes interacting in the world arena.

Castro himself, recognized that if his effort to come to power had occurred in the early 1950s, it might very well have been repressed. The fact that it occurred while the Soviet Union was beginning its major challenge to the United States in the late 1950s, allowed Castro to combine the radical anti-American nationalism with the international communist system. That particular alignment option for the radical anti-American nationalists is a declining option in the years ahead. So whether or not Castro presides over the transformation or reform of his own regime, or whether it occurs inevitably after his demise, has no major significance because it will happen regardless of his actions, because the international rivalry is in the process of fundamental change, making concomitant changes in Cuba inevitable.

Cuba can no longer serve as a detonating devise for an armed conflict between the United States and the Soviet Union.

On the other hand, Cuba can be of immense significance in the evolution of the international system in the twenty-first century. What we now understand as occurring is the repositioning of states, economies, and regimes for the emerging economic, cultural, and political environment.

In the economic sphere, the world is clearly moving toward growing regional economic arrangements which have become necessary for the maintenance of both the economic markets for large corporations and for the sustenance of ever-more concentrating urban populations. This regionalization of economic relations will nonetheless have an uneasy relationship with the continuing nationalist trends that will exist within those blocks, and the United States will face the intensifying challenge of accommodating national economic interests versus the transnational regional interests.

In the cultural sphere, there will be a concomitant stress between the growing regionalization and globalization of mass cultural values bottomed on commercial entertainment values versus the national and internationalist cultural values based on customary, localist practices and religious normative standards. These cultural clashes suggest that there will be both regional and national differences which will divide the groupings seeking to work out their economic relationships.

In the political sphere, all of these forces will be played out in the complexities of managing the national and regional interrelationships. In this context, the way Castro ends his regime, or in the way the post-Castro transition occurs, can have enormous significance for how the Western Hemisphere regional relationships develop. If Castro's transition can be brought about in such a way that it does not rekindle the fires of radically secular particularisms, then one of the threats to a cooperative relationship of democratic regimes based on traditional values can be contained.

If however, a Castro transition is not managed with the concerns of the new era in mind, then it will have a significance not for the revival of some globalist rivalry, but for the efforts to create a cooperative economic and political relationship in the Western Hemisphere which will protect the traditional values of the American nations.

What we are arguing has a double fold: the first is the ending of the twentieth century international system, and the Cuba problem is a relic of that disintegration. Nonetheless, the deeper problems that existed, not only during the twentieth century model, but before it began, are still present. These problems essentially are the cultural and political responses to the modern capitalist international economy. On the one hand, there is the gnostic movement which from its right wing brings about a totalist state based on a Hegelian *geist*, and on its left, brings about a totalist state based on a materialist atheistic revolutionary anti-metaphysic. These values and attitudes remain strongly embedded in the world culture despite the fact that the Soviet capability of protecting the materialistic wing of that tradition has been greatly eclipsed. Therefore, it cannot be ruled out that this challenge to the new regional groupings and their inter-relationships cannot and will not be revived in the twenty-first century.

Castro's Cuba and its transformation may be particularly significant to whether or not the left wing gnosis gets a new lease on life in the system of the twenty first century. If Castro in following one of the options for the transformation or revitalization of his regime's ideology is successful, then it will be the seed for the continuing challenge to constitutional democracy in the emerging regional order of the Western Hemisphere. On the other hand, there continues to exist the cultural challenge of the West's traditional religions to the reductionist massifying and alienating aspects of the transcapitalist economic interests. The traditional distaste for the subservience of the essential spiritual aspirations of mankind to the demands of economic interests have been best protected within constitutional democratic regimes, sustained by peoples with a sense of their dignity, human rights, and transcendental destiny.

To the degree the democratic transitions of Latin America can continue in the direction of representing these civic values in a constitutionalist regime, then the disruptions that may occur as a result of the inevitable adjustments to the increasing large scale requirements of the modern economy may be managed in a mutually productive and culturally acceptable manner.

Should the new regional economic arrangements prove to be too disruptive of the cultural, economic, and social fabric however, then the prospects for radical gnostic movements returning forcefully to the international scene, particularly under the guise of ethnic and other particularistic nationalisms, would seem likely. It is probably therefore, with these considerations in mind, that the United States must move to assist a post-Castro Cuba to enter the American system of states as a nation which will be able to protect itself culturally and politically while it prospers economically.

What is clear from this analysis, is that the historic U.S. interest in promoting the independence of Latin American states in general, and that of Cuba in particular, is also linked to the establishment of a democratic regime and an open economy.

Most commentators somehow envision that once Cuba breaks out of its dependency on the Soviet Union, and breaks away from the grip of the communist apparatus, that it will revert to its condition of the 1950s, as a de facto U.S. dependency. This belief assumes that Cuba is a fundamentally dependent regime, and that it cannot escape being dependent on one regime or another. Yet all are agreed that dependency is inherently wrong in the damage that it does to the collective national psyche, in the manifestations of retarded development, and in the basic deprivation of those most human of all aspirations: autonomy and independence; in short, the ability to exercise free will. In fact, Castro seems to be seeking to diversify the economic base of his statist regime by reaching out to Latin America, Asia, and Europe.

What Cuba needs perhaps, is a third way, a Japanese model. Off the coast of a great power, with few raw materials and a backward infrastructure, the Cubans have, until now, chosen a political approach to power rather than an economic one. After thirty years, they are not politically influential and their economy is in ruins. Japan, on the other hand, having chosen an economic approach to power, is now economically strong and politically powerful.

The Cubans need to overcome their confusion about capitalism, and realize that what they had in the past, was an oligarchic precapitalist situation. It is hoped that the Cubans learn the same lesson that the Eastern Europeans have learned from the East Asians, and implement economic policies which will encourage free market decision-making and break the Cuban economy's crippling dependency on an ossified and inefficient state bureaucracy.

In this context, Cuba needs to view the United States not as a potential master, but as an ally desiring what it should desire as well: a workable democracy and an economic and social climate of freedom and independence. Any other relationship has proven unhealthy in the long run, and has hurt the United States as well as Cuba. While the United States should naturally be desirous for the installation of a regime favorable to it, what it really needs to do is reassume its historic identity as the ally and facilitator of Cuban democracy. It is in this guise that the U.S. can most effectively lay the demons to rest which Castro has conjured, and begin the process of reconciliation which the two countries truly need.

Like the Japanese, the Cubans may learn that the best road to self-sufficiency lies in accommodation with their great neighbor, and active constructive participation in the affairs of their region. Cuba, in many ways, has been a metaphor for Latin America as a whole. Like the other countries of the region, it may find that its best bet for independence and self-autonomy may lie in its defining itself in the context of Latin America, and not as a pariah set against it.

Selected Bibliography

Allyn, Bruce J. et al. "Essence of Revision: Moscow, Havana, and the Cuban Missile Crisis" *International Security* winter 1989-90, vol. 14, no. 3. [pp. 136-172].

Anderson, Benedict. *Imagined Communities: Reflections on the Origin and Spread of Nationalism.* London: Verso Editions/NLB, 1983.

Barron, John. "Castro, Cocaine, and the A-Bomb Connection" *Reader's Digest* March 1990.

Blasier, Cole. *The Giant's Rival.* Pittsburgh: Pittsburgh University Press, 1987.

Bonsal, Philip W. *Cuba, Castro, and the United States.* Pittsburgh: University of Pittsburgh Press, 1971.

Bourne, Peter G. *Fidel: A Biography of Fidel Castro.* New York: Dodd, Mead, & Company, 1986.

Carbonell, Néstor T. *And the Russians Stayed: The Sovietization of Cuba.* New York: William Morrow & Company, 1989.

Castro and the Narcotics Connection. Washington D.C.: The Cuban American National Foundation, Inc., 1983.

Clissold, Stephen. *Soviet Relations with Latin America 1918-1968.* New York: Oxford University Press, 1970.

Cohen, Saul Bernard. *Geography and Politics in a World Divided.* New York: Random House, 1963.

The Cuban Government's Involvement in Facilitating International Drug Traffic, Joint Hearing Before the Subcommittee on Security and Terrorism of the Committee on the Judiciary and the Subcommittee on Western Hemisphere Affairs of the United States Senate, Miami, Florida, April 30, 1983. Washington D.C.: U.S. Government Printing Office, 1983.

Cuba's International Foreign Policy 1975-1980: Fidel Castro Speeches. New York: Pathfinder Press, 1981.

Cuban Studies vol. 8, no. 1, Jan. 1978, pp. 39-40.

Dinerstein, Herbert S. "Soviet Policy in Latin America" *The American Political Science Review.* 1967.

Dominguez, Jorge. *Cuba: Order and Revolution.* Cambridge: The Belknap Press of Harvard University Press, 1978.

_____, *To Make A World* Safe For Democracy. Cambridge: Harvard University Press, 1989.

Douglass Jr., Joseph D. *Red Cocaine: The Drugging of America.* Atlanta: Clarion House, 1990.

Draper, Theodore, *Castro's Revolution: Myths and Realities.* New York: Praeger, 1962.

Ehrenfeld, Rachel. *Narco-terrorism and the Cuban Connection.* Washington D.C.: Cuban-American National Foundation, 1988.

Erisman, H. Michael, *Cuba's International Relations: The Anatomy of a Nationalistic Foreign Policy.* Boulder: Westview Press, 1985.

Falin, Valentin. "The New World Disorder? the Collapse of Eastern Europe: Moscow's View" *New Perspectives Quarterly* vol. 7, no. 2, 1990.

Falk, Pamela S. *Cuban Foreign Policy.* Lexington: D.C. Heath, 1986.

Fidel Castro: Nothing Can Stop the Course of History. Interview by Jeffrey M. Elliot and Mervyn M. Dymally. New York: Pathfinder Press, 1986.

Fontaine, Roger W. *Terrorism: the Cuban Connection.* New York: Crane, Russak, & Company, 1988.

Geyer, Georgie Anne *Guerrilla Prince: The Untold Story of Fidel Castro.* Boston: Little, Brown & Company, 1991.

Gonzalez, Edward, and David Ronfeldt. *Castro, Cuba, and the World.* Santa Monica: Rand, 1986.

Gonzalez, Edward. "The Cuban and Soviet Challenge in the Caribbean Basin" *Orbis* vol. 22, no. 1 Spring 1985, pp. 73-94.

Gunn, Gillian. "Cuba in Crisis" *Current History* March 1991. pp. 101-104, 113.

Hollander, Paul. *Political Hospitality and Tourism: Cuba and Nicaragua.* Washington D.C.: The Cuban American National Foundation, 1986.

House Foreign Relations Committee, "Cuban Involvement in International Narcotics Trafficking" Washington D.C. 1989.

Hudson, Rex A. *Castro's America Department Coordinating Cuba's Support for* Marxist-Leninist Violence in the Americas. Washington D.C.: The Cuban American National Foundation, 1988.

James, Daniel. *Cuba: The First Soviet Satellite in the Americas*. New York: Avon Book Division, the Hearst Book Division, 1961.

Kagan, Frederick. "The Secret History of Perestroika" *The National Interest* Spring 1991.

Kass, Ilana. "Gorbachev's Strategy: Is Our Perspective in Need of Restructuring" *Comparative Strategy* vol. 8, no. 2, Spring 1989.

Kass, Ilana, and Fred Clark Boli. "The Soviet Military's Trans-century Agenda" *Comparative Strategy* vol. 9, no. 4, Oct.-Dec. 1990.

Kimura, Hiroshima. "Soviet Focus on the Pacific" *Problems of Communism* May-June 1987.

Levesque, Jacques. *The USSR in the Cuban Revolution: Soviet Ideological and Strategic Perspectives 1959-1977*. New York: Praeger, 1978.

Lockwood, Lee. *Castro's Cuba, Cuba's Fidel*. Boulder, Westview Press, 1990.

Manara, Luis V. *Russian Missiles in Red Cuba*. Miami: Truth About Cuba Inc., 1968.

Martí, José. *La Edad de Oro*. Cuba: Editorial Juvenil/Editorial Nacional de Cuba, 1964.

McGaffey, Wyatt, and Clifford R. Barnett in collaboration with Jen Haiken and Mildred Vreeland. *Twentieth-Century Cuba: The Background of the Castro Revolution*. Garden City, N.Y.: Doubleday & Company, Anchor Books, 1965.

Mesa-Lago, Carmelo. *Dialectica de la Revolucion Cubana: del idealismo carismatico al pragmatismo institucionalista*. Madrid: Biblioteca Cubana Contemporanea, Editorial Playor, 1979.

Montaner, Carlos Alberto. *Fidel Castro and the Cuban Revolution: Age, Position, Character, Destiny, Personality, and Ambition.* New Brunswick: Transactions Books, 1989.

Moore, Carlos. *Castro, the Blacks, and Africa.* Los Angeles: UCLA Center for Afro-American Studies, 1988.

"Moscow Continues to Batter Carter Administration" *Soviet World Outlook*, ed. by Mose L. Harvey, Fay D. Kohler. Miami: Advanced International Studies Institute) vol. 3, no. 8, August 15, 1978,

Padilla, Herberto. *Self-Portrait of the Other* trans. by Alexander Coleman. New York: Farrar, Straus, Giroux, 1990.

Pastor, Robert. *Condemned to Repetition.* Princeton: Princeton University Press, 1987.

Prizel, Ilya. *Latin America through Soviet Eyes: The Evolution of Soviet Perspectives during* the Brezhnev Era (1964-1982). Cambridge: Cambridge University Press, 1990.

Rangel, Carlos. *Del Buen Salvaje al Buen Revolucionario Mitos y Realidades de America Latina.* Caracas, Venezuela: Editorial Arte, 1976.

Redondo, Regino Diaz. Endeudamiento y Subversion: America latina Entrevista a Fidel Castro. Mexico: Collecion Enlace-Girjalbo, 1985.

Ripoll, Carlos. *José Martí: Thoughts on Liberty, Government, Art, and Morality: A Bilingual Anthology.* New York: Eliseo Torres & Sons—Las Americas Publishing Co., 1980.

_____. *José Martí, the United States, and the Marxist Interpretation of Cuban History.* New Brunswick: Transaction Books, 1984.

Rostow, W. W. *The Stages of Economic Growth*. Cambridge, 1971.

Rubin, Barry. *Modern Dictators*: Third World Coup Makers, Strongmen, and Populist Tyrants. New York: McGraw-Hill, 1987.

Rubinstein, Alfred Z. "Soviet Success Story: The Third World" *Orbis* vol. 32, no. 4, Fall 1988.

Ruiz, Ramon Eduardo. *Cuba: The Making of a Revolution*. New York: W. W. Norton, 1970.

Russian Military Expenditures. Washington D.C.: Committee on the Present Danger, 1991.

Shannon, Elaine. *Desperados*. New York: Viking Press, 1988.

Smith, Earl E. T. *The Fourth Floor*. New York: Random House, 1962.

Szulc, Tad. "Can Castro Last?" *The New York Review of Books* vol. 37, pp. 12-15. May 31, 1990.

_____, *Fidel: A Critical Portrait*. New York: William Morrow and Company, Inc., 1986.

Tsypkin, Mikhail. "The Soviet Military: *Glasnost* Against Secrecy" *Problems of Communism* May-June 1991.

Valenta, Jiri. "Cuba in a Changing World: The U.S.-Soviet-Cuba Triangle" *Testimony for the House Foreign Affairs Sub-Committee* April 30, 1991. Washington D.C.: Cuban-American National Foundation, 1991.

Valladares, Armando. *Against All Hope*. New York: Alfred A. Knopf, 1987.

War and Crisis in the Americas Fidel Castro's Speeches 1984-1985. ed. by Michael Taber. New York: Pathfinder Press, 1981.

Weyl, Nathaniel. *Red Star Over Cuba.* New York: The Devin-Adair Company, 1962.

Index